BASINGSTOKE BOY

JOHN ARLOTT

Basingstoke Boy

The Autobiography

Fontana
An Imprint of HarperCollinsPublishers

Fontana
An Imprint of HarperCollins*Publishers*
77–85 Fulham Palace Road,
Hammersmith, London W6 8JB

Published by Fontana 1992
9 8 7 6 5 4 3 2 1

First published in Great Britain by
Willow Books 1990

ISBN 0 00 637737 8

Set in Palatino

Printed in Great Britain by
HarperCollinsManufacturing Glasgow

CONTENTS

ACKNOWLEDGEMENTS

The author's grateful thanks are due to his wife, Pat, not only for typing but for being monumentally patient about alterations – and for remembering where everything was. Thanks are also due to Tim and Beverley Jollands; the watchful John Gatrell; old friends in Jack Donovan, Leo Harrison, David Rayvern Allen, and Neville Rogers; Alan Smith and Michael Doggart at the publisher's office; Stephen Green at Lord's; and Arthur Attwood (Basingstoke) and Roger Mann for their help with photographs. None of them, however, may be held responsible for the opinions or errors.

INTRODUCTION

This is an introduction to an attempt to look at the life of a man who, in general, enjoyed it, through his own eyes, but in the third person. Perhaps, too much reading of autobiographies, and other 'personal' writings, fostered a dislike of the use of the third person. Far too much writing appeared to suffer from the intrusive 'I'; which seemed often to infect it with conceit, self-satisfaction or, far more rarely, an almost equally unhappy mock modesty. That produced a personal resolution, some twenty or more years ago, to discontinue its use completely. In that period it has twice been included in his copy, but each time inserted by a sub-editor.

In commentary it was a different matter; it is impossible – surely? – to give an impersonal commentary, even though the matter is not autobiographical; and the approach is basically objective. Thus, it seemed fair, in an admitted autobiography, to stand back and look at the subject as objectively as possible; striving to explain; to give the reader as clear and as unbiased a view and account of opinions or actions as they seemed at the time or – pardonable in the third person? – at the subsequent time of writing.

It must be admitted that some wise, and literarily informed, friends thought it at best unwise, possibly destructive of the autobiographical aim, even horribly self-conscious, to use the third person. On the other hand, to have written in the first person would have destroyed a habit of many years. Perhaps it will fail; fall down half-way, or continue to a self-destructive end. No help to labour the point in a subjective way; let the creature stand to be examined; or self-examined.

To take a leap from start to finish, this volume ends where and when it does with the completion of what some people chose to call 'The D'Oliveira Affair', which was probably the most important thing J.A. ever did in his life. By it, and with a clear mind, he was able to put back into the game of cricket something of what he had taken out of it and – more than that – something of what it had given him – two different things. So, from thereon, he might state where he stood in terms of common humanity, for he was facing a degree of maturity, understanding of what life was about, and of his purpose – if any – in it. That seemed to him the time to pause, draw breath and re-shape his thought about his life and, probably more important, about life in general. He was then forty-four, passing into the state where to look back was nostalgic; to look forward was a matter of contemplation, rather than planning – in so far as it had ever been that. So he briefly stopped writing and began to think afresh about what had already happened. Hence the end of *Basingstoke Boy* – an end full of gratitude for those early days, that place, those parents, relations, and his friends.

John Arlott
Alderney
April 1990

Chapter 1

A MINOR BASINGSTOKE EVENT

About four o'clock in the morning of 25 February 1914, Mrs Saunders, the Basingstoke midwife, delivered Nellie Arlott of a fat baby boy. The child weighed something over 7½ pounds; and an unposed, nude photograph (taken, in the manner of the day, by a local photographer) shows the infant prophetically idle. For many years only hearsay evidence of its progress or regress is available: certainly, though, the child grew up in fascinated awareness of its family.

It was the son of William John Arlott, generally known as Jack, son of John Arlott. Indeed, although the baby was christened Leslie Thomas John, all three generations were known as Jack or John. Old John was a short, lean, physically hard man, born in Silchester, who ran away (?) to sea as a boy. He claimed to have served in the ship on which Edward VII went round the world when he (Edward VII, not John Arlott) was Prince of Wales.

Old John used to relate that, as a boy, he went to Aldershot to work for a baker who put him into lodgings paid for out of the child's meagre wage. On Saturdays he had to be down at the bakehouse by half past three in the morning to load up for the long country delivery round. Reluctant to leave his bed early – a family failing – he was several times late, and the baker threatened the elderly widow who was his landlady that, if she did not get the boy to work in time, he would be lodged elsewhere.

So she warned him, 'If you are not in by half past eight on Friday nights you'll be locked out.' Soon afterwards on a wintry January night, though, the temptation of a smoking-concert at the local working men's club proved too strong. He fell asleep in the stuffy atmosphere, and did not wake until nearly half past ten. He ran all the way to his lodgings, only to find the doors closed. When he hammered at the door, his landlady shouted down, 'You can stay outside and perhaps that will teach you a lesson.'

Cold, tired and frustrated, he howled up to her bedroom window, 'If you don't let me in, I'll throw myself down the well.' After several minutes without response he went to the well, rolled the boulder off the cover, opened it up and tipped the stone down into the water with a huge splash. At once he saw the flash of a match and the lighting of a candle in the landlady's bedroom. She bustled downstairs: he hid behind the door and as she hurried over to the well, he ran into the house, bolted the door and called out, 'Now you stay out there and get some of your own medicine.'

In the kitchen the dying fire was still warm, and he sat down in the armchair to wait until he thought it time to let the old lady in. After – for a boy – a late night, he dozed. When he woke and struck a match to look at the clock it was half past three. Hurrying out to the backyard he found the landlady in the woodshed, in only her nightgown, cold, stiff and dead. 'So that was why I ran away to sea.' He used to tell the story once every three years or so at Christmas, terrifying his grandson with the fear that Grandfather might still be locked up for killing the old woman.

Father always said it was a story Old John had heard aboard ship and repeated in the first person. Certainly he had been in the Navy; he was extensively – even luridly – tattooed. He had, too, served in naval ships covering the China coast. In the little hut where, for ten minutes or a quarter of an hour of his brief midday break, he dozed in a hammock, there were Chinese pots and silk embroidered pictures.

He had a son whom he tried without success to bully, and four daughters, three of whom he cowed. When his grandson reached the age of ten he was ordered to report at half past five on Fridays at the bottom of Chapel Street, where 'the men' were paid; there he received his weekly twopence, for which he was truly grateful, but which was withheld if he did not turn up on time. If he stood in awe of his grandfather, he also found him stimulating, not quite like other boys' grandads. He was a determined little man: when he wanted to hang a picture, he employed a six-inch nail; and, in the asbestos bungalow to which he eventually retired, that often produced spectacular results in the next room.

He was violent in his responses, broke ponies ruthlessly, 'trained' a series of fierce mongrel dogs. He drove himself hard, too, working relentlessly into his seventies, keeping pigs, chickens and goats and tilling a tough two acres. One summer evening he determined to mow his entirely unnecessarily large lawn and – characteristically – to finish it before he stopped. Eventually he finished: he lay down utterly exhausted and woke three hours later cold and feverish. The chill he sustained affected his bladder in a fashion which so shamed him that it broke his heart; he simply died of shame.

His son, by contrast, was quiet: unassuming but firm. From his childhood he used to go early, before breakfast, to one of the 'big houses' in Cliddesden Road where, for a few pence a week, he cleaned boots, shoes and silver, cleared and laid fires, swept out yards. From the time he passed the school-leaving examination at eleven, he, in the manner of the nineteenth century, served a long and completely thorough apprenticeship as a plumber.

There he developed a quite masterly skill with his hands which, after him, jumped a generation plus one grandson. A few subsequent weeks of work, and he set off for the Midlands – Coventry and Wolverhampton – where he became a highly capable metalworker. Then, for such was the career he planned, he presented himself at the hardware department of Harrods (a name undoubtedly picked up at one of the 'big houses') and asked for a job. 'What can you do?' he was asked.

'Anything to do with metal.'

A rapid but intensive interrogation – chiefly involving identifying the source of manufacture of pots and pans without being allowed to touch them – proved satisfactory. For the next four years he worked at Harrods, demonstrating that goods brought back to the hardware department did not require replacement but merely 'attention'. From that period came his immensely thorough knowledge and love of the music hall. Then, in 1910, one of the Harrods' salesmen, named Parker, decided to open an ironmonger's shop of his own in Meads, a suburb of Eastbourne.

Mr Parker was a clever man who made no attempt to conceal the fact. He had been clever to choose Meads; such a smart place, you know. Young Arlott – Will, as his mother called him – was impressed. He was deeply flattered when Mr Parker asked him to come down to Meads and do the servicing as at Harrods – and perhaps gain experience of serving behind the counter when there was no servicing on hand and the proprietor wanted to go out – on business, of course.

So it fell out that the new assistant was behind the counter when a young woman of Meads Village – the nearby square of cottages with allotments in the middle – came in to buy a coal shovel. Eventually the two began 'walking out'. He was a smart young man, sporting a spiky waxed moustache as was the fashion of the time; short – about 5 feet 7 inches – but as an enthusiastic swimmer at the Devonshire Park baths, muscular and extremely well proportioned. Jabez Wolfe, one of the earliest men to swim the Channel and a physical giant, was the swimming coach. On one gala night, in the comic lead, Wolfe picked up a newspaper boy (Arlott) and threw him fully dressed, newspapers and all, into the bath, where the lad surfaced, cap still on, through a floating surface of papers.

Meanwhile, the courtship went happily and properly along. The young couple became engaged, and were planning marriage, when one morning, Jack – as his fiancée called him – went in to work, but found no Mr Parker; neither did anyone else come to unlock the door to the ironmonger's shop. Mr Parker was, simply enough, bust, and was not seen again in Meads.

The young couple decided to make a match of it fairly quickly, and, in April 1912, they were married by the local – Meads – curate: one Theodore Woods, who used to play interminable games of chess with the bride's crippled father, and who later became Bishop of Winchester (it is not suggested that the three events had any but coincidental relationship).

Immediately after the wedding they went to settle in Basingstoke, where they spent the rest of their lives in, so far as their closest observer could tell, a steady love based on deep affection, mutual respect, the sharing of responsibility, a sense of humour and a considerable zest for life. Their son is not merely utterly grateful for their care and kindness but increasingly aware of the rare quality of the love they bore one another (and him).

Her maiden name was Nellie Clarke, daughter of Thomas Clarke from Brockenhurst. He had been a foreman for a firm of contractors building a dam in the Scottish Highlands. A tall, powerful, rugged man, much like William Ewart Gladstone in appearance, he contracted rheumatic fever from sleeping in tents in the mountains and went back to Eastbourne and his bed until he died in 1917. His wife was a sturdy country girl from near Evesham; she bore him twelve children – six boys and six girls – never lost one, and lived into her eighties.

Their daughter, Nellie Jenvey Clarke (all their children had Jenvey, their father's mother's surname, as their second), was an extremely pleasing woman: fair-haired, blue-eyed and rosy-cheeked. Fairly tall for a woman (five of her six brothers were over six feet), she was probably about 5 feet 8 inches, with a shapely figure which was aided by the corset she wore in the fashion of the time, but lamented, even if she did not actually curse it.

Two memories of her come constantly to mind; once she stood looking uphill when the sun took her fair hair and irradiated it, as it seemed to a small boy, like a fairy crown. The other recollection is of Mondays – washing day – when she was up early and, all through the long morning of scrubbing, wringing and hanging-out, she sang; she had been a church chorister, but now she simply made happy music. For a school- or pre-schoolboy, lying in bed above, it was enchantment: all unpremeditated. The mood was sometimes shaped by the kind of work she was doing – washing, mangling or smoothing – but, in the main, she simply sang. A hymn would be followed by a music hall song, something from an opera or comic opera, occasionally a snatch of plainsong; if anyone had asked her what she had been singing she would have had to cast her mind back to recall it. One piece in particular used to recur, never heard anywhere else before or since, in her upstairs listener's memory. It was from a song of the Russo-Japanese War (1904–1905) – and leaves no doubt where British public sympathy lay at that time. The single stanza, the only one she ever sang – though often repeated, sometimes with variations – was surely the

15

only one she remembered, but it made a deep impression on a child's mind:

Yo San, my little Yo San,
Yo San, my sailor boy.
He has gone out to fight
For the truth and the right,
And the glory of dear Japan.

Memories of schooldays still echo with that spontaneous, effortless, sweet song. Like her husband, she too had passed the school-leaving examination at eleven and had gone out forthwith into the world of work. She went into service, at first in the Anglican religious house near her home; then, gradually, up the social, and – crucially, if infinitesimally – the financial scale.

So into marriage, for which by Victorian lights – or, dammit, any others – she had been well trained. She could cook – which, by the measure of the time, included baking bread and cakes, making jam, pickles and other preserves. She laundered immaculately – to the standard inculcated by the nuns; she knitted, darned and mended, and did straightforward needlework. Above all, she was a happy person, and extremely perceptive: for years she would puncture her son's deepest laid tricks and stratagems with a broad smile and a cheerful but deadly accurate 'I know you, my son.'

The young husband, despite his anxieties, had no real difficulty in finding a job as a fitter with Thorneycroft, and the newly married pair moved into a terraced cottage quite near the works, in May Street, an obscure corner of Basingstoke. Now the cemetery where Old John was the registrar was filling up; the council acquired land for another and installed him in the lodge there. After about a year, Nellie became pregnant and, despite their happiness, they were worried by the threat – indeed, the probability – of war. With that in mind they were grateful for Old John's offer of the original, and now empty, cemetery lodge. The rent was low, but, more importantly, it offered Nellie a certain base against the possibility of war and her husband joining up. It was a fairly fantastic building – built, hopefully, in the style of a Swiss chalet – but by no means a bad working-class house for 1913: three fair-sized bedrooms, biggish dining-room and kitchen, plus the registrar's office, which was also the sitting-room, an outside lavatory and tool-shed in the backyard; no bathroom, of course: that was a rarity then, but there is still immense warmth in the childhood memory of that huge iron bath pushed up close to the roaring fire in the dining-room. Now – February 1990 – as this copy is being prepared for press – the *Southern Evening Echo* headlined 'Help sought for Arlott home renovation', a feature which begins 'Thousands of pounds are going to be spent on restoring John Arlott's Basingstoke birthplace to its former glory.' Apparently the old place has been much vandalized inside and out but, nevertheless, was sold by the Basingstoke Council to a lady from Dummer for £50,000. Perhaps when renovated it will be given a blue plaque!

Anyone who has travelled by rail on the Southampton to Waterloo line will know the house: on the way to London it appears on the left; the cemetery with many, often odd, trees overlooking the main town on the right, is itself dominated by the ruined arches of the ancient Chapel of the Holy Ghost. There their only child – the writer of this book – was born, took his first tastes of the world and grew up in an only slightly morbid innocence.

One day in 1915, Father's mail consisted of an 'invitation' to report to the local recruiting office. He duly presented himself, only for Captain Llewellyn to take one look at him and say, 'You shouldn't be here: you're a reserved man – at Thorney's aren't you? but never mind; now you're here, you had better stay.' Dad was too – innocent? fearful? patriotic? sensitive? – simply to walk out. Instead he went home, as he was told, picked up such necessities as washing gear and underwear, walked back to the office, was despatched to Aldershot and did not set eyes on his family again for four years.

The family, as usual, worked out its own kind of solution. Father had four sisters; three of them – Kit, who was impatient, Norah, who was solemn, and Lillian, who had a twitch but was humorous – were painfully thin; the fourth, Edie, was plump, because, it was said in the family, she used to stay with her aunt, when she had free run of the dripping pot. She was also gentle, placid and kind; her husband, Bill Baldwin – a butcher's clerk-accountant who could play the piano – was also summoned to the war, so she moved in with Nellie for the duration. So far as memory serves, it was a quiet, happy household, with much affection lavished on a little boy by two lonely but healthy women. If they were distressed – as they must have been by their husbands' absence – they never showed it, except that, sometimes, after they said 'good-night' to the boy, his pyjamas were wet with their tears.

Nothing remotely approaching argument ever happened; neither – as was confirmed by older observers afterwards – did either step out of the line of matrimonial fidelity.

Nellie – Mum – used to wait with radiant anxiety for the at-least-weekly letter from the man she now built into her son's consciousness as 'Dad'; who used to include a passage at the end of his letters addressed to 'My dear son'. Thus it was that the boy – precocious little beast – learnt to read by the time he was four, two years before he went to school.

Aunt Edie went to work at John Mares' clothing factory: she was a button-holer, which meant that she spent her extremely dextrous working time cutting button-holes with a peculiar instrument called – believe it or not – button-hole scissors, and then stitching round them. Mum looked after the boy, kept the house tidy, did the cooking and dug the allotment, where she grew cabbages, potatoes, broad beans and – always for Christmas – Brussels sprouts.

Father was paid the 'bob a day' of the private soldier (private, hell, nothing was ever less private); the two women got the next-to-nothing of the soldier's wife, yet they never grumbled. The trains rumbled or snorted past, only a few yards away, and by night the turntable groaned and screamed, but only once did any of the family ever travel by rail during those war days. When Grandfather Clarke died, in 1917, Mum took the boy down to the funeral at Eastbourne; he was caught crawling upstairs 'to see Gran' – who was lying in domestic state in his bed. The child was captured and, of course, carried away before he achieved his objective. Yet, oddly, that old man – or the character evoked by family talk, with the aid of a few photographs, in the mind of a child only three at his death – remains to this day impressive. He created in his grandson

18

a loyal Gladstonian, in whose home the 'Old Man' is still vener-
ated, in Staffordshire figures, steel engravings, Stevengraphs and
statuettes.

Otherwise it was life within a tiny, tight circle. Across the road
was the Rising Sun where landlord Butt's family were always kind;
but 'the girls' would not be seen in a pub without their husbands.
There was not another house within a quarter mile. Yet this was a
magic world, created by talk, ideas, hopes, dreams.

Old John was a godsend: he was always at hand to do any really
heavy work and, old as he was, and short, he had immense wiry
strength. He looked exactly like the sailor on the Players' cigarette
packets, with his pointed beard; and he feared no one. He could
bully Aunty Edie, but not Mum: 'Don't you speak to me like that,
Mr Arlott,' she said one day.

'Don't call me Mr Arlott, Nell,' said Old John, 'call me Dad.'

From that date, if not in charge, she was accepted as his equal.
The other women, especially Dublin-born Grandma Arlott, were
amazed; the equality was never mentioned but simply apparent.
His devoted loyalty and generosity to the two 'girls' and the little
boy – and, by implication, to his own loved, absent son – never
wavered. He read as much as they permitted of their letters 'from
the soldiers' as avidly as they did. That drew him almost, but not
quite, into the circle: still, when he left them it all became safely
complete; no one needed to say anything, it simply was so; something felt; founded on the bond between the three there and the
two men away.

In one way the bad days were yet to come. Armistice Day was
relief from the real fear – of the men's death – otherwise it was, for
everyone, a time of near hysteria not paralleled by anything in
more recent times; coloured by the never-lifted consciousness of
the many who had died. Then came the first dawning realization of
the long wait ahead. Troop ships simply did not exist in the numbers needed to bring back the thousands of soldiers from Palestine, Egypt, and further east, from Mesopotamia and India. The
warnings in Father's letters from Hyderabad, written with more
hope than expectation, gradually sank in. 'They say we are starting
back next month' – or 'week.' The disappointments – the fact that

19

no cable or telephone facilities were available to the troops, meant that he could only write: 'Expect me one day on the troop train, probably from Southampton.' That train – often two or three of them – would pull into Basingstoke station in the afternoon. The waiting women and children from the town and the countryside around would flood forward, looking, withdrawing but, even in their disappointment, buying cups of tea for the lucky men who were there, who would sometimes, with a great cheer, smash all the cups on the platform. This gave rise to a laughable, difficult situation: the station buffet manager had to weigh his sales of tea against the occasional loss of cups. His anxiety used to become almost comic, especially when his impassioned plea, 'Don't break the cups, mates, will you – *please*,' simply put the idea into their minds.

Then, day after day, week after week, came the long, slow plod back home. 'Never mind, son, he'll probably be there tomorrow.' The hope never broke; indeed, the waiting all became something of a ritual, bound up with talk of the Dad who was tinglingly real to the woman, an almost fictional – but still exciting – creation so far as the boy was concerned.

Then one day he was there: Dad. He was leaning out of the carriage window, waving as the train slowed into the station; he pulled slowly past; Mum and boy turned and ran, caught up with him; he leapt out and embraced them both. 'All right, Jack, we'll put your stuff out,' shouted the mates he would never see again. His arms bound the three together; he smelt strangely – of tobacco, khaki (presumably), blanco; but it was Dad. Suddenly all were crying, all three; Dad tried, as the train pulled out, to say good-bye to the others, but nothing, no one else, mattered: the three clung together. Then the walk home up the path so frequently and recently of disappointment. Another life was starting for three people.

Not better, not worse, you understand, but simply and completely different; utterly new. It was a widespread euphoria of the time; wives walking round displaying their safely returned husbands; children showing off their new-found dads. There, in that funny little lodge on Chapel Street, it was all as good as they had dared to hope. If the spoilt brat was no longer the sole object of one parent's attention, he was half the care of two; both of them inclined to indulge him. At almost exactly the same time, too, Aunt Edie had her Bill back; they shared the third bedroom at the lodge until, after the death of Grandma Arlott, they went to look after Old John.

For a growing boy the discovery of Dad – the real Dad, not the man of the letters and the photos – was immeasurably exciting, while, as hindsight demonstrates, Dad himself was captivated and, in truth, a bit less firm than Mum.

On the practical side, though, jobs were not ten-a-penny; the war had gone and, with it, the industry it had demanded. Thorneycroft's yard held all too many lorries and their components that would never be sold.

Old John fixed it all, muttering complaints and blaming anyone, right and left, whether they were to blame or not – even Lloyd George did not escape criticism – for letting his boy be out of work after he had saved the country. In fact Dad had served competently but quite unspectacularly in the RASC, in Mesopotamia and India, repairing, often, Thorneycroft lorries, some of which he had worked on at Basingstoke and, occasionally, to his fury, some he had botched up in the first place to get away on a Friday evening. Now the matter was different.

'Be my assistant,' said the old man. 'We need a chap at the old lodge: take on there.' Mum had her reservations: strong ones; Dad pointed out that it would probably be only for a few weeks, months at the most. It proved to be for the rest of his working life. He watched the post-war slump come and go and, from that, absorbed his almost obsessive determination never to be out of work; a belief he impressed, with at least initial success, on his son.

Jack Arlott was now thirty-one. War and the tropics had sweated every ounce of spare weight off him, and even hardened him physically – and he had been a fit man when he left. One day he took his son – hereinafter 'the boy', as his parents always called him – to the local baths to teach him to swim. He stripped off magnificently, with rippling muscles, in fine proportion. He dived in and covered several fairly spectacular lengths of the baths with what he called a 'trudgeon' stroke, and then gave his lesson keenly, patiently and genuinely helpfully. This led to one of his disappointments: he had had malaria several times during his service in the East, and that evening he suffered a frightening attack of ague. Several times in ensuing years he tried again in the hope that he had shaken it off, but without luck.

He was a gift for any wife. Not only was he affectionate, faithful and infallibly kind – perhaps, even, somewhat too happy to take orders – but he was also of quite amazing value in the house. Not only did he mend shoes, do all the plumbing, electrical fitting and decorating – in which he was neatly helped by Nellie – and repair virtually everything about the place but, over the years, he made all the major items of furniture in the house, in oak, without ever using screws or nails – all morticed or plug-and-socket: dining-table, sideboard, beds, armchairs, dining chairs, bookcases; working furiously to have an item finished, every year, in the week before Christmas; twice, indeed, owing to interruptions, on Christmas Eve.

His hobby, enjoyed with his usual interested care, was music; again, an ability not inherited from his father or mother, nor inherited by his son. He had been a useful violinist in his late teens, learnt other orchestral instruments and soon joined the local North Hants Iron Works (brass) Band. He once claimed that he could play – 'after a fashion', as he insisted – every wind and string instrument, though not the drums which he found uninteresting, except the brass bass and the string double bass, which were both too big for him to handle, and the piano, because he had never had the chance. One of the first things he did in his retirement was to buy a piano and learn to play it.

In addition he laboured prodigiously in his garden; so that Nellie – as was her boast for him – never bought vegetables or garden fruit in her married life. Every vegetable in season was available, and – the essential ingredient – in ample quantity; as insurance, there was generally even enough for some to be given away.

Such were his efforts that through the long days of summer he tended, increasingly with the years, to look exhausted; whatever the doctors may have diagnosed, when he died, a few years after he began to draw his pension, it was, quite simply, of hard work.

It was not easy to live, even in those days, on his £2 2s 6d a week. Every Friday night he handed his wage-packet to his wife; they debated expenditure. There was the weekly slate club payment to be made; the insurance contribution; the Christmas club; something to be put aside for holidays; eventually the boy was given his pocket money, and then Father. Yet somehow they found enough sometimes to go to the cinema, or to see some visiting 'show'; for Mother to go to a whist drive. Occasionally, too, when Mother had run short by Friday lunchtime – they proudly had nothing on credit and never borrowed – she would despatch the boy to collect sixpence from his father for 'six penn'orth of stewing steak'; and Father always had it; and, as a measure of the times, that six penn'orth was enough for three healthy appetites, eked out, of course, by a plenitude of vegetables from the garden.

Chapter 2

REALITY?

Ahead, though, lay reality – or was it real? Yes, if, that is, reality was the world outside home and the family. Certainly the nearest he had known to reality.

Old John – Grandad – emphasized its importance by pointing dramatically into the future with the finger of his left hand, of which all above the top joint was grimy-grey bone. 'What happened to the rest, Grandad?'

'A rat bit it off in the ship.' There was never any evidence of the truth of the statement, but it was tremblingly exciting.

'The boy's six. Time he went to school.' So, in boots, because 'shoes give boys weak ankles', he went to school. School was Fairfields; Dad had been there thirty-four years before, when it was simply 'the Board School'. Now it had more dignified titles: Fairfields Infants School, Fairfields Senior Boys and Senior Girls. With an almost intoxicating blend of terror and excitement he set off. For the first day Mum took him; bobbed to the headmistress and left him to her mercies. She was a Miss Dodson: tiny, corsetted to a high bust, her head held high – and, surely, uncomfortably – by a net-and-wire collar, autocratically pince-nezed. Nowhere else could she have towered over all; there amongst the children she was a firm, but understanding, giant. It was something of a miracle for a spinster, now past middle age, to take so many and such different children from so many different kinds of households, and at such a difficult time as the post-war muddle, and yet to run a happy school.

Handed the boy, she despatched him to Standard One; he went, tense and wondering.

Did he know his ABC? 'Yes.'

'Yes, Miss – say it.' He did – and the ABC.

Could he read? 'Yes, Miss' – learning. Simple reading book satis-factorily negotiated. More difficult reading book: satisfactorily handled by the insufferably precocious child.

Could he add up? 'Yes, Miss.' Examination revealed that that was sketchy; this was not really a mathematician. To Standard Four for intensive arithmetic; also scripture, in which he scraped through. Art: appalling. So, largely, it was to remain in terms of standards in a highly indifferent academic career. For the moment, however, all seemed fairly well.

During that year, one enduring aspect of his entire life was deeply implanted. Opposite the school was the cricket ground – May's Bounty – named after Lieutenant-Colonel John May, the bibulous local brewer, who gave it to the town and the local gram-mar school. During the war, it had been used for various activities, important, no doubt, but quite unconnected with cricket. One summer afternoon, though, the boy came out of school and, hear-ing unfamiliar noises coming from 'the Folly', as the ground was called locally, he went, curiously, to see what was happening. There he saw men, some of them in white clothes, throwing balls at each other in netting cages and hitting them away. It was intrigu-ing; he continued to go there, though there were not always men there. The appeal to omniscient Dad elicited the information that they were playing cricket. Then, one day there was no netting; the men were all in white, throwing and hitting; and suddenly one of them hit the ball up in the air, amazingly high, and another, run-ning round under it, caught it. Then there was much more hitting and running and stopping and throwing. It was all puzzling, won-derful and, so far as his childish brain could assimilate, beautiful. He pestered Dad until an old (tennis) ball materialized; and Dad had shaped a piece of wood for a bat. Dad, though, was a swimmer, not a cricketer; he could bowl underarm, straight, but not like the men. It all helped, though; soon, too, he dared to sneak into the Folly and watch, silent and in some trepidation; but amazingly, no one shooed him away – as most people did to boys in places where they had no business. Gradually the purpose of it all – or its basics – began to sink in. One day, too, Dad produced a hard red ball – they called it 'compo'. It hurt the boy's hands but Dad explained that was the way it had to be. The seed was sown.

No one in the family ever seemed conscious of any deprivation; life was generally easy and happy. Of course, there had to be 'discipline'. Once, when he was sent shopping, he stole sixpence out of the change. Quite apart from any moral criterion, that was downright stupid: Mum was not the person to miss a deficiency as great as sixpence was to the family then. In face of the evidence, and both parents, he confessed.

'He'll have to be thrashed, Jack; we can't have a thief.' Slowly that gentle creature took off his leather belt and swung the boy across his knee. The 'victim' was not merely crying but positively bawling by the time the first blow fell. Four more followed, boy howling all the time. Then the blows stopped. Sustaining the howls in case any renewal was contemplated, he slid off the knee: looking up, he saw his father was quietly weeping; another look, so was Mum. All three in tears about a fairly non-violent hiding for a boy who deserved it. Suddenly Mum stopped, looked at the other two and, through her tears, burst out laughing with 'What a damned silly thing, three of us all blubbing – never knew such rubbish.' She handed out a friendly box of his ears which he accepted happily enough; Father rubbed a hand through his hair, and the boy sloped off on some less nefarious purpose.

Often when he was out in the 'grounds' – that is to say, the cemetery – he would hear his father telling sightseers about the ruins of part of the tower of the thirteenth-century Holy Ghost Chapel and the guild Chapel of Holy Trinity (1524) which stood there. This prompted him into many questions. It was most truly an unusual place, that cemetery; full of ancient gravestones with legible engravings dating back to the eighteenth century, with strange devices – skulls, shields and a few coats of arms; the towering arches of the 'ruins'; unusual trees, yews of course, but one splendid weeping willow, ancient hollies and boxes, and a massive 'Christmas strawberry'. Many schoolfellows invited to play there backed away in well-brought-up horror; but he found it all fascinating, and was sufficiently – morbid? – to attempt to peer through the keyhole of the mortuary when he knew it to be occupied. It was probably well that Dad early observed this phase of curiosity and blocked the hole on the inside.

Beside the eccentric lodge was an iron bridge over the entrance drive where the black-plumed horses used to sweep, stamping, up the steep slope. On the west side, the ground sloped down through strange grasses to the boundary wall; opposite, the tiny 'Quakers' Ground' had a soothing air of quietness and privacy. At the back of the house was the yard containing Dad's workshop, where he worked by candlelight during the winter evenings; a level higher was the chickenhouse by which he kept the family in eggs for most of the year, and he made a loft for the boy's pigeons which may have been known as 'homing' but never stayed: presumably, to them, home was somewhere else.

Across the drive was the shed which housed the family bicycles. In 1921 the family biked to Eastbourne – 'best part of a hundred miles', Dad reckoned – for a holiday with Grandma Clarke. The boy rode on the carrier behind each parent in turn. The thought of that journey still revives the memory of walking sluggishly up a steep hill, encouraged by the assurance, 'Not far now,' and then, all at once, over the brow, to be enlivened by a lifetime's first view of the sea.

The next year the parents cycled down alone: he travelled with Old John, who had just acquired 'the car', a strange AC three-wheeler, entered through the front which lifted like that of a hansom cab, and steered by a joystick. In the 1920s – or even earlier – it must have been a fascinating transport museum piece.

On that holiday, the boy pestered Old John to take him on his night fishing trip; allowing him no peace until he gave in with the warning, 'Well, if I take you, you'll have to put up with it: I shan't bring you back until I've finished.'

'All right, Grandad, all right; thank you.'

Maternally well wrapped up against the night air and, in truth, tremendously excited, he set off in the strange little tri-car; down to the beach and the fisherman who was taking Old John and two more anglers on their excursion. The boat was small, open, and driven by a reeking oil – paraffin? – engine. Sternly enjoined in advance to 'Sit still and keep quiet,' he contained his excitement as the little tub set off. Soon, though, a whiff of the awful fuel gave him doubts, and then positive qualms. It would be all right, of course, as soon as they stopped for the men to fish, the engine would be stopped then. But it was not, it kept running gently to 'keep her into the wind'. The first vomit was convulsive and prolific, those which followed, smaller but more painful. The fumes went on; he had never been so wretched.

'Oh, Grandad, please can we go home?'

'No, you can't; there are two other men here who came to fish; you knew if you came, you came for the whole trip.'

Did logic – or a sense of fairness – seep through? He did not argue or plead: he simply lay in the bottom of the boat, and puked; in the end, on nothing. In his misery he pulled out his grimy handkerchief to wipe the spew from his face. At that time, though, he was collecting and begging 'confetti' – the punchings of the local bus ticket collectors – and the day had been quite productive; his handkerchief was full of it, and now his pawings smeared grotesque, multi-coloured patterns across his vomit and sea-water sodden face. He must have looked genuinely comic if anyone had been sufficiently detached from the fishing to look. It should have taught him a lesson: not to demand to be involved in everything, particularly matters of which he was quite ignorant. Alas, it did not, but if that terrible night had any compensation, it lay in the fact that he was never seasick again.

In that same ten days – the allotted holiday period of the time – he heard one of the family legends, told by Grandma Clarke – and impressive even to Old John, himself addicted to telling less credible stories. Her son, Uncle Frank, a tall, lantern-jawed man, had volunteered for the Army at sixteen. There was no need to conceal your age at that time: if you were big enough you were old enough – and in. So, by seventeen, Frank was in the Grenadier Guards, and at the first Battle of the Somme. Incidentally, he was a mighty left-arm thrower, cured of cricket by his wartime experience, but capable of throwing a cricket ball – or a hand-grenade – the hundred-plus yards of the distance between the lines of trenches in that war – and highly unpopular with the occupants of the dugouts near the sallyports from which he operated.

After that terrifyingly costly encounter of the Somme – in terms of distress and lives, against little advantage – many of the troops were shell-shocked, the young Frank among them. They were hustled to the back areas where one parade was asked, 'Anyone here from a south coast seaside town?' Frank put up his hand and became one of the batch of shattered soldiers sent down, just as they were from the battle line, to the cattle trucks which took them by night to Calais. There they were herded on to an old paddle steamer which had been a pre-war pleasure boat and, all standing and weighing the boat deep into the water, were despatched to Margate, Ramsgate, Deal, Dover, Folkestone, Hastings, Eastbourne. 'I was the only one for there,' he used to recall, 'so I suppose I must have been lucky they stopped for me, because there were a lot for Brighton.' It was barely a touch at the barbed-wired pier: time for him to jump and struggle on, and the boat was gone. He negotiated the pier, recognizing, but too exhausted to worry about, the fact that it might be mined, and made his way through the darkness of the December night, along the deserted front to Meads Village, to the house where his mother sat alone, dozing over the fire. He walked into the house saying, simply, 'Mother.' She looked up and saw her tall son's face in a shell-helmet – he had nothing else to wear on his head – and clothes smeared with mud and blood, looking pinched and miserable. Convinced she was looking at his ghost, she fainted. When she came to, she was in his arms, that grisly countenance and accoutrement even closer and more terrifying: she screamed and fainted again. Frank went out, roused – and at first horribly scared – a neighbour, and brought him in to convince the old lady that it was her son, alive. They celebrated, in tea, but meanwhile the neighbour dashed down to the pub and brought back brandy and, ever afterwards, she used to keep a bottle of it in the house – in case it happened again?

It was a delightful place for a boy, Meads Village, at the Beachy Head end of Eastbourne; almost feudal in its village-ness; the terrace of cottages built round the central allotments with their vegetables, plants and fruit trees, safe from thieves because they were all overlooked by their owners; or perhaps because people did not steal so much in those days. For a boy on holiday or – for one significant period – convalescent, it made a pattern of contentment: slow moving; the dairyman's and the baker's and the grocery man's horses plodded round that yellow grit road with their carts so placidly that even Meads Street outside seemed a different, noisier place. To return there now is to find a village of ghosts: no Verrals, no Corners, no Lucks, no Clarkes, no Harveys: essentially a different kind of place; no longer the humble, ordinary, respectable, strongly accented Sussex artisans, but all smart.

Eventually, though, it was right to be back in Basingstoke; it was home. It still is, but the Basingstoke of sixty years ago was an ordinary enough, country market town, not the six-times-greater planned London overspill town of today, which is not better, nor worse, only completely different.

After a year – though under age – the boy moved to the Senior Boys School, with some pride which was soon corrected by clipped ears, a kicked bottom and, from time to time, a bloody nose. There was, though, much to be learnt, and some good and diligent teachers to impart it. First, Miss Attwell, a burly lady with a rather shaggy and dusty bun of hair, a straightforward look and manner, and a devotion to teaching boys, including both those who did not want to learn and those who were altogether too keen and cocky. Mrs Taylor, the headmaster's wife, was even burlier; she was tall, bustling, North Country, straight as a die, with a sense of humour and the immensely rare capacity for imparting that attribute: a great teacher by any standard. Then her husband, Mr Taylor, nicknamed with schoolboy cruelty 'Snuffy': balding, conscientious, serious, he was determined to have discipline but was not aggressive, so he caned on the hands from a sense of duty and without pleasure; he thoughtfully kept a just and tidy school. His son, Selwyn, became a surgeon of some distinction, a civilized man, equally thoughtful, and a respected figure in the Wine Society.

Miss Tregarthen: now, there was a different matter. A trim and, undoubtedly, by adult standards, attractive Cornish redhead, she could be charming – to adults. To an innocent boy she first revealed adult treachery. During the summer – grass-cutting – season it was his delight to go out every morning to talk to 'the men', the motley gang mustered by Old John to cut the grass of the two cemeteries; the elders, with scythes, mowing the level stretches, the younger, with rip-hooks – sickles – clearing the uneven hummocks of the 'old place'. It amused them – most of them fathers – to talk with a prattling and, obviously, admiring child, and they would often give him what he called grass snakes (in fact, slow worms) which they came upon during their work. One day he decided to take one of the creatures to school. He put it in his jacket pocket and could not resist the temptation to show it to Ernie Jones during the first lesson – Miss Tregarthen's. They were so engrossed in admiring the beautiful creature that they did not realize the lady was approaching until, voice rising, she was almost upon them. Hastily he thrust it into his pocket.

'Arlott, give me what you were playing with.'

Silence; surely she would not want his grass snake.

'Give it to me, I say, at once.'

'No, Miss, please.'

'Give it to me, at once, I say!'

Silence.

'At once, or I will send you to the headmaster to be caned.'

So he gave her his snake.

She screamed; then: 'Go out to the headmaster and say I sent you to be caned.'

The headmaster duly administered two blows on the palm of each hand. They hurt, but what was appalling was the injustice of it all. He had tried not to give it to her, but she had insisted. He had been caned for doing as she told him, and his grass snake was lost. He had learnt about injustice. The world was never quite the same again.

There were no PT classes, no organized school games: nothing like cricket. The big boys used sometimes to play football in a mob game, their steel-tipped and studded boots striking sparks from the asphalt playground. There was the 'Rec' across the road with its big see-saws and towering swings, but they were not for the little boys. The big ones ran along the see-saws or stood in the middle as they rocked. The really brave ones risked the swings – and they were really high – twelve feet. Standing on the chain-hung seat they would work up speed until, at its highest pitch the chain curved and then as it reached the bottom of its arc, they would jump off and run under it as it came down so fast as to send it 'over the top', sometimes wrapping itself twice round the crossbar, when another of the bold would climb up and unwind it.

Primarily, this was a time of learning for the boy: school lessons, so necessary for the scholarship which was the family hope for him, and dutifully – indeed, eagerly – accepted as an aim and ambition. Also, learning about cricket, at first simply by watching. Soon, though, other boys were to be seen fielding out behind the players in the nets; questioned, they said their fathers took them along for fielding practice; that probably anyone could come, but not in boots like those. So, determinedly taking plimsolls to school and changing into them under the Folly fence became a regular summer routine. Sometimes, too, one of the men would drop an item of information, and one day Mr Butler himself, the 'pro', vouchsafed about a newcomer that he bowled big leg-breaks; informative, but the important fact was that Mr Butler, himself, had spoken to the boy.

Meanwhile, study was enthusiastic, so much so that the school decided to enter him for the 'County' scholarship a year early, which lifted endeavour even higher. There was only one possible result: some erratic bouts of temper, feverish nights and, eventually, symptoms never revealed to him but which were diagnosed as a 'nervous breakdown'. This was treated with plentiful doses of Parish's Chemical Food and Ovaltine at home; recovery was aided by some mild cricket when out.

In the following year, it was decided to enter him for, not one, but two, scholarships – belief in his recovery being strong – the County once more, and the Aldworth Charity, which carried an extra pound a year in book money, involved an extra morning's examination in religious knowledge, Church matters, the Catechism, the Prayer Book and *The Pilgrim's Progress*, and ended with an hour's *viva*. On this occasion, the last was conducted by the Bishop of Winchester's chaplain, who weighed in on the Catechism (all too easy) and then on the Bible, where he was fairly searching, but not unanswerable. Bunyan – simple, nice story – was child's play to the horrid child. Then came the Prayer Book, on which he had gone to special lengths and indecent pains. The interrogation was deep and grew deeper. Suddenly the chaplain's eyes lit up: it was a contest. 'Tell me,' he said, 'where does this come from: "Thou art a merciful God, full of compassion, long-suffering and of great pity. Thou sparest when we deserve punishment and in Thy wrath thinkest upon mercy."'

'A commination Denouncing God's Anger and Judgments against Sinners, Sir.'

After a couple more like that, the chaplain surveyed the horrid child with – surely – a mixture of enquiry and distaste. He rooted briefly in his Prayer Book and came up with 'What about "Are you persuaded that the Holy Scriptures contain sufficiently all doctrine required of necessity for eternal salvation through faith in Jesus Christ?"'

'Service for the Ordering of Priests, Sir.'

'Do you know the entire Prayer Book by heart, young man?'

'Most of it, Sir.'

'What about the Bible?'

'No, Sir, a lot of it I don't understand, Sir.'

'What don't you understand?'

'Lots of the Revelations of St John the Divine, Sir.'

'No, young man, neither do I – good luck.'

Well, the boy passed, won the scholarship – with its extra pound a year – and the first 'highly commended' in religious knowledge in the Aldworth examination since 1902; nothing similar ever happened to him in any examination again.

It was success: everyone at home thought so. The Grammar School lay ahead, but he still had not tasted reality.

Chapter 3

GRAMMAR TIT

That the boy should go to Queen Mary's School had long been the height of his and his parents' ambition; the scholarship added lustre to it. It was to prove an emotional five years, with – like any schooldays – excitements, depressions, friendships – some deep and long enduring – and at least one deep, tainting hatred. For the moment, however, it was heady excitement; even the taunt of 'grammar tit' – not so common, not so bitter, as it had been in some earlier days, but still a term of abuse – seemed like an accolade: he wore the black cap with its small, silver metal dove – symbolizing the Holy Ghost – with pride. Again, like all schooldays, his were formative of every main aspect of his subsequent life – except the sexual and the vinous.

The school, an offshoot of the ancient Guild of the Holy Ghost (1214), was certainly in existence in 1548; and is one of only two named for 'Bloody Mary' Tudor. The Guild had escaped Henry VIII's suppression but suffered that of Edward VI, though the school continued until Mary restored the Guild and gave the school her name in 1554. It was known through the county as Basingstoke Grammar. Despite its antiquity it was of little historic importance apart from the fact that Gilbert White – of Selborne – was a pupil there when the Rev. Thomas Wharton the Elder (1688–1745), who became professor of poetry at Oxford, was headmaster and his two sons, Joseph (1722–1800) and Thomas (1728–1790, the Poet Laureate) were pupils. It did not survive that phase of Government policy designed to kill off the grammar schools, but was merged with the local primary under the name of the Chute School, while the over-sixteens moved to a mixed sixth-form establishment called Queen Mary's College.

In the mid-1920s, though, it was a country grammar school – accent on 'country' – for about 120 day boys. It had been moved more than once since its foundation, and was by now housed in a gaunt three-storey reddish-dun brick building – still to be seen in Worting Road as a technical college. During the nineteenth century it had accommodated a few boarders but the dormitories were now empty, wildly insecure and, most certainly, a fire risk; all the rooms in the building had a dusty, punch-drunk look which, in its way, was a good thing since only damage far beyond ordinary wear and tear was noticeable.

The great, clumsy, double seat-and-desks had taken immeasurable punishment without sign; the lockers were built into the walls and, apart from the masters' fairly forlorn desks, these, and the great stove, constituted the entire formroom furniture. The staffroom was a poky hole with a common table and one chair per teacher. The two 'laboratories', protected from cricket balls or footballs by wire netting over the windows, would have made any true scientist shudder, even in those days. The central washbasins were the traditional place of summary punishment. The headmaster's house was part of the same building, cut off from the herd by a glass-paned door, which rattled perilously when he slammed it in his morning temper. At the back, a steep, sloping, crudely turfed field did duty as recreation ground, football and – incredibly – cricket pitch. An occasional gardener kept the headmaster's garden and the 'lawns' about the entrance gate something less than trim. 'Old Harris' was the amazingly ancient, scruffy, bearded, Rabelaisian and likeable caretaker, who cursed the boys, grumbled about the headmaster, took appalling chances with his stoking of fires, and awed – or horrified – most of the staff.

The pupils were a mixed bag of country and day boys. The country boys travelled anything up to eight miles by bike, or by train from more distant villages. There was no provision, not even hot water, for the country boys at lunchtime. They brought sandwiches, and sometimes onions, which reeked happily about the place, and left their crumbs and – rarely – uneaten food on their desks to attract the mice and – so he alleged – rats, which roused Old Harris to vast heights of blasphemy.

The school morning and afternoon were both relieved by 'break': ten minutes of often violent release, strictly timed and to be exceeded only for the purpose of a fight, when the contestants, with one 'second' for each, might continue – frequently with the attendance, or window-spectatorship of the headmaster – until it ended. The only first-aid available was a ducking under the taps at 'the basins'. It would, most certainly, have seemed primitive by the standards of the second half of the nineteenth century in more urbane settings. For something over a hundred boys in about 1926, though, it was real life.

In that place its staff were to shape those boys far more positively than might seem possible in a day school: at least it can be said that the output was not standardized – or was it? Perhaps they had a few characteristics in common, but not many: that would have been impossible at the hands of such a motley and, to be truthful, sub-standard crew of teachers; recruitment had not quite recovered from the First World War. A gallery – a kind of living Madame Tussaud's – of those teachers must be firmly stamped on the mind of every boy who went there.

First came the headmaster, Charles Wilhelm Percivall, presumably, from his second name, of German origin; a Prussian, it was said, and undoubtedly he had all the traditional characteristics of those people. He was asthmatic, which was not good for his temper. His house adjoined the school at the washbasins, the ritual setting for less than major canings. It used to be suggested that this central location, in an echoing brick area, was selected for propaganda reasons because a caning there could be inescapably heard all over the school: there would be a pause in lessons while classes mentally counted the strokes. A teacher would order a boy 'out to the basins' and when the headmaster could be heard wheezing as he approached, the offender could be sure of wholehearted punishment.

Percivall enjoyed caning, and carried his heavy bamboo cane – thick as his thumb and about three feet long – awkwardly but conveniently down the hem of his gown. He would survey the offender through partly closed eyes; then came the orders 'Get down,' which meant touch toes, whereupon he would whip up the coat tails and administer as routine three or four powerful, swinging strokes. The resulting bruises on the buttocks would be red on the first night, gradually growing grey-black and fading over about a fortnight. Any boy sent for the 'whack' who was due to play a game for the school in the afternoon was spared – in an ironic joke – until next morning, or, in the case of a Saturday match, until Monday.

A six-stroke punishment was always administered before the entire school, including the staff, who stood round the platform in the hall in varying degrees of indifference or embarassment, and was prefaced by an unctuous sermon which must have increased the suffering. This at least the young Arlott escaped; it was only administered for serious offences, such as cheating, cribbing or truancy; no one was ever able to walk away from it. Most would fall forwards, others staggered through the nearby fifth-form room and to the basins, where friends would generally run water over their heads or hold them while they vomited.

One murky November day, the head walked out to the bogs where he found two boys bolted in a cubicle. In a terrifying voice that could be heard from afar he ordered them out. They came timidly: two weedy twelve-year-olds, Percy Pudduck and 'Bunny' Lunn.

'What were you doing?' They hung their heads humbly. Three times more he asked them, then ordered them into his study. Asked once more, they still did not reply, so he gave them a fierce four apiece and, as they stood, awed and silent, he said, 'You will both be expelled – now then, what were you doing?'

'Lighting a firework, Sir,' panted Pudduck, through his tears. (The headmaster had lately laid down a strict injunction against fireworks and they had been dumb at the thought of his anger.)

Percivall burst out laughing. 'Get back to your classroom; you need not leave,' he said, and walked away chuckling. Later, other boys explained to them what his suspicions had been; the two were amazed.

Percivall taught mathematics, clearly, competently, without humour or warmth; he had rowed for his college at Cambridge and kept his oar over his study mantelpiece. His wife was a soft, plump woman who spoke little within hearing of the pupils. His son and daughter were alarmingly timid.

The first time he caned Arlott – three strokes – the boy straightened, about to burst into tears, when he found himself looking into the headmaster's eyes. He saw something there that he hated for evermore: impossible to say what it was, except evil. The tears were pushed back; he had found an enmity which – dammit – he cherished for many years. It was unhealthy, and had many reverberations. For instance, when he grew up and could – more or less – afford cigarettes, he bought the expensive, oval-shaped Passing Cloud which the headmaster had affected: an attempt to pull level.

The final development, probably – possibly – psychologically therapeutic, was of the kind that everyone knows does not happen, that is the pipe-dream dénouement; but it *did* happen a full thirty years later. The secretary of the school's old boys' association rang up.

'Will you speak at the Old Boys' Dinner?'

'Yes, if you want.'

'But, you see, Percivall is coming. Will you propose his health?'

'Health, be damned; you must know what I thought of him.'

'Yes, but you see, he asked us to ask him, and we talked it over in committee and decided you were the one to tell him what we thought of him.'

'Are you serious? Because if I propose his health, I shall tell him.'

'Good, that's just what we want.'

There followed several weeks of intermittent thought, doubt, compunction; then the final conclusion that, if a committee of contemporaries wanted it done, it should be done.

It was an odd evening, of fearful, yet gloating, anticipation. Percivall talked casually to several people across the table, apparently insensitive to the lack of warmth in their replies.

The toast to 'Our former headmaster' was called and, long pondered, it was delivered ad lib and remains – give or take an adjective or two – clear in the memory. Some unease there was, uncertainty, doubt, but, behind it all, a kind of semi-drunken exhilaration, so, into it:

'Gentlemen, many of you will remember personally the subject of this toast; for them, no description is necessary. For others, the purpose of this speech is simply, with the knowledge of your committee, to recall a single incident in his life. One day in 1929, this speaker was sent out to the basins to await the inevitable. He did not relish the prospect. He was to play for his house in a soccer match that afternoon and, as some of you will recall, the disciplinary tattoo made football impossible. He therefore, in cowardly but, surely, wise fashion, hid behind the coats hanging in the lobby by the basins. After a few minutes, the door of the upper third opened, and out came a frail, timid, twelve-year-old named Woodcock. It was clearly his first time at the basins and he shifted uneasily on his feet, obviously wishing he could fade into the wall. Presently the old, familiar, asthmatic wheezing could be heard, and the glass in the door to the headmaster's house shook in its frame as he slammed it shut.'

(At this juncture Percivall shifted in his seat, realizing what was coming.)

'He saw Woodcock and said, "What are you doing here?"

' "Mr Pearce sent me out, Sir."

' "What for?"

' "Talking, Sir."

' "Then we shall have to teach you not to talk, shan't we, Woodcock?"

'No reply.

'Then, loudly, "Eh, Woodcock?"

' "Yes, Sir."

' "Get down, Woodcock."

'The boy got down; the headmaster whisked up his coat tails, gave the cane a few preliminary swishes and brought it down. As he did so, Woodcock stood up and the cane hit him across the back of the legs.

' "That doesn't count, Woodcock; get down again."

'He got down; again it swished down and, this time, landed squarely across the ass.'

(Now the atmosphere was not good. He wished he had not embarked on it all; but too late, now, to pack it in.)

'Another stroke across the behind.' (Starting to hurry now; uneasy.)

'As the third stroke came down the wisp of a boy straightened up again, took it across the back of the legs and fell over. He lay on the ground weeping.

'"Stand up. I've told you once already, Woodcock, that doesn't count. Get down again."

'He got down. The third "counting" stroke landed and he fell on his face, sobbing. Percivall turned him over, gently enough, with his foot. "Get up, Woodcock, you fool."

'The headmaster looked down on him for a moment and strode off into the fifth form.

'That, gentlemen, is an accurate, eye-witness account of a happening which until now neither of the people concerned realized was seen by anyone else. This cowardly witness was unseen and, after the custom, unseen meant unpunished; he played for the house that afternoon.

'That may remind you, gentlemen, of the headmaster whose toast is now proposed: Charles W. Percivall.'

The toast was drunk in a mutter, almost silently. Then there was some applause, a little of it strident, but some sad shaking of heads. Mr Percivall did not reply to it, but he left hastily and, so far as can be ascertained, never returned. One man said 'Oh, Christ; but at least he knows now what we thought.'

It is best to think there is no pleasure in revenge, but that, unhappily, is not quite true. In any event, at this point in the narrative that was still a thirty-year distant dream; for the time being, only the wounds were reality. Once in schooldays it approached a flare-up. After a caning – four – he turned to walk to his desk – where the victims used to lean up on their elbows to ease the pain – and, not very clear in his state of semi-shock, collided with the headmaster. Once more they looked into one another's eyes; his fist closed; there was, by now, little difference in their heights. It could not have lasted as long as it felt. 'I beg your pardon, Sir.' Percivall can now be regarded as out of the system, almost unnecessary to introduce again into this story, but therapeutic to have done so.

The number two was 'Pete' Ballard, MA Cantab, a burly, quiet man who taught Latin, which he had obviously learnt with a delight which had evaporated in face of many years of the indifference – even scorn – of generations of adolescents. Still, though, once in a while, he would recapture it, describing the Appian Way, the Praetorian Guard, or the creation of the army by Augustus; then, just as he warmed to his theme, some fool would snigger and he went back into his shell for weeks. He was a keen cricketer, a well coached batsman, who, if tactfully tempted, would talk about it. He maintained discipline in form by bringing his knuckles down on the top of an offender's head: it was terrifyingly painful. It was a help to be in his house, for which he felt an immense, though largely painfully concealed, affection and loyalty. Sometimes he would try desperately to show a boy how he could most effectively do his best.

Then there were the Pearces: 'Boney' and 'the Major'. Boney (W.G.) was young and raw, BA London; not very good nor self-confident but eager to build himself higher in the esteem of the boys than he could ever be among his contemporaries. He turned out at cricket and football but never contrived to talk himself into any peak of ability in the eyes of those merciless boys. He was intensely fond of his fairly pretty and highly protective wife. The Major owed his job to late – very late – wartime recruitment from outside education: he took scripture, oozily but with little conviction. He knew how bad he was. Heaven knows what he can have been or in what part of the Army, for he seemed to have no mental merits nor any hint of military character. He lived in a most attractive house where he looked after the garden with immense care.

Wilson: now, there the school stepped into post-war modernity. He was a graduate of Oxford and had played for the University – though he did not win a Blue – at rugby football before the war. He bore most horrifying red blisters around his hairless eyelids as the result of wartime mustard gas attack. He had been a captain, but unlike some he never boasted about, nor cared even to discuss, the war or his part in it. On a mean allocation of periods – or so it seemed to the pupils – he taught history and English with some zest. He was responsible for sport, for which his enthusiasm was such that he could persuade even fat, reluctant boys like Arlott to complete the cross-country course. He had a cheerful Scottish wife, a large rambling house and, which filled the entire school with admiration, a huge Vauxhall tourer which he drove about the town capably and at the highest speed compatible with his standing: a lift back to school in his car was an honour. He was the loved master. Meeting him many years later, when he held a quite ordinary administrative position in the BBC, was to find him by no means prosperous. He no longer seemed godlike, indeed, a little tragic, but he was still a truly kindly, likeable man.

The science master was named Smith – no more than inter-BSc – a slightly comic figure with a large red nose, knobbly knees and no great mastery of his subject; but he compensated – almost – for these shortcomings by the impressive christian name of Thurley, and a quite beautiful wife. Indeed, she was probably the most devastatingly lovely young woman in the town, and was generally credited by lascivious schoolboys with being the cause of Thurley's general air of exhaustion.

Miss Hannah, the French mistress, was another wartime recruit. A tiny, bitter, bent Eurasian with a hooked nose and dusty clothes, she belonged to some minority religious sect, on behalf of which she extorted a levy from several generations of schoolboys who lived in awe of her. She was a tyrant, and mean with it. Her favourite weapon, against a boy whose only offence was not knowing something, was 'Wait till I see your father, I'll tell him about you, you idle boy.' She once sent an entire form to the basins for the cane because, asked in turn, not one of them knew the fact – which she had never taught them – that, in a certain context, *en* meant 'of it'. Even Percivall could not bring himself to cane for that. She hated boys, more particularly the healthy ones, and treated them all spitefully. Yet, even those who disliked her most will – must – admit that she was the most superb teacher of French, instilling it by none of the more generally recognized teaching methods, but communicating it in unforgettable fashion.

The first violent shock of grammar school life was administered on the second day by Mr Garrett, who taught singing on Saturday mornings. He looked like a musical comedy Frenchman: tall, with bushy white hair and spiky moustache, a butterfly collar and generous white silk tie. On this particular morning he stood on the platform during prayers, seeming to listen intently to the hymn-singing – it was 'Onward Christian Soldiers', a reassuringly familiar noise.

At the end of prayers he took over the young rabble of the lower third in the main hall which doubled as that form's classroom. 'Let us go on with that hymn,' he said in his – affected? – French accent. He struck chords on the piano: the form sang. He looked surprised. 'Go on singing; don't stop, sing loudly.' Everybody did that while he walked softly along behind each row of standing boys. Eventually he came up behind Arlott, paused for a moment and then, in a tone of horror, said, 'It's you! What is your name?'

In surprise and fear, 'Arlott, Sir.'

'Arlott, go away. Never come near my singing class again,' and dropping to a tone of contempt, 'Go to handwriting.'

That, the boy soon discovered, was the writing class, held high upstairs in the second form and presided over by a bored master, generally content, unless pandemonium broke out, to read a novel or mark papers. There he found all the other out-of-tune scholars, grimly scribbling away, as most of them were doomed to do for the first two Saturday periods for the rest of their schooldays. The alternative was to join the cadet force, run by Major Pearce, drilled by an understandably sad sergeant from the local drill hall and 'commanded' by an imposingly uniformed Mr Percivall. Preferable to the other two possibilities, the writing class was not bad and certainly did his handwriting good.

Between them, for all their shortcomings in schoolboys' eyes, the teachers made his education interesting. English, history, French, Latin, geography were all right; science and, for an obvious reason, maths, except arithmetic, learnt earlier, were the blind spots.

A genuine influence was George Willis, a jeweller in the market-place, several times mayor of Basingstoke and its leading historian. He was, too, a senior trustee of the Aldworth Scholarship; he saw each holder, and went through his report with him, at the end of every term. A kindly man and an idealist, he would be pleased with the subjects at the top of the list, scripture, English, history, geography, Latin, French, and generous in his congratulations. Then, though, the standard slipped and, when he reached 'behaviour', saw fifteen hours' detention and read 'noisy' or 'unruly' or 'tries to be funny', he seemed so hurt that the boy was filled with remorse, resolved each time to do better, but never did.

Friends made it all. John Carter was quiet, thoughtful and opening partner at cricket for form, house, all too briefly school, and, later, club. He and Arlott shared an education in reading (far outside the school syllabus) and, to an amazing extent within a meagre budget, travel (within England, of course) and the theatre. Jack Donovan shared a desk in form, and was a devout Catholic, wise beyond his years, relaxed, a huge but superb athlete with a pretty wit and an unfailing sense of proportion: that friendship has endured without effort and with humour on both sides. Ron Prickett was Arlott's partner in soccer, especially soccer theory, mischief, formulation of obscene stories and rhymes, and in improvised – 'anything for a game' – cricket.

Games were desperately important. Apart from running – bulk militated against that – they were all a source of delight. Fives was punishing but absorbing; a game to get the teeth into. Cricket was the finest of all and, after trying everything – wicketkeeping, fast bowling, wrist-spin – he learnt what he might do. It was occasional finger-spin but, above all, defensive batting: going in first and staying there. It worked well at form and house level; 1930 would be the summer in the school team.

First of all, though, came the football season of 1929–30. It was now accepted that the boy, having shed much of his puppy fat, could play at full-back, where his long kicking and willingness to charge and tackle were useful. He, however, had other ideas. In 1926–27, George Camsell, of Middlesbrough, had broken the League goal-scoring record with 59 goals and, in solemn consultation with Ron Prickett, his fellow theorist, it was decided that Camsell ought to be studied. Late in the season Middlesbrough came to play an evening match against Reading. It was a seventeen-mile cycle ride but a serious duty for the students. Camsell proved a personable, well built, lithe and lively redhead. The secret of his goal-scoring was clear even to those two boys. Indeed, it was so obvious that soon every League centre-forward was doing it, and in the following season 'Dixie' Dean broke the record with 61 goals (which gave rise to the Donovan dog – perhaps puppy – Latin tag 'Dixit Dean multos goalscorit') and, as a result, soon all the clubs – led by Arsenal with Roberts – had a stopper centre-half to prevent it. The centre-forward simply lay well upfield, just on-side between the two backs – the centre-half played upfield in those days – and someone for Middlesbrough, usually Jackie Carr, would angle the ball between them; Camsell ran on to it like a stag and drove it past the goalkeeper. Indeed, Jackie Carr used to strike the through-ball and then squat on his haunches while Camsell scored and trotted back with the ball under his arm.

It was not yet, though, apparent at school level in Hampshire. Hence it would be introduced. Pete Ballard's house had Jack Donovan, a skilful footballer capable of laying on the pass, and the quite unstaglike Arlott happy to lumber after it through the backs and, sometimes, belt it past the exposed goalkeeper. During the seasons of 1927–28 and 1928–29, it worked not only at house but at school level – if the ball could be brought to Donovan, as usually it could.

That, however, was not simple against Peter Symonds School of Winchester, much larger than Queen Mary's and, it may be surmised, possessed of a coach who instructed its players in tactics. In addition, by 1929–30, Jack Donovan had departed for the Great Western Railway where he was to make for himself a considerable career. So the good through-ball never came and, by the middle of the second half, Peter Symonds led by seven goals to nil, and all the wretched Arlott could do was chase futile long punts which went through to the bored goalkeeper, who amused himself by bouncing the ball round the frustrated mock-Camsell, dodging his bull-like lunges until he cleared the ball downfield. This he did successfully, even contemptuously, until he made the stupid mistake of walking straight into the despairing gallop. The result looked spectacular: the goalkeeper stood on his ear while his erstwhile dupe walked the ball into goal. The refereeing master disallowed the 'goal' and gave a free kick for a foul. There was no further chance for any Queen Mary's forward. The headmaster happened to be watching and, next morning, sent for Arlott and told him that, because of his brutal behaviour towards the goalkeeper, he should never play for the school again.

Cold disappointment was followed by hot anger; he would leave the school. Mum and Dad were wise, counselling, 'Put up with it until you get your school certificate, then you can tell him anything you want.' That would not do; they clearly recognized the depth of his feeling, and gave in when it was apparent that he would not, physically, walk back to the school.

He was a fool, of course. He took the Cambridge 'externally' and, fool again, estimating that he had done enough to pass the geography examination in the first hour (he was relying on arithmetic and geography to take him through the maths and science group) he walked out to watch Reading's Cup tie. Of course, he was failed in geography, not for lack of knowledge, but for what had to be seen as a bad-mannered gesture. Neither would he take it again. Had he done so, a Cambridge senior school certificate might have taken him far further up the employment scale; perhaps to a civil service job; who can guess? He might have 'succeeded', and never have lived the happy life he eventually enjoyed; which is a foolish coward's justification for his folly.

Schooldays were ingloriously, if relievedly, over; Mum and Dad must have been desperately hurt, but they were philosophical about it, and kind. They talked about many subjects in the evenings and, for the first time – when he was not playing cricket or otherwise engaged – he began to know them as adults. Dad, kindly, thoughtful, made available his bookcase full of many in the Nelson's Classics series, the Penguins of the time. They gave the boy his first, and quite extensive, knowledge of Dickens, Scott, Ainsworth, Bulwer-Lytton, Wilkie Collins, Charles Kingsley and – often pleasurable relief – Captain Marryat. Dad talked, too, of his service days in India and Mesopotamia; airing his wonderings about life there and, above all, the odd dichotomy between Army life and that background.

Mum had added politics to her many household interests. After joining the local women's Liberal association, she had become first a delegate to the national conference and then the local election agent. In that capacity she was the first agent to have a Liberal elected for Basingstoke, a certain Lieutenant-Commander Fletcher. When it was reported that he had 'crossed the house' and joined the Labour party, she sat long silent at breakfast before concluding, 'Well, we shall never get another Liberal in for Basingstoke now.' So far her prophecy has proved correct. There were other game attempts, notably on behalf of John Foot. Lloyd George came down to speak for him; Mum went up to meet the great man at Basingstoke station, and took the boy. Mum curtsied and introduced 'My son'. Lloyd George put out his hand, but the boy was at first frightened to take it for fear that touching the most vibrant human being he had ever encountered would give him an electric shock. Lloyd George came back to the cemetery lodge; spread Mum's home-made jam on her home-made bread; drank tea, talked amiably and then walked up to the committee rooms, where Mum mightily impressed her offspring by directing the former Prime Minister on his speaking schedule.

She was always a clear-minded woman with a quick sense of humour. Sallying out from domesticity gave her fresh confidence and an altogether greater range of interest. Soon the entire family was reading more widely. Crucially, too, Dad could not resist the impact of 'the wireless'. He built, first, crystal sets, and the earliest radio sound – for that family, of a banjo band – seemed briefly a miracle. Then, though, came valve sets, conjured out of strange materials into absolutely new shapes and concepts. It was all strangely wonderful but, for the boy, so much else was happening, and at such speed, that it was impossible for him to judge what was really important.

Chapter 4

THE ADOLESCENT

The school years were not, thank God, all school; nor adolescence
all pimples, though both were significant ingredients of life.
Undoubtedly, the two major influences on his adolescence were
books and cricket. To an insatiable reader the boon of the school
was the library, a collection only to be described as catholic, and
none the worse for that. It yielded such diverse influences – and, if
only for days or hours, they were influences – as 'Sapper', Percy F.
Westerman, John Buchan, Jeffery Farnol, 'Saki', Richard Jefferies,
Robert Graves, John Masefield, Joseph Conrad, which sounds like
the progression it was. At that time there were two complete blind
spots – Richard Aldington and Thomas Hardy. Happily, they came
later – Hardy much later – when the mind could assimilate them
properly. Verse was an early appetite, but not poetry, which also
came late, when it could dawn. John Carter was the fellow devotee;
he introduced a latish supper as a substantial and civilized part of
life for the pair of them. Otherwise they sat reading for hours of the
evening in silence.

One of the happiest discoveries was the marriage between reading and cricket. That happened in the winter of 1924, sparked by a
dog-eared, grimy, jettisoned 1922 edition of *Wisden*, that yellow
'Almanack' once described in the press as 'The primrose-hued har-
binger of Spring'. That copy – a revelation to the tiro – became the
foundation of what is now a complete set of the original editions. It
led directly to the writings of Neville Cardus with no remote idea
that he might ever become a friend except through the pages of his
books.

The first 'important' cricket event of his life came in 1926. The
family holiday was contrived by dint of swapping houses with

Uncle Frank. He stayed in the lodge (now the new lodge in Worting Road, since Dad took over from Old John as superintendent registrar). Meanwhile, the family took his flat in Warwick Way, between Victoria station and – significantly for the boy's purpose – the Oval. It was significant because the day before the holiday was to end was the first day of the Fifth Test between England and Australia. It was, too, an historically important match: the Ashes, which Australia had held since 1920–21, depended on it. The four preceding Tests had all been drawn and this one was to be played to a finish. With all the single-minded persistence of a twelve-year-old, he began well in advance to pester his parents to let him go to it. It was not certain that he would manage that – largely because the press put the idea in jeopardy by forecasting huge crowds, with gates closed long before the start, and so on. Fortunately he had struck early and gained tacit approval before that alarm was raised, but it was a close-run thing.

Eventually he set off at eight o'clock in the morning, armed with sandwiches, money to cover admission, and other reasonable needs, but under strict instructions not to persist but to come straight back if the crowds proved heavy, and to beware of men – like lemonade sellers – who would cheat boys if they could. As the tram rumbled down Vauxhall Bridge Road, excitement moved inside him. Then he was there. There was a queue, slow-moving, but moving: he joined it, passed into the ground, resisting the temptation to cheer, collected an economical glass of water and was lucky enough to find a seat in the front row barely inside the boundary on the Harleyford Road side; thinking that if many more people came in, they would sit in front on the grass and it would be possible to see over them.

A number of the players came out for a net. The man next to him said he would keep his place: the nets were tempting, but the fear of losing that seat spoilt their allure. So, back, almost chewing the scorecard in the agony of waiting. The first sign of a real game was the appearance of the two captains, Herbie Collins and young Percy Chapman, who had taken over from Arthur Carr, and he genuinely did look as splendid as the newspapers said. There was no public address system then but the new captain signalled unmistakably that he had won the toss, and England would bat. It is difficult to describe an experience looked forward to with something near superstition; as if something were bound to go wrong, so that the game could not actually happen. There, though, were the Australians, Collins first, but attention on the mighty Gregory as he strolled to his mark, and then Hobbs and Sutcliffe came out: it was going to happen.

Gregory began; and as he started his run, all the terror stories of 1921 rushed back into the mind. Hobbs, though, seemed to have no great trouble; he was not hurried. Of course, Gregory must have lost something of his earlier pace: he was now thirty-one; in fact, this was his birthday. All such were known facts; although he had never set eyes on them before, these men were not strangers to the boy. From reading the often clumsy sporting press of the time, he had a full collection of clichés about every one of them, a language only slowly diluted by more perceptive writing. Indeed at that very time Neville Cardus was initially urging the language of sports writing into literacy, a process which is still not complete. Moreover, although 'the wireless' was making its way into every household, commentary had not been thought of; television, of course, was non-existent. Hence, though the young of today may find it hard to believe, for a boy in a provincial town the newspapers were virtually the only source of sporting news and ideas, and most households took only a single newspaper.

At the other end, the second Australian bowler was Clarrie Grimmett, neat, almost furtive, as he buzzed down his low-arced leg-breaks and googlies; though they did not, at that juncture, seem to worry anyone. All at once the new, the impossible spectacle, was familiar, understood, right. Yet much – an encyclopaedia – was still to be understood. This man, Hobbs, the great one, he played in such ordinary fashion: there was nothing exciting like Mr Crate or Mr Chesterfield hitting their huge sixes on May's Bounty at Basingstoke. Only when one looked at Sutcliffe, painstakingly precise, was it possible to understand that Hobbs was doing it all with the untroubled, easy air of a man pottering in his garden. Unquestionably, Sutcliffe was a great batsman, fine in temperament and technique; but this unremarkable man at the other end was all but disappointing in making it all so simple; he pushed or stroked or flicked the ball away, and had 37 of the 53 in under an hour. All seemed so reassuringly English when, in what seemed an affront to the natural order of things, the cheerful-looking Mailey bowled a full toss, which hit Hobbs's stumps – and dared to laugh. Sacrilege? – no, Hobbs laughed too, and gave a wave as he turned away. Mailey went on spinning elatedly and when Woolley and Hendren – already romantic figures – went all too soon, consolation for the partisan young came first from the staunch solidity of Sutcliffe and then the in-character, youthful aggression of Chapman.

This was English cricket history: after the young Chapman came that sage elder of the game, Wilfred Rhodes, recalled to the colours two months before his forty-ninth birthday. All went according to character. Chapman was stumped going down the wicket to Mailey. Sutcliffe was impregnable until, hit in the face by one ball, he was bowled by the next, which he did not seem to see; Mailey again. Rhodes soldiered pawkily on, falling on to the back foot to Mailey, and Maurice Tate had a big biff (23 in a few minutes).

All of a sudden the innings was over: England were out for 280. That was not many compared with 475 for 3 at Lord's; and Australia had made 494 at Leeds. 'Ah, good,' said the man along the bench, 'we shall see both sides bowl,' which sounded like treachery. Less so at the sight of Larwood racing in and sending the ball far, far faster than the boy had ever seen anyone do before. Surely enough, he had Bardsley caught at the wicket, sparring; and, after Macartney played on, he ran out Ponsford with a high-speed return and clean bowled Andrews. At the end it was 60 for 4; and, forgetting the instructions to leave early, the boy sat, slightly dazed, for some time before he climbed on to the tram, full of – no doubt exaggerated – descriptions of the day for his parents. There was never any real chance that he might be allowed to see the cricket on Monday . . . Tuesday . . . Wednesday . . . and, after all, it was to be played to a finish. Even as he launched into his *spiel* he knew he was beaten. They just laughed: good-naturedly, but they laughed.

So, for a couple of days he trailed around Basingstoke behind whoever was going out, his mind on that match; anxious to pick up scraps from the stop press of the newspapers of people arriving on the trains from London. In the end all was well. Australia made 302, a lead of 22, but then came the great opening stand of Hobbs (100) and Sutcliffe (161); 172 of them on the Tuesday morning when, following overnight rain, they mastered the varied Australian spinners on a turning pitch. The next highest score was Tate's 33 not out, but they set Australia 415 to win. Larwood and Rhodes, fast and slow, young and old, put them out for 125 and the matter was unexpectedly rapidly settled.

Then came a long wait, eked out, it is true, by doings on May's Bounty where Hampshire, from time to time, sent a strong club and ground team. Far too strong for the club side: it was not serious; much harder stuff was Basingstoke against good club opposition: but not, for boys, important.

A little before this time, a long-standing problem was solved. The old posters used to show the local cricket team as 'Hampshire and North Hants'. He had been puzzled as to why none of them – if it was a composite team – ever appeared in the Northants side, about which he read in the newspapers. Gradually he perceived that that team's home matches were played at Northampton, Kettering, Peterborough and Wellingborough. Until then he had hesitated to ask what might be seen as a silly question. Now, though, he felt bold enough to ask Dad, 'Who are North Hants who play at Northampton?' Informed that it was Northamptonshire, the first of his major cricket mysteries was solved: it has been followed by an unending stream of more and more mysterious non-understandings.

In 1927, holiday was with Grandmother Clarke at Eastbourne, just along the road from the Saffrons ground. Sussex were to play Lancashire, the reigning County Champions and current leaders, with their team full of famous names, on the run-in to the Championship. It was going to be possible to watch every minute of it. Lancashire won the toss and batted. The opening Sussex bowlers were the Rev. F.B.R. Browne and Maurice Tate. Francis Browne was headmaster of St Andrew's School, immediately behind Grandmother's house at Meads; a tall, rangy man who was known as 'Tishy' after a racehorse of the day reputed to cross its legs, because he bowled off the wrong foot – and he did – big inswingers at a lively pace. Tate was at his mighty best; with heavy shoulders, powerful arms and wide hips. His big feet, like Tishy's legs, were cherished material for that great cartoonist, Tom Webster, but they had been battered during his prodigious labours of the 1924–25 tour in Australia.

Lancashire won the toss and batted; theirs was a genuinely heavyweight order, leading with Hallows, Watson, Ernest Tyldesley and Makepeace, and all-rounders as good as Iddon and Sibbles batting at numbers seven and eight. The Sussex bowlers must have anticipated a hard day; in the event they found it all remarkably easy going. Browne made an initial penetration with the wickets of Hallows (7) and Tyldesley (0) before Watson (22) and Makepeace (28) embarked on the only real stand of the innings. Once Arthur Gilligan, not so fast as he had been prior to his heart damage, but still a useful seam bowler, had Watson taken at slip by Bowley – who made the catch look ridiculously simple – resistance consisted almost solely of Harry Makepeace. He was a redoubtable double-international, who played in four Tests against Australia and, in 1920–21, scored a century (117) at Melbourne, the highest score in a losing side; while at soccer, three of his four caps were against Scotland in Scotland, tough assignments but he thrived on the hard way. Short and hollow-cheeked, he was quick and sound in footwork and eventually a shrewd county coach; he had a dry humour and was the subject of some pure Lancashire stories by Neville Cardus. Now he held out for two hours until Bowley picked him up. Bowley, too, collected a couple of wickets with his high-tossed leg-breaks, while Tate took three in the final mopping-up.

McDonald, opening the Lancashire bowling, lived up to all the adjectives: lean, dark, sprinting light-footed in, and bowling, with an immense flick of the wrist, at high-bouncing pace; he blasted out Ted Bowley. Sussex were doing little better than Lancashire until Holdsworth (159) and Arthur Gilligan (103) came together on the second day and put on 188 for the eighth wicket; only three others made double figures in the Sussex total of 371.

When Lancashire batted again, Tate's bowling was a revelation, his pace off the pitch terrific, as he took five of the first six wickets. His bowling was watched – gratefully at not being shooed away – from the edge of the sightscreen. His late swing and occasional movement off the pitch made the ball, from his arm, disappear behind the umpire and then reappear: such a ball bowled Malcolm Taylor (many years later, when with Dorset, such delightful company). When Charlie Hallows, the mainstay of the Lancashire batting all season, played a startled stroke at Tate, the ball leapt at him and bounced back off the bat for a simple caught-and-bowled. Tate's match figures were 9 for 49; Browne's 8 for 50; and Sussex won all too easily by an innings and 196, a result which appeared to have cost Lancashire the Championship. Nevertheless, afterwards, when the crowd gathered in front of the pavilion, Leonard Green, who must have been an extremely disappointed man, made a most gracious and generous speech congratulating Sussex.

For that, perhaps, Lancashire deserved not to lose the Championship. Nottinghamshire needed only to avoid defeat in their last match – against Glamorgan who had not won a game all season – to take the title. Yet Bates (136) and Bell (57) set a Glamorgan first-wicket record stand of 158; Mercer (match figures 7 for 82) and Ryan (9 for 95) bowled them out for 233 and 61 and Glamorgan achieved the most amazing result of the season to win by an innings and 81.

The third 'big' match – cherished at the rate of one a year – he was able to see was between Hampshire and the West Indies of 1928; again, completely different from those before.

Basingstoke to Southampton and back on three days and a shoe-string consisted of one lift in a neighbour's car, one rail excursion and a road coach. On the first morning, the neighbour was nearly late – if he had been, it would have created a vast gap in experience. Constantine began the West Indian bowling – unforgettably. No doubt the other opener, Griffith, was fast – that is in the record books – but Constantine was the personification of fast bowling. He bowled the first of the Hampshire heroes, George Brown, convulsively, for nought; the doughty Alec Kennedy for 12; and, as all Hampshire found hard to believe, beat the mighty Philip Mead for sheer pace to find him lbw. Ronny Aird was caught, pushing out, and Constantine had taken 4 for 24. (Stories were heard later of some acid leg-pulling between some of the Hampshire giants.) By midday, when Griffith bowled Hosie, Hampshire were 88 for 5; and the Hon. Lionel Tennyson, grandson of the Laureate, who became the third Baron later that year, joined the thoughtful, patient Jack Newman. 'Lordship', as the players were to call him, was now rising thirty-nine, well past his Test-playing days, generously addicted to the fleshpots, not particularly fit, and carrying an unathletic amount of weight. He lumbered cheerfully out to the wicket, stern jutting, cap-peak pointing to the sky. The two batted for the rest of the day.

As always, Tennyson drove mightily, hooked – sometimes varying that stroke with one reminiscent of a man swatting a fly, one of which flew for six to long leg – pulled usefully, occasionally, but not often, edged, blocked when he had to, and generally went on his probably surprised but cheerfully dominating way. Jack Newman was his usual patient, sound and professional self and they batted steadily.

Now there was opportunity, too, to enjoy the utter glory of Constantine's fielding, surely the finest in the history of the game. Deep, he would run round the boundary square to the line of a fast-moving ground-stroke and, as he ran over it, bend, sweep it up between his feet and return it all in a single flowing movement. Close in, he took a low, unreasonably sharp slip catch off a faster ball from Challenor to put out Newman. Once, when he was bowling, Philip Mead played back defensively: Constantine hurled himself down the pitch, and all but caught the ball as it dropped in the crease; Mead's jaw fell open. The West Indian was simply so fleet, sure-handed, ambidextrous, quick in reaction, over ground and in every action. He had the perfect build, not too tall, long-armed, incredibly smooth in movement; cricket was not only in his needle-sharp brain, but also in his every instinct. There can, surely, never be another quite like him. He also delighted by a unique cricketing parlour trick: when someone played a ball from him into the field within reasonable range of his crease, he would turn and walk back towards his mark; the fieldsman would throw it at his back and he would catch it, apparently blind, between his shoulder blades.

The Hampshire men scored another 87 next morning: a stand of 311. Lionel Tennyson had made the highest first-class score of his career: 217 at over 50 an hour, with a six and 27 fours. Jack Newman made 118 before the tail curled up at 429.

Still the game and its time were less than half-done, but one of those people who always knows about these matters said Alec Kennedy had told him the pitch was a real 'belter' and it would all end in another draw, and so it proved. Yet it was most certainly not without entertainment.

The perky little Roach made a lively start to the West Indian innings, hitting all round the field until he was out to what the man who knew everything told us was Kennedy's 'cut-away' ball. In yet another 'highest' in the match, Martin went on in subsequent partnerships with Hoad and Browne to make the largest individual West Indian score of the tour. Challenor, something of a father figure of West Indian batting, made nought; while Constantine, though bright, was also brief. The Hampshire spinners, Newman and Boyes, senior and junior, right-arm and left (four and five wickets respectively), worked their way quite slowly through the main batting but took the last five for 29 after lunch on Friday to give Hampshire a lead of 26. So there was time to watch Constantine again, and, although there was virtually nothing to play for, he still bowled wholeheartedly fast and excitingly. He had George Brown and Ronny Aird again, but Lionel Tennyson came to bang a few heartily extrovert runs before the day ran out.

That match was the last of the three annual cricket events that were to prove, in many ways, formative. Not merely the course of the play, but the players made a deep impression. Jack Hobbs and Maurice Tate were to become the subjects of nostalgic biographies; Arthur Mailey, Harold Larwood, Harry Makepeace, Ted Bowley, George Brown, Philip Mead, Jack Newman and Learie Constantine all became cherished and relished friends.

At the time, though, there was much to be done; starting work, for instance, which demanded fresh and serious thought. Dad solved the initial problem of conditioning with a job of office boy to George Paget, the Basingstoke Town Planning Officer. It was not truly work, but the gentlest possible – too gentle? – introduction to it. In a single room at the top of the stairs on the first floor of Goldings – a roomy 'gentleman's residence' lately acquired as the headquarters of Basingstoke Borough Council – was the Town Planning Office. There was space, but little to spare, for the TPO and an office boy who would do the typing as best he could. The typing was little enough, and could easily have been done by one of the girls in the other offices. The wages were ten shillings (50p) a week, and it must be suspected that George Paget wanted an office boy only to answer the phone in his absence, for the sake of the company, and the service – fetching his coffee from downstairs and his cigarettes from the shop down London Road. He chain-smoked, without ever removing the cylinder from his lips, a most economical and slightly sinister brand called 'Rhodesian'; they came in boxes of fifty which cost 1s 10½d (9p) a box. For his parlour trick, though he did not regard it as one, when the ash fell while he was colouring one of his planned 'areas', he would, with a single sideways puff, blow it clear before it could fall on the wet paint. Wispily grey-haired, with a moustache dyed ginger by nicotine, nowadays he would be, thoughtfully, a serious non-smoker.

On an altogether more important level, he was one of the early town planning enthusiasts and students; somehow, simultaneously, an idealist and a pragmatist. Never a wordy man, he was sometimes persuaded by his office boy's interested burblings to expand on that then infant study of planning. 'Oh, Mr Paget, how wonderful to think that all this land is going to be preserved and kept for the best possible purpose.'

He blew the ash off his cigarette, gave a friendly sideways look and, in his slight Yorkshire accent, said drily, 'Yes, until some rogue with enough money wants to change it.'

He came from Sheffield; had played good amateur soccer there and talked interestingly about that game, as well as many other matters. In the course of less than six months, he imparted some well received wisdom, much good humour and something towards maturity. Then, though, came the really serious matter of

earning a living. The job of 'diet clerk' at Park Prewett, the local
mental hospital, was advertised in the *Hants and Berks Gazette*. It
carried a salary of £1 a week, with tiny but positive increments:
dizzy financial heights. Application; interview with dry mouth;
testimonials required; job offered and most gratefully, even
proudly, accepted. Hard, real life had begun; Mum and Dad were
delighted. George Paget smiled congratulations, sheepishly
pushed a crumpled £1 note into the boy's hand, and turned
abruptly away from his gratitude.

There followed almost four years of partly muddled, morbidly
fascinating, desperately worrying hard work in a vast establishment where life existed on many different levels. These were the
1930s, and unemployment was not only a serious economic threat;
for a young man, in Basingstoke, 'the sack' carried a stigma. Thus,
employers used the threat unscrupulously. The diet clerk's was a
monotonous, but demanding, job. It involved calculating, and hurrying out to the provision stores, the baker, the butcher, the
amounts of each item of food needed each day by each ward and
department. A jungle of mental arithmetic: 42 female patients at 5
oz of meat a head; 54 male patients at 6½ oz each; tea by the peri-
odic quarter ounce, and no time to check. Working flat out, it
meant nearly three hours of figures a morning – including Saturday – and dire consequences for an error. Once he got a meat issue
wrong, working on a wrong basic figure – no one checked – and
was 'warned for dismissal' if there should ever be another, similar
error. For that reason he went into the office on every public holiday and even on the first day of his annual holiday, to check with
stores manager, baker and butcher before the issues went out. The
other eight men in the hierarchy, up to the eminence of 'Clerk and
Steward', were all on superannuation – which meant they were
less likely to be sacked – but then they did not have to work out
some thousand calculations a morning. That prospect of security
in such insecure times was tantalizing: security, yes; to stay in that
world of petty office jealousies, no; and yet . . .

Of course it was not all diet sheets. Some afternoon hours working for the doctors were absorbing, and often amusing. They were
mostly Irishmen, qualified but without the capital to buy into a

practice. They lived in the hospital, in fair physical comfort; were given to whisky, hockey, casual sex with members of the nursing staff, and could not wait for their annual escape to some long-planned holiday. They were cheerful, generous and often highly informative, feeding the young man's morbid curiosity and answering his questions about mental illness – and other exciting medical matters.

In this time of unemployment in the North, there was an influx of recruits, Yorkshiremen especially, from the pits and the mills into mental nursing. They studied, often doggedly against natural inclination, and many of them made good careers. Their other capabilities were reflected in music – they raised the standard of brass and orchestral playing in the hospital far higher than ever before – and in sport. They made the hospital football team much stronger, much tougher, and it was both exciting and salutary to play with them; but they particularly lifted the standard of the cricket.

Charlie Tunstall as an opening batsman was little below county standard. Austin Fretwell as a genuinely fast bowler, slim but with a magnificently flowing action; the Gledhill brothers as all-rounders; and the Welshman, Tom Beddoe, as wicketkeeper, were all well above local club standard. Their hospital duties meant that not all the better players were available on every match day and it was an education, as well as a pleasure, to play in the hospital eleven with them. Their disciplinary standards were high, but they did a novice's cricket immense service and imparted some lessons which lasted a lifetime of play.

Another ingredient of that dawning education was the teaching of the egregious Ernie Eldridge, the patient whose duty was the cleaning of the male nurses' mess room and, more important, the billiard-room. Rabelaisian in rage and sometimes bubbling to the extreme brink of violence in his unpredictable, and usually unnecessary, anger, he was a quite remarkably fine snooker player: the male nurses delighted to play with him. Once or twice a week he used to rattle up a hundred break, but when it ended short of clearing the table, he would erupt into a storm of oaths. Yet he could be a most patient teacher if he was not playing himself, though he never managed to teach the quite remarkable degree of spin which used to send his cue ball screwing in such exaggerated curves or changes of direction. He would have given any of the professionals of today a good, if sometimes explosive, game.

In other directions, too, the lad was growing up, and progressing from the fumbling into the romantic phase of courtship. Peggy Nelson was a quite tiny, blue-eyed, blonde Ulster girl. She wore, so far as could be ascertained, on her country expeditions at least, two pairs of extremely tight knickers. Her address was, unforgettably, Roses' Lane Ends, Co. Wicklow: as romantic as the brief and utterly innocent relationship between the two. Much of it consisted of walking, hand in hand, along the narrow, grassy lanes in the neighbourhood of the hospital; semi-inarticulate protestation, not simply of affection, but of adoration; the first, fine, careful rapture. There was not, though, much room for that kind of idealism in a boarding establishment for between two and three hundred healthy – indeed, lusty – and mainly single young men and women, all being instructed and working in medicine. Knowledge soon dawned, and Park Prewett was quite capable of dealing with it.

Away from that establishment was a separate existence, based on the school friendships with Ron Prickett and, particularly, with John Carter, who was now spending a protracted and envied, though alarmingly solitary, period in the little attic which was the sixth form of Queen Mary's, working for an external London BA degree.

The two still shared their long, heavy reading and supper evenings, and opened the innings for Old St Michael's cricket team. In the football season, Ron Prickett played outside in a left-wing partnership with J.A. which, at times, became so complex in its tactics that, while it sometimes baffled opponents, all too often proved self-defeating.

The peak of all this was the annual holiday with John, which consisted of taking poky bed-and-breakfast rooms in Russell Square boarding houses and, from them, sallying out every morning to a day's cricket selected over breakfast with the guidance of the morning papers. That covered matches not only at Lord's and the

Oval but also, in different years, at Southend, Leyton, Tunbridge Wells, Canterbury and Hove. Sometimes the journeys involved hurrying back – twice, even, sacrificing the last few minutes of cricket – for the second half of the day's programme: a visit to the theatre and supper. It was the time of the Aldwych farces, of Austin Melford, Sidney Howard, Jack Buchanan, Bobby Howes. A seat up in 'the gods' usually cost sixpence, at most a shilling; and, after a half-pint of ale in a pub, a meal (teetotal) at Lyons was no more than half-a-crown. Regarded by parents with slight disapproval, this was the life of Riley, providing memories to be talked over, digested, and re-digested, through the winter.

One of those cricket days in particular gave rise to many hours of deep and puzzled discussion. On Friday 5 August 1932, the break-fast-table debate decided – quite wrongly as it turned out – that there could be a good finish to the match between Essex and Nottinghamshire at Leyton. The timetables indicated that it would be a long journey, allowing less than the usual lingering over the meal. It was long indeed, revealing impressively, as mile after mile of bricks and mortar was unrolled, the vast extent of 'greater' London. Eventually the very urban, though hardly urbane, ground was reached, with its grey ammunition boxes for seating and an ice-cream man's monotonous refrain, 'OosezaniceiceWallses?'

Notts had led on the first innings by 94 (290 to 196) and had scored 53 for no wicket overnight. In the morning they lost Walter Keeton and Charlie Harris fairly soon, but that quiet man Willis Walker made his way steadily through the morning, latterly with the luckless 'young George' Gunn. Arthur Carr, the Nottingham-shire captain, was nothing if not positive. He told his batsmen that, in the hope of winning, he proposed to declare at lunchtime, and he did precisely that, even though Walker was 95 not out.

So, on a straightforward wicket, Essex wanted 298 in four hours to win. Their batting was weakened by the injury to Jack O'Connor but, though Notts, with two fast bowlers and one of brisk pace in the fashion of those days, bowled 75 overs in that time, Essex never shaped at the objective.

Interesting, though – or even more than that – was the Notts bowling. They began with Harold Larwood bowling to his normal right-arm fast field, and Voce – fast, left-arm over – to his usual leg-side setting. They had bowled two overs apiece when Arthur Carr set an intensive leg trap. Bafflement of eighteen-year-olds.

'Voce can't bowl two consecutive overs.'

'Is Larwood going to bowl off-spinners?'

'No, the wicketkeeper is standing back.'

Then, in an awe still clearly recalled until today: 'He's going to bowl at his head.'

Sure enough, Larwood bowled fast and short. There was not enough life in the pitch for the ball to get head-high and none of the batsmen had much difficulty in playing him. Voce, with his normal left-arm inswing, had Dudley Pope and Jack Cutmore caught by the wicketkeeper and Denys Wilcox at mid-on. Essex made a safe 203 for 4 and the game was left drawn, with the two young men still baffled. Such of the press reports as they saw in Basingstoke said nothing about the tactic – if indeed it was one – and there was no further opportunity to study it until the end of the season, when Nottinghamshire were due to play Glamorgan at Cardiff.

With two 'public days' off in store, and by dint – with some trepidation – of persuading the office boy to check the diet sheets, it was possible to bicycle to Reading and catch the milk train into Wales to be there for the Wednesday and Thursday. It was the first time out of England for both the young ones. They were thwarted in their main interest when Notts won the toss and batted (thank heaven for that fail-safe second day) and they went on and on. Eventually, after much patience, it all happened, and even more spectacularly than the young explorers had dared hope.

Nottinghamshire – Walker well, Carr in militant fashion and Shipston excitingly – put together 386. The real excitement, though, came on the second day. Those two likeable, solid technicians, Arnold Dyson and Emrys Davies, founded the Glamorgan innings, facing Larwood and Voce circumspectly, but after they had gone and Maurice Turnbull came in to join Dai Davies, the action rose to a peak. Turnbull, most tragically killed in action late in the Second World War, was good enough to play nine times for England – always harder, they said, for a Glamorgan player to get into the Test side than for those of other counties – as a batsman and fearless short leg. His deficiency lay in batting against flighted spin; his strength, in dealing with pace, for he was a quick, bold hooker and a militant driver. He was a boyhood hero – an unusually gifted all-round sportsman. He played cricket for England, rugby football and hockey for Wales, held the South Wales squash rackets championship, and was one of the finest batsmen and, arguably, the best captain Glamorgan cricket ever had.

In this match, he proceeded to master Larwood and Voce, then in their pacey prime, to a rare extent. His partner, Dai Davies, batted soundly, but Turnbull made 205 in five hours; the ultimate assessment of that innings is that Larwood eventually ceased to drop short, or to bowl at his leg stump.

What the two had watched was, of course, the beginning of the fast leg-stump attack, which, when it was used in Australia during the immediately following 1932–33 season, was called 'bodyline'.

Conversations long afterwards, with Arthur Carr and, more explicitly and logically, with Douglas Jardine, made it clear that the deliberately planned tactic was successful for four fully appreciated reasons: Larwood and Voce were extremely accurate in their high-pace leg-stump attack; Australian wickets at that time were appreciably faster than English, which accounts for the fact that the two looked so ordinary at Leyton and Cardiff; there were no really fast bowlers in Australian domestic cricket who might have allowed their batsmen practice against such pace; and, finally, Don Bradman, against whom the tactic was primarily aimed, was believed to be vulnerable to a fast attack on his leg stump. Nevertheless, and although Australia were beaten, he was top of their batting for the series with 396 runs at 56.57.

Later, it felt like having been present at the making of history which, after a fashion, it was; significantly it was lassooing a boy into the most absorbing and profound of games. He was only too willing to be captured, though it never occurred to him that he would ever be close enough to it to live within its ambit.

In complete contrast to all this was the ordinary club cricket played for Old St Michael's, which had once been the choir team of the local parish church. It was indeed so remote a contrast that it seemed barely to belong to the same game. Yet it was educative in allowing the opportunity to experiment on live victims with all the basic tools of the game: pace, swing, finger-spin, wrist-spin; even, as an interval in laborious struggles in the field, a terrible attempt at wicketkeeping. The nearest approach to success – with some degree of satisfaction – lay briefly in a burst of bowling as fast as possible; later, in off-spinners; but, most of all, in going in and, through a state of almost strokeless resistance – if indeed it was even as positive as resistance – not getting out. It was, though, a most companionable existence. Old St Michael's had no ground of their own – the nearest approach was the meadow behind the 'Rising Sun' pub across the road. Yet playing on a fresh ground each week was to be among old friends – for fixtures were arranged with the same teams every year – and many villages were happy with a home match which saved travelling, and ended near their own pub.

The background to it all was Basingstoke; nothing like the sprawling Basingstoke of today but a friendly, bumbling country town of some 12,000 people, in which almost everyone knew almost everyone else. It is worth recalling that, when the idea of making it a 'New Town' was broached, that wise man, George Willis, having listened to the arguments – often most passionate on both sides – observed that no one could argue from knowledge because never before had there been such an exercise as this pro- posed rapid conversion of a small town into a large one. No one could tell what the outcome would be, he said, but if Basingstoke submitted to being the material for such an experiment, then, experiment or no, it would be irreversible. He was, obviously, cor- rect, but he was far too nice a man to have felt any pleasure in his grave at being right about the dire outcome he had half prophesied. The essential weakness of the plan lay in the fact that the people who came in to settle the place were strangers. It was no surprise that they felt warmth and even nostalgia for their original homes when they found themselves in the monotonous duplica- tion of houses which were all too soon described as 'the slums of the future'. Much of the damage was by unwitting official vandal- ism. The former town had four buildings of distinction: all dwelling houses, of no great size, and obstructing no reasonable development; all four were demolished in the construction of the blur which is 'modern' Basingstoke.

The old place – like so many in everyone's childhood memories – was at its best in the period about Christmas, when the lights from the shop windows shimmered across the – invariably – rainshiny streets. Moreover, all the shops – even those of the same type – stocked different varieties of their goods; there simply was less standardization. Hosts of representatives from small firms prowled those shops, of which each owner wanted something 'different from them down the road'. So the term 'window-shopping' had real meaning. The market-place in particular was splendid, with its naphtha flares, its varieties of meat, fish, fruit, shoes, cheap clothes, sweets, while the cheapjacks hoarsely provided the background of sound.

Of course it was not in the least sophisticated. Especially on Sunday evenings, as the motorists drove back to London from the coast, a considerable proportion of the population was not merely content, but delighted, to watch the variety of cars, motorcycles, and all types of horsedrawn carts, traps and, at times, wagons – such as some of the village cricket teams used for short journeys to away matches – as they made their noisy but varied way along the main road of the town which ran through the market-place, where the connoisseurs of traffic matters used to congregate.

The business area of the town, with the exception of the railway complex, consisted of Winchester Street and its continuation into London Street, plus the upper, or southern halves of Wote Street and Church Street, all of which ran into the Market Square. There was a secondary centre – if that is not too exalted a title for it – at the bottom of Wote Street, and the terminus of the old Basingstoke Canal, facing the Barge Inn; a late-night resort for drunks, later to become the bus station. The little side streets, like Potters Lane and Victoria Street, were lined with tiny terraces which, at the time they were knocked down, housed old people who were moved into 'modern' homes a mile or two out of town: as a result, they lost sight of their old friends and gossips, shops and pubs and, in many cases, simply faded away in loneliness. It was not a happy result;

more a plan for anonymity. Those councillors who had controlled the town in earlier days were reactionary and, with the exception of George Willis, mainly Tory tradesmen; but they had character and, therefore, they produced a Basingstoke of some character, quite unlike the impersonality created by those who later 'planned' and moved on.

It was a place of do-it-yourself entertainment. Musical comedies, and sometimes straight plays, were mounted by amateurs. At soccer, Basingstoke once won the Hampshire League, and their 'blood' matches with Thorneycrofts engendered immense, but orderly, partisan enthusiasm. Basingstoke and North Hants played the best class of club cricket. The occasional match for them as an odd, picked-up body, only too anxious for a game, was a bonus for J.A. but no indication that he belonged on that level. The swimming baths were primitive enough, but a warm-weather pleasure; the two cinemas, a glimpse of a distant – surely not real – world.

To a great extent life still revolved about home. Mum called herself a 'plain cook' and constantly lamented having 'too heavy a hand for puff pastry'. She had, though, the knack of producing, on a shoestring family budget, food of profound flavour. The steak and kidney puddings were superbly rich. A rapid trip down to the barrow of 'Happy Bob' at the bottom of Wote Street to buy the fish he fetched at a shuffling gallop several times a day from the station – fresh herrings 'straight from Grimsby', kippers, sprats, winkles, whelks, whiting, huge cod steaks – provided the hearty high teas of those days. The fowl Father raised would now be called 'free range' but then they were just chicken, and something of a luxury. The fairly regular beef aitch-bone was roasted on Sunday, cold on Monday, minced or stewed on Tuesday, and anything left was apt to appear in a mysterious guise – 'made out of my head' – on Wednesday. Or there would be liver with its deep rich gravy. Old John kept pigs, and those huge hot joints, fantastically fatty and too rich for a boy's taste, made fine cold eating. Fruit cake, mince tart – a family favourite all year round – bread pudding heavy with fruit, pies filled with apple, blackberry and apple, gooseberry, blackcurrant, loganberry – according to what Father had ripe in the garden – or Mum's jam – especially the strawberry and the quince – satisfied the family's sweet tooth. Dad made wine of varying flavour and strength; Old John, who always considered himself a teetotaller, knocked it back, with only rare adverse effect, by the tumblerful. Most of the boy's pleasures were simple: starting to collect books, at first pamphlets and booklets given away with comics or penny 'bloods', shelved in an old boot box, then, courtesy of Dad, on a shelves of his bookcase, produced from timber pieces; reading in bed by candlelight; bridge in a 'school' with John Carter, Ron Prickett and 'Monk' Mills. They were, distance emphasizes, happy days, and although it would never have occurred to those dashing teenagers, extremely innocent ones.

Work was a different matter. In the office at the hospital there were two reasonable men but they were a minority, too junior to have any effect on those who created the mean and petty atmosphere. The idea – a young man's need – was to escape to a life that would be 'manly': what about the police? That, though, was not simple; it would involve an interview which meant absence from the office; that would be recognized for the attempt to escape which it was, and malcontents were not viewed favourably at Park Prewett. So the application had to be timed to fit an interview into the annual holiday. Surely there could be no harm in indicating dates of availability for interview as a footnote to the application form? but he wondered.

Then, where to apply? The Metropolitan Police did not find favour at home. A country force, from observation, meant having to work all hours, and being constantly moved. So, what was needed was a pleasant, largish town where first-class cricket was played, which had a good theatre and was close to the sea. So off went applications to Bristol, Brighton and Southampton, timed to arrive a fortnight before the start of his holiday. Bristol and Southampton both called for interviews – thank heaven, within that special fortnight – while Brighton named a date which was a week too late. Interviews over, waiting was an agony. Then came the offer of acceptance by Bristol; a daring three-day wait, and Southampton said 'Yes'. The choice had, of course, to be Southampton: near home, the force had a strong club cricket side, and there was county cricket during much of the season. A courteous apology to Bristol – with gratitude at its heart – and an even more polite acceptance to Southampton. Then the long suspense for one who did not realize they were waiting for a vacancy on a training course before the summons. It came. Writing out a resignation from PP was humbling, uplifting; and then, under some sour smiles but no congratulations, away.

Chapter 5

COPPER

He had never before been away from home for longer than a week or two of holiday, apart from convalescence after whooping cough, with Grandmother Clarke at Meads. Some appalling doubts: what if everything was too strange? or he was not capable? Encouragement from home: gifts of a dressing-gown, sweaters, socks, warm shirts. A couple of parties with friends; a lift to the station in a neighbour's car. At the beginning of September 1934 he left. The train pulled out of Basingstoke station: no longer home now – nor ever again? A mixture of exultation and sinking stomach; the need to do something; there was not long to wait; a plutocratic gesture – a cab to Police Headquarters, and it all began to happen. Within a few minutes of ascertaining that he was indeed the man who had been accepted, and after due examination of his credentials, his father's probity and his mother's respectability, he became Probationary Constable 94, Leslie T. J. Arlott of Southampton County Borough Police Force.

A room was arranged in Silverdale Road, opposite the Dell football ground, with Mrs Warden, the aunt of a member of the CID (the police authority vetted all policemen's lodgings to ensure against unsavoury or criminal involvement). With a carefully chosen and altered uniform (Southampton was supposed to be the best-dressed police force in the country), the purchase of two pairs of boots without realizing how important they were, the issue of notebook, staff and handcuffs, he had become a uniformed policeman stationed at Portswood on the north-east of the – then – borough. The wage was £3 2s 6d a week, plus a shilling a week boot money and six shillings rent allowance: princely by a country boy's standard in 1934.

Now he entered a world where everyone was informed, self-reliant, and he was the clueless clot. He spent a fortnight walking the beat with senior PCs – he was the youngest man on the Division by twelve years – and his elders were fairly, but not infallibly, decent about the fact that he was an infernal nuisance, keeping them from their normal illicit behaviour such as turning in to friends' houses, drinking, sleeping – usually in cars – or gossiping – strictly forbidden. He picked up a lot about the habits of coppers if not about police duty in that first idle fortnight before he was despatched to the provincial Police school at Digbeth in Birmingham, which proved no slight shock. The PT was the first revelation – not merely 'jerks' or toe-touching, but running in step round the gymnasium for what seemed like hours – but was only forty minutes – urged on by such orders as 'Keep up the step or I'll send you back to your force medically unfit.' There were boxing bouts in which a 'round' generally went on until one or the other fell: one reluctant gladiator would whisper to the other, 'For God's sake knock me down and finish it,' though deliberate falling was invariably spotted and resulted in a re-match. A broken nose remains as a trophy of one of those contests: it was inflicted by 'Larry' Gaines with a haymaker which started near the floor, was never seen, and threw J.A in a somersault across the room. The PT was followed immediately by swimming with, undoubtedly, the intent to produce cramp: 'Please, sir, I've got cramp.'

'Good, stay there and let the life-savers practise on you.' Those who could not swim had to learn; those who could had to take, and pass, the life-saving examination.

Nearly all the hundred-odd 'Pro. Cons.' were in the same boat, the majority about twenty and away from home for the first time, though the ex-soldiers – most of them guardsmen – were older and tougher. It was not funny: discipline was administered by Chief Inspector McWalter, and seen through by the sadistic Bulstridge – a civilian PT instructor – and the more refined but equally savage Sergeants Whale and Swift.

No, it was not funny, but it did make for the most splendid camaraderie. Cribbing and every sort of 'helping-out' was the general scheme. One alliance consisted of Arlott, 'helping' with arithmetic and dictation; George Nicholls, former Grenadier Guardsman, uniform smartening and foot drill; Bob Kemp, formerly of Otter swimming club, who had accompanied Temme on his Channel swim, life saving; the Scotsman, Eddie Hope, first aid; Austin Malia, law. The young men were boarded in stations all over the city, so that, for the early – 8.30 – parade, with all clean and shining, they had to be up at half past six. The day in school finished at five; there was time for a quick high tea, and then off, on four nights a week, patrolling with a Birmingham regular until ten, when the Brummy would leap on a tram for home, leaving the greenhorn to find his way back to his own station as well as he might. The mid-day meal for these lusty young men, their normal hearty appetites sharpened by the cold autumn and winter weather, consisted of two full meals apiece in Woolworth's cafeteria in the Bull Ring. It had to be quick work, not too much badinage with the waitresses, when the two journeys, queuing and eating had all to be crammed – *mot juste* – into one hour. There was time, though, for glorious Saturday night and Sunday parties, explorations and eventual return to stations generally, except for one former Irish Guardsman, more or less sober.

The last night party – officially organized but more or less unbuttoned – was an all but sentimental occasion; not only from relief, but also from a feeling of trials shared. Most of the class, of a hundred or more, would bring their copies of Moriarty's *Police Law* – which every policeman needed and which must have made its author a packet in royalties – for the others to sign, together with the name of their force. In those times, quite small towns – Winchester, Rochester, Canterbury and, for that matter, Southampton (two hundred strong) – had their own separate forces, which seemed in its way to humanize the whole matter. A copper on that course, travelling through another police district, would recognize, or be recognized by, another who had been there. As a result he would be asked, 'Look round to my place, I shall be off at one,' or two, or whenever, and be given a drink, and would see on a shelf that 'Moriarty' with those faded signatures from years before. If it was hard, it was recalled in tranquillity with some relish.

No, it was not funny; neither was humour encouraged. One day

Sergeant Swift was quizzing the class before the visit to the city mortuary.

'Any of you ever seen a corpse?'

Several hands went up; the sergeant surveyed them.

'Yes, you, Arlott, how many corpses have you seen?'

'About four or five hundred, Sergeant.' (A lie.)

'Crikey, where did you work then?'

'In a hospital, Sergeant.'

'How long for?'

'About four years, Sergeant.'

'Four or five hundred dead in four years – I shouldn't have liked to have been in that hospital.'

'No, I shouldn't have liked you to, Sergeant, it was a mental hospital.'

The class relished the release of tension in laughter. For a moment it seemed as if Swifty was going to use power – disguised as discipline: he thought, and did not; but he did not forgive. Thereafter, his constant greeting was 'Hallo! here's the one from the lunatic asylum.'

Most police forces have – or had, especially when so many of them were much smaller than now – their particular interest and pride, proficiency in which was usually regarded – all else being equal, or nearly equal – as a passport to promotion: it might be uniform, a brass band, a bridge team, football, an annual operatic performance, swimming, water polo or boxing. No doubt the Birmingham police excelled in some or all of those activities but, in those days, it was simply the hard force. Advancement was by cases, which was taken to mean convictions: it was a force hating, and hated by, its public. It was said that no one from, or with close relatives in, Birmingham was ever recruited into that force; indeed, those police themselves invariably referred to the people of the city as '. . . . Brummies' (the adjective varying between the merely contemptuous and the spiteful). That, of course, was in 1934, but at the end of the training course, a group of those who were departing next day to other forces raked together some of the best-liked Birmingham recruits, sympathized with them, and received some quite rueful, almost touching, farewells.

Southampton was altogether different, regarded by some as a soft outfit: the quasi-official line was that, in a district where the public was not harried, the police would be accepted and would receive help – information – in cases of serious crime. That seemed, then at least, a valid argument, and it is a fact that, at all levels in Southampton, the young officer was warned, 'We don't want a lot of this "nick 'em all" Birmingham stuff: let people live.'

A beat policeman in a semi-urban division was something of a solitary. Except for long, complicated report-writing, only the half-hour refreshment period of his eight-hour tour of duty was spent in the station or in the company of colleagues, unless he was on a – rare – joint or mobile patrol. Night duty in Southampton on a beat such as Bassett could be extremely lonely. In such territory as on the Bassett Wood Estate, a man pushed into and left in the under-growth, unconscious, could lie there for days without being dis-covered. That was a risk recognized, accepted and put out of mind at a very early juncture, otherwise the job would have been impos-sible. Once an hour the constable 'made a point' where he might be met by his sergeant or, in this instance only very rarely, his inspec-tor; even the sergeant rarely turned up more than twice a night. Thus, at the town end of the Division – 'two' beat – the designated points might be 'odd hours Stag Gates, even hours Rockstone Place', physically an easy stroll over a small area but with much and important prosperity. At the other end, on 'four and five' – Swaythling and Bassett, often linked on night duty – it might be 'Stile Inn ten-thirty, Bassett Cross Roads eleven-thirty, Hampton Park Hotel one-thirty, supper two-ten'. This meant, ins and outs included, quite eleven miles: under the 'chaser' sergeants who added, sadistically, 'And do not take a bike,' a murderous walk in sodden overcoat and cape on a wet winter's night.

That was little more than another phase of physical toughening. At twenty a young man accepts such processes relatively easily. Neither was the work difficult: there was no problem on the men-tal side that the Digbeth syllabus had not adequately covered, and anything forgotten or needing confirmation could be looked up in that copy of Moriarty – autographs and all. The true difficulty lay in settling into a fortuitous grouping of twenty-seven men, many of whom had merely snatched at the police force as a job after the First World War. In fact, with the exception of 'Nick' Carter, twelve years the rookie's senior, every man then on the Division had seen war service, and all were married. They were not only of a different generation, they were a different kind of people: widely different, too, from one another, but all old soldiers in one, or both, senses of the term. The new recruit set off, too, on the wrong foot; he had, by dint of striving and with some luck, finished at the top of the examination at Digbeth, and someone in the Chief Constable's office had made the fact known. In a police force, as in any tight community, gossip sweeps through like a forest fire. For a few weeks it was an easy jibe: 'How's the top boy, then, eh?' Then one day a sergeant, not recalling his name, asked, 'Where's that bloody Basingstoke boy?' and that stuck for many a month. Some of those older men went out of their way to be friendly and helpful, but the fact was that he did not really belong; no one of his age and type possibly could genuinely have belonged in that community.

The inspector in charge was Bill Robertson, a mild man. It was amazing that one of such limited and, in fact, dim unmanly mentality should have achieved such seniority; everyone of similar rank was at least shrewd and generally tough. It was suggested that his wife wound him up in the morning so that he ticked until evening.

The senior sergeant was 'Tiny' Watson, an extremely large, stupid and self-important, yet also self-pitying, ex-marine. When he decided to teach his equally – proportionately – huge wife, 'Tusker', to drive their elderly and too small car, word spread around the younger members of the force, who came even from other divisions to hide in the bushes on the common overlooking their house in Kitchener Road and watch the farce. The Watsons' manoeuvres were sluggishly funny; their high-voiced conversation riotously comic; for they did not see eye to eye on anything, certainly not car-driving, and their indignant squabbles approached bursting-point. The high peak was reached on the day when they came up towards their house, voices in crescendo as to what to do, and Tusker, in masterful fashion, suddenly trod on the accelerator, swerved at high speed into the entrance drive and tore on, bursting through the back of the match-board garage and into the back garden. The laughter from the surrounding undergrowth must have carried to Tiny's ears, so he cannot have been surprised when, coming on duty that night, he found the story common, ribald, knowledge throughout the force. Sadly it marked the end of the Tiny-Tusker motoring scenario. Rather surprisingly, Tiny's son proved an intelligent, even sensitive, policeman in the Hampshire County force.

The outstanding officer in the Division – indeed, in Southampton – was 'Jas' Chambers, a heavyweight sergeant, nimble on his feet and in his penetrative mind. He solved, single-handed, some complicated systematic crimes. He knew he had quite the sharpest brain in the force and unfortunately could not refrain from pointing out the fact; this, as in any organization, was not popular, or he would have won quicker and higher promotion. He had a good sense of humour and was not ungenerous to the young; he retired to a biggish pub in Bournemouth, but never achieved as much as his intellect justified.

The third sergeant was Fred Bellas, whose violent complexion bespoke an astronomically high blood pressure. He was full of wisdom about police duty and even more – and this is not the same thing – about being a policeman. He often imparted his knowledge obliquely. Once in the early hours of a December night, he asked, 'Have you done your Portswood Road backs?'

'Yes, Ser'nt.'

'Lately?'

'Straight after supper, Ser'nt.'

'All right, no need to Sergeant me all the time. I'll walk you along there.'

'Right, S. . .'

'Yes, right, you're learning.'

With many other sergeants, that invitation would have foreshadowed an attempt to catch out a constable, not with Fred Bellas. They walked until, pausing, 'What's that, then?'

'Back of Bounds' warehouse, Ser'nt.'

'What did I tell you?'

'Sorry, S. . .'

'Right; could you get in there?'

'Yes, easy.'

'How?'

'Slip the bolt on the big back door, but it is bolted – tried it earlier on.'

They had come to a standstill opposite the warehouse.

'Where's the office?'

'Middle right of here.'

'Any safe?'

'Yes.'

'Any good?'

'No, could rip the back off with a tin opener.'

'Anything in it?'

'Hey, what's on Sarge?'

'Just interested in how well you know your division, lad – anything in it?'

'Well, yes, at this time just before Christmas and a Thursday night, most of the vanmen's takings.'

'How much would that be?'

'Oh, plenty, about a thousand pounds.'

'Yes, perhaps a bit more, eh?'

'Perhaps.'

'Yes, not worth it, is it?'

'Now, what do you mean, S. . .?'

'Not worth it. Remember that bloody fool Joe Wilkie – done, pension and all, and did a stretch, all for a few packets of fags and a couple of bottles?'

'Shame, nice guy.'

'Yes, but that thousand quid isn't worth it either, is it? Now if ever you know where there's a hundred thousand to be got as easily as that, let me know, and we'll do it together, and go to South America on the loot.' They walked a quarter mile in silence, then, 'All right, lad; I'll book you back of Bounds, three-ten.'

'Thanks, Sarge – I mean, just thanks.'

'OK, lad.'

That conversation was to come to mind years later. An old hand con man's two sons had done a big job and gone to South America: he wanted to join them, but he did not want to go empty-handed.

He did a sucker in London, booked a passage to South America via New York, came to Southampton and had actually gone on board a little over an hour before the ship was due to sail, when Scotland Yard rang Southampton CID and asked them to pick him up. He proved only too easy to find: proudly confident, he made no attempt to hide on board – if he had, he could have made it difficult to find him in the time available, but there he was, large as life, in the first-class lounge, taking a pink gin. The series of expressions on his face as the arm was put on him remain in the memory as a most agonizing sequence. He seemed to have aged years by the time he was put in the police car. When it stopped at the Dock Gate the sergeant – George Adams – went into the Docks Police office to clear an extra passenger leaving. The miserable man looked feverishly over at J.A.: 'Lose me, mate, will you? I could just get on that boat.'

'Sorry, don't be daft.'

Why the devil did George not come back? The old man pulled a fat wallet out of his breast pocket. 'Look, mate, there must be five grand in there; you just go across to that pisshole over there with it, and I'll get back on my own.'

Both paused. Then, with a sympathetic grin: 'You don't understand, and it doesn't mean what you might think it means, but it's not enough.' He looked deadly sick again; thank heaven George came back just at that moment. The old con man died in prison three years afterwards.

Fred Bellas had a sense of humour, too: not common among police sergeants. Once, the Chief Constable – then John Thomas McCormack, a very old Irishman indeed – being unable to sleep at about half past two in the morning, phoned his chauffeur and told him to drive him round the entire police district; he did not see a single policeman. He could prove nothing, but he could act. He changed everyone in the force to a new division, just to shake them up. It certainly gave the small-time villains a great time to operate unrecognized by the new local watch. Fred Bellas and several of the Portswood constables were sent down to Headquarters: small beats but plenty to do. The sergeant, who had a free hand in nominating points, set three of the night duty to make theirs near Holy

Rood – centre of the bottom of the town – at four in the morning. Picking up all three of them he walked them a few yards down the High Street, stopped and leant against the wall of the Bank of England. When they were all doing the same he remarked, 'Blimey, we should all get commendations if some villain broke out of here now, shouldn't we?' Of course, he had planned the joke, but it relieved the tedium of the night.

The last of the sergeants was Wilf Cottell, content with that rank, past police ambition and more interested in his reading; he was nobody's fool, and an inherently kind creature. Unusually among sergeants, he realized how heartening his company could be on a remote beat on night duty when, at the top of Bassett, for instance, he could be the only person the constable saw between about midnight and five in the morning. Wilf would walk the PC twenty or thirty minutes to the next beat, chatting amiably all the way. He could be helpful, and he had a lovely daughter, Joan, a somewhat statuesque girl with corn-coloured hair and a sense of humour. She was an immense early weakness; perhaps too pure for a young copper, but a friend for many years.

On bad winter nights, too, Wilf would greet the PC on a distant beat with a grin and 'What ho, young feller – air like wine, eh?' leaving him with, 'Now don't freeze; keep warm; I don't expect anyone will pinch your beat if you get away into the warm somewhere.' He was right: shop-breakers and their kind abhor cold and dirty nights. There are, of course, obvious reasons, mainly discomfort, for a good breaker to avoid a wet winter's night.

Tiny Watson's character was the complete antithesis of Wilf's. If Tiny had anyone junior in his section whom he did not like – which meant any young man or one he could not browbeat – he would book them on a distant beat, refuse them a bicycle and visit them only twice a night – once before supper, once after. He would pull up on his own bike and, with a terse 'All right, I'll book you three-thirty, Bassett Church,' wheel ponderously round in the road and ride back to the station, where he sat in his overcoat over the fire and steamed. Once when he ordered the arch misery of a month of night duty in winter – Bassett and Swaythling and no bike all the time – hate for him became obsessional. At the time Chetwynd

Drive, a remote, unmade, unlit road under construction, was being excavated for sewers. Tiny had not turned up for the half past three point, so 'half past four, bottom of Chetwynd Drive' seemed a certainty. The young copper blew out the contractors' warning lanterns, threw the three protective barriers into the trench, which was some ten feet deep, and lit a cigarette. Tiny would turn up, see the young man smoking, ride down on him, fall into the trench and break his neck – or at least be injured and too heavily concussed to recall what had happened. In 'rescuing' him, the young policeman would so trample the muddy ground and the lanterns that any possible clue to contrivance would be obliterated. In evidence he would say he saw the sergeant wobbling along half asleep on his bike – as was his known habit – suddenly swerve and carry barriers and all into the trench. It was ready in good time; with trembling hands he lit the cigarette, leant casually against the only remaining barrier support and waited . . . the sergeant never came.

There was the first break-in; the indignant, hurt householder, his sense not merely of loss but of violation; the thought of some strange intruder handling the very stuff of the family's life. The business of quiet consoling, taking statements, writing a detailed report, with descriptions of the property missing; no detection of the crime, of course, but a good piece of – utterly useless – report-writing.

Then there was the recurrent case – mystery is not too strong a word – of the man with the newspaper: that was all anyone ever seemed to remember about him. Did he wear different clothes for every job? Did his hat shadow his face? His method was simple. He approached a house in an ordinary residential area, always with a folded newspaper under his arm. The house was usually semi-detached. He walked up to the front door and knocked or rang the bell, once, twice, or three times. Then he inserted the end of the fine, sharp jemmy he carried in the newspaper between door and jamb and with practised skill gently broke the lock. The door slowly opened; he raised his hat, walked in as if invited and instantly moved behind the door, pushed it closed and bolted it. That was discovered by one householder returning home: when she returned with help he had gone – that was the nearest he ever came to being caught. Once in the house he swiftly and tidily emptied prepayment gas and electricity meters, and unerringly discovered the drawer where loose money – saved for insurance, rates, milk, rent or other household expenses – was kept and took it all, but always cash, never any identifiable property. In a period of some five years or more, he was never caught and no useful description was ever obtained. Sometimes he operated as many as three times in a week; sometimes not for several weeks – did he go away and work some other police district? It seemed not; the MO – *modus operandi* – never came up in exchanges of information. At what point, it was wondered, did he produce the newspaper and put it under his arm? Several times men carrying folded newspapers under their arms were stopped – to their amazement and disturbance – but none had a jemmy and all were, reasonably(?), eliminated from enquiries. One line of thought suggested itself quite early: what did he do if anyone answered his knock or ring at the door? That could never be ascertained. Quite extensive enquiries in places where he made a successful break-in failed to reveal anyone who remembered such a caller; or did he slip paper and jemmy out of sight when he heard anyone approaching the door? Perhaps his enquiry was so innocuous that it simply passed out of people's minds. Or perhaps, if the door was answered, he took himself out of the neighbourhood for some time. He was responsible for a large proportion – in incidence if not in property value – of the reported crime in that peaceful out-division.

There was, it was once thought, a gang which broke into upper-middle-class houses while the family was at dinner – usually when they were entertaining, which would disguise any noise. Undoubtedly, their method was to steal a car and take it to some chosen, ill-lit area where they broke into the previously chosen house by an upstairs window – probably with a ladder – and took jewels or other immediately obvious and portable valuables. They left within minutes, drove the car to a quiet place where they had left their own car or an accomplice was waiting, and drove away. They did not go too often to the well – or perhaps they were caught somewhere else – but they made a fair killing, in terms of value, in their five or six jobs in the Southampton area.

A few years earlier policemen had gone in pairs Below Bar at night, when drunken seamen off ships had gone on the spree – sometimes violently; and when the crew of the *Leviathan* came ashore, the peace was often riotously disrupted. The former had waned and the latter was stopped by a single organized sweep of police which saw over a hundred of her crew in the cells when she would have sailed next morning; ever after she sent a tender ashore to fetch the crew, to the great sorrow of the local prostitutes and bar-keepers.

There was no pattern of crime. It cannot be too strongly emphasized that Southampton in the 1930s was quite strikingly free of evil, and especially of violence. Indeed, for a young policeman it was disappointingly free from any kind of 'action' or real excitement. Any crime of the least interest was seized on by a sergeant or someone in the CID. Even being recruited to catch a flasher, too fast on his bike for Ernie Rampton's ageing wind, was only too easy, and they were such pitiful characters. For the young constable, police duty resolved itself into door-trying by night, parading the main streets or striding main roads by day, interspersed with such mild mischief as calling in on friends for gossip and, or, drink. It was probably as safe and peaceful a time and place as there has ever been for the English police: even the atmosphere of football matches was decorous. It became so dull that the thought entered his somewhat placid and idle mind of trying another police force and even another job – a suggestion which filled his highly security-conscious father with alarm.

It was, though, all too dull when, like a tonic, John Creighton arrived. There had been some little talk of him when he first joined, but he quickly went away to training at Digbeth. Now, with him, life at Portswood changed. Creighton was one of the eight-man increase in the force and his arrival in the Division was an immense relief; all at once, life seemed sensible – even relishable, companionable. He was a lean six feet tall, with an intelligent face, a neat moustache, and an inherited knowledge of police duty. The son of a Birmingham sergeant, he became rapidly and fully aware of the difference between the two forces. The friendship was quick and proved long-lasting: the two young men were delighted with each other, with their similar senses of humour; the powers within the Division were less than pleased. Quickly it was ensured that the two were never on the same section; soon they were not even allowed the same days off. They were, though, not defeated. By dint of giving up a little sleep they were able to arrange their sorties in various borrowed motorcars to all kinds of places and at all hours, though they had a bad moment when the unpleasant Sergeant Appleton flagged down their car on Bitterne Road as they were returning home from a night out in Portsmouth at half past seven in the morning. It was a providential stroke of luck that they spotted a stolen car along the road, pushed the driver into the verge and locked him up.

Eventually their very youth – which largely prompted the hostility of their senior officers – caused them to be harnessed on duty. Rather laughably, a flasher hit on a new method: he would pick a row of housebacks fenced with match-boarding strip – of which there were many on those suburban estates – and would ride his bicycle along, fairly fast, to the end, which gave a clear escape; as he did so, he ran a walking-stick along the fencing – causing a loud drumming noise – and, at the same time, shone an electric torch on his erect male organ. Thus, one whole side of a street was 'treated' to that unilluminating spectacle within a few moments; while the offender did not give a sight of himself adequate for identification, or even a vague description. All this sounds ridiculous; in general, the public found it gloriously funny, and so did the younger policemen, but their masters did not see the joke – some twenty or more complaints were entered in the crime register every time he did it. The inspector and sergeants worked out a routine, choosing streets suitable for this operation and posting one, eventually two, men there to wait for the ingenious cyclist to justify their choice. Three times he did, and three times the constables posted there proved too slow to catch him. So, reluctantly, it was acknowledged that probably only Arlott and Creighton on the Division were young and fit enough to match his pace; even so, the flasher next 'struck' at a new time, while they were, perfectly legally, at supper. After that, the two were sent in plain clothes to patrol the backs of

Ripstone Gardens leading out to the steep downhill of Shaftesbury Avenue.

It was November; the weather was bleak; no inspector or sergeant would come to check for fear of scaring off the offender, so the pair of observers took the opportunity to spend the evening with Bill Morgan and his wife in their warm sitting-room. They were enjoying coffee there when, suddenly, they heard the drumming noise. 'Hell, it's him!' They dashed out to the back garden as he raced past, threw their bicycles through the back gate and set off after him. Shaftesbury Avenue is a very steep hill indeed, down at the Ripstone Gardens end, uphill at the other; and their quarry had a flying start. They raced neck and neck, down, up and then, to their alarm, he turned left towards the main traffic junction on Portswood and St Denys Roads. They were closing on him by the time he swung out there and, desperately, they charged him across the front of a tram whose alarmed driver, providentially, had the presence of mind to apply his power brake as three men and three bicycles piled across his great timber front bumper bar. They were congratulated on their success, and fortunately were not asked why they had ever fallen behind the exposer, but they were again booked on to different shifts.

They were up to every kind of what the inspector described as 'devilment' that would attract young men. The older constables on the Division – no doubt recalling their own youth – were generally sympathetic and occasionally issued helpful warnings. The sagest counsel, though, came from Fred Bellas: 'Just watch yourselves; if you get into real trouble there will be no sympathy, it'll be out; but so long as there is nothing to pin on you you'll be all right.' Then, all at once, the pressure was off: three more of the young intake – Pro. Cons. Wallace, Ansell and Glass – were posted to the Division; so was Bill Drayton, ten years older than the young men, Bachelor of Arts of the University of Oxford, a prodigious student of beer and monumentally idle. The 'powers' had their hands more than full, and virtually surrendered the fight so far as petty sniping was concerned. A few of the older men were moved to other, inner divisions as the leavening of younger constables came in. In the space of little more than a year the entire character of Portswood and its police were changed. Now, too, it was apparent that war was coming; while for PC 94 the mental pattern of life was also changing.

Chapter 6

AMATEUR AT WAR
IN SOUTHAMPTON

A fairly frequent though short-term visitor to Mrs Warden's lodging in Silverdale Road was 'Johnny' Malan, then fourth officer on a Union Castle boat, who had a considerable interest in the landlady's daughter, Mary. One day at a pub with J.A. and John Creighton on one of their rare free mornings together, he came up with news of a short-service commission in the RAF, which paid a far better wage than the police force and produced a thousand-pound pay-off at the end. The chance seemed more than worth exploring and the three set off, forthwith, for the RAF recruiting office, where they received a friendly greeting and filled in application forms, with all personal details, including past and present employment. The recruiting officer read the forms through, told all three to sit down, and settled to his correspondence. In due course, Johnny was waved in for his medical; but, as the other two awaited the call, the duty inspector from Police Headquarters, Bill Turner, arrived, took one look at them and announced: 'You two are under arrest for attempting to opt out of restricted employment,' (or some such official-sounding gobbledegook). 'Go over to my office at once.' Once there, 'Don't you two young idiots know you are in restricted employment? The Superintendent is not best pleased with you – get back to your division, and don't be so damned daft again.' They slunk off, met Johnny down the road and took a drink with him. A good man; his full name was Adolph Gysbert Malan, later known as 'Sailor' Malan, ace of the Battle of Britain, a distant cousin of Dr Malan who was Prime Minister of South Africa, but not of the same political outlook.

Terry Delaney was as Irish as his name indicates. Also of that middle-twenties age-group, he worked in the local public library, and was addicted to beer, football, cricket and the young life. Terry had a quite ordinary – indeed tatty – basement flat which he used to lend to left-wing friends for political meetings and used for parties and occasional courting: importantly, unlike young coppers' lodgings, it was unsupervised and allowed complete freedom. For J.A., Terry represented also a recall of the old bookish habits, and they formed a friendship which was to last until his death.

War broke out; the police force took on a fresh look. The old Chief Constable left and was replaced by a man who was no improvement. However, he had been briefed to start a War Emergency department, and appointed the young man to it on the basis of his slight typing ability and knowledge of French. Life had somersaulted yet again, and it did not remain still. From the boredom of the pre-Creighton period, he was now involved in immense activity.

At the same time, an attachment to Dawn Rees, a nurse at the Royal South Hants Hospital, became serious and led to engagement and eager anticipation of marriage. Dawn was Celtic in colouring – some Irish but, as her maiden name indicates, more Welsh – she had black hair, big blue eyes with almost impossibly splendid lashes, a rosy complexion, full lips and a fine flash of well-made white teeth. In build she was sturdy: a bustler who made a most competent, no-nonsense nurse and, later, a fine, practical, compassionate mother, with a sense of justice and of humour, a generous, convivial and efficient hostess. While she was apparently worldly-wise – and she was certainly shrewd in practical matters, especially those connected with nursing – she was in truth extremely innocent.

Dawn's mother, daughter of the wealthy owner of a chain of butchers' shops, estranged herself from her family by marrying a Welsh-born Canadian army dispatch rider. However, she did her best to bring up her three children, of whom Dawn was the eldest, in snobbery. She greeted her daughter's marriage in 1940 with a telegram regretting that she had married beneath her, which was little cheer for a wartime bride. Her father and her parents-in-law, though, were prepared to laugh, and the bridal party – for which the groom was unconditionally excused from all police duties for the day – was happy and prolonged. The two contrived a slightly belated honeymoon in Ilfracombe, but otherwise it was duty, not as usual, but as it now shockingly and regularly became. Dawn had qualified as a State Registered Nurse and became night sister at the Southampton Children's Hospital. J.A.'s duties in the police emergency department were from nine to half past six and, also, every other night, he was required to sleep in Police Headquarters on air-raid emergency duty. All this meant that they spent much less time together than most young couples in normal circumstances; but these were not normal circumstances, and they were desperately grateful for the time they were together, indeed for the very fact that they were together.

Soon, too, the air-raids became more frequent. It is difficult to piece together, or at least to evaluate, the emotions, developments, events of that time. Love of a young wife was mixed with fear, chiefly for her: never knowing whether she would be there, or even alive, at the end of a tour of duty. Southampton, as a matter of historic fact, had more 'incidents' – and air-raid warnings – than any other place in Britain. The first raid on the town came by day, when the couple were at home. After some dithering, they took cover; then could not resist coming out to look, and were rewarded for that piece of madness by seeing the legendary Polish fighter squadron drive away the German bombers, an event which produced an euphoric effect, to be rapidly dispelled by the well organized, systematic and heavy night bombing. In the same raid a huge food store in Southampton Docks was hit: it was full of butter and burnt for several days, while an appalling mess of molten yellow fat ran across the dockside to clot in the sea. Within weeks, the new flat which had been a young couple's pride was in truth very near to the receiving end. It was not a direct hit, which was a considerable comfort because it meant that the contents remained intact, apart from the glass and other splinters embedded in the furniture. Fortunately, too, both were on night duty when the bomb, fourth in a 'stick' of six, fell. It was a chilling experience to return 'home' – by luck within two or three minutes of one another – to contemplate the destruction of a superficial dream. It was no more than a trifle; it was not possible to come back from the death and maiming of the raids and regard damage to property as a matter of real importance. What was important was that they were both alive. Now they needed to find somewhere to live before nightfall: that proved simple as did so many problems in that period when such difficulties were seen as everyday. Terry Delaney solved it: 'Go and stay at Bumble's place.'

'Bumble' was Hubert Humby, a short, dark, constantly preoccupied member of the public library staff; sensitive, literary and intelligent; no more than an acquaintance, but in those times that concerned no one. He had been bombed out a few days before and had taken the furnished house of a fireman who had been transferred to the West Country. Seen at the library that morning, his response was instant: 'Glad to have your company in these devilish times. There are the keys – can you manage to move your stuff in?' So, no sooner bombed out than rehoused. It was a pleasant, modern, semi-detached house in Bassett Green Road, with ample rooms for two couples. Bumble's wife, Doll, was an amazingly young-looking, nervous, but bright woman. The four hit it off well enough – when they were there.

It was an odd, unnatural existence, between nursing duties, police duty and air-raid stand-by in one family; fire-watching, library work and auxiliary nursing in the other. It was a bicycle life: riding home, generally through the blackout in that 1940–41 winter, wondering whether one would find one's spouse there, or any company at all. Rations were stretched, augmented from the garden and the preserve cupboard at Basingstoke – where he visited as often as he could take his wife with him.

When bombs fell, everything was activity, though it soon became completely orderly, controlled activity – as a rule. One night he left his office as the alert sounded to stroll, as usual, unhurriedly over to the control room in the Civic Centre. On the way he passed young George Brown, son of the great Hampshire and England cricketer, a constable in the mobile section. 'What are you up to, then, George?'

'Got to drive the Chief Constable up to Red Lodge; he doesn't like it down here when it gets hot.'

'Lucky chap, enjoy it.'

As he entered the Civic Centre, a bomb dropped a few yards away. The three or four men who were inside the door dived for cover: the stick of four – big ones – thundered on. As the dust slowly settled they gratefully made their way into the control room. That personable, young George Brown, though, was dead; a direct hit on his car – before the Chief Constable reached it.

Southampton was, indeed, hard hit; the great V of the Test and Itchen rivers of Southampton Water was a simple, even inviting, target for any bombing aircraft. First the incendiaries marked it in detail and then the heavy stuff pounded down, magnifying the destruction and spreading the fires. The police in the target-area towns were under instruction that in the event of any military withdrawal they would remain behind, to render support of a pacific kind to the occupying force to control and protect the civilian population: though not too much was said about that. At one juncture, though, it was decided, after four days of intensive night attack, and with buildings burning steadily, that, if the bombers came again, the town would be abandoned. It was a gut-racking piece of knowledge. That night one couple took a tender and terrified farewell; when the alert sounded, it seemed that the end of all things was near. The bombers did not come – not that night – and for the rest of the war life seemed, if not safer, richer, a bonus.

Now, too, having acquired a smattering of Norwegian and German – enough to find out the name of a sailor's ship – he was translated to Detective Constable, Special Branch. The Special Branch was a free gift in his life. Unlike many of his colleagues, he obtained his information from extremely tidy sources. Now, this enabled him to spend much of his time – say an average of two hours a day for several years – in Southampton's extremely pleasant art gallery, in quasi-privacy, where he read to his heart's delight, wrote a little, and generally idled. He did not evade work – he merely telescoped it while, in a way, he formed a small part of his consciousness. Odd as it may seem, however, the great change in his life occurred in the time to be passed on air-raid emergency stand-by.

What followed still seems amazing, recalling an old cricketing expression used when, for instance, a rabbit batsman has driven a fine fast bowler for four or six: 'No one more surprised than the striker.' No single development of his career, certainly for the next six crucial years, was planned, premeditated, nor even vaguely foreseen. He was far too naïve for that: he simply did not belong to the class or type of person who planned a career. His kind took it as it came: it simply occurred. In normal peacetime conditions, it could never, by the wildest stretch of the imagination, have happened to him; and if many people then in the forces had been in competition, they could have done it all so much better. That does not mean that for those immediately post-Dunkirk months, life was more comfortable in a police uniform than in khaki. Often, when he was lecturing in military establishments, the word was 'This is the safest place.' They suffered, then, petty but dragging irritation; but their time, their bad time, was to come. The advantage of the police service was always that regularly, if not constantly, the conditions, even the comforts, of a normal life were available. For him, though, those following six years were so bewildering, so surprising, and so crowded that, if the chronology of the following few pages is confused, the facts reported are accurate and their order barely relevant.

Of course, his success, such as it was, was primarily a product of fear, and no one realized that more clearly than he. The whole place reeked of fear as the bombs blindly thumped out their tattoo; everyone was frightened; each tried to hide it in his or her different fashion: J.A. needed to be by himself for a time. Bridge, as partner of the Detective Inspector, helped to provide some sort of shelter or stimulus, but that did not last, even if it was useful to play with the Detective Inspector.

The influence of Terry Delaney and Bumble drove him back, increasingly, to reading; for a while, to a considerable extent, it filled in that terrible time of the stand-by. Office duty finished at 6.30; going out, or drinking, was forbidden, sleeping was pointless, so the time had to be filled in. It was impossible to leave the control room so long as the alert was on; even afterwards, the alarm might well sound again: that covered the night, at least until midnight. Then, often, the alert would remain on until four or five in the morning, tying control staff to the table: a situation which allowed dozing but no sleep, no return to the office, no undressing, no crawling into that funny, scruffy little bed: so he read, read, read.

Anyone with literary taste must find it a very strange medley of authors: Belloc followed Chesterton, both romantic, then a little of Wells; he moved on to George Bernard Shaw, Arnold Bennett – desperately easy to read; J. D. Beresford, Oliver Onions, Francis Brett Young, Siegfried Sassoon; not, oddly, Robert Graves, but an immense interest among those First World War writers was Richard Aldington, who was to remain an influence for an entire lifetime, and to become a friend. Of course there was the most skilfully amusing P. G. Wodehouse, the companionable J. B. Priestley. Somehow, though, there was not complete satisfaction. He turned to verse; it would be silly to call it poetry, because it was not – yet – though he did not perceive that fact then. John Betjeman led him through topography, but not yet to poetry; George Rostrevor Hamilton through epigram and wit led to an appreciation of his poise, his polish, his critical capacity, but provided an object lesson in the fact that verse is not, by any means necessarily, poetry.

Then, one day, out on an investigation in a police car, he drove up to Bordon, went into a pub there where he needed to make an enquiry, and got into conversation with two men who were taking an amiable lunchtime beer. They were Douglas Goldring and Tommy Earp, both of whom had been young poets of slim volumes; widely different in many ways, yet fundamentally similar in their quality of civilization; as neighbours through wartime shifts they had become close friends. Encountered a second time in the continuing enquiry, they were hospitable, friendly, illuminating, undoubtedly a little flattered to have found a disciple; he delighted in their company and in listening to their talk. On subsequent visits, with no police car, getting there the hard way – train and bus – was still excitingly worthwhile. They opened up another world; Goldring, in particular, because although he was never a popular author, he had made – just – enough money in the inter-war years by writing books about things he wanted to write about and places he liked to live in, especially around the Mediterranean. Tommy, a scholar of Exeter College, Oxford, was a student of history, particularly of London and Paris, and had a splendid turn of wit. Douglas had known D. H. Lawrence, Richard Aldington and Robert Graves overseas, and talked with unfailing interest about them. Those two, aged far beyond any question of military service, had got out of London and were living extremely economically in a village just outside Bordon. They were quite amazingly generous with knowledge; aware of, and imparting, a formula for living far removed from the police force. Now those hours of the night, reading, studying, meeting a fresh kind of hunger, of extended knowledge, wisdom and understanding, made J.A. a new, wider-minded and a bigger creature.

Still in summer there was cricket, cricket known now with a new understanding; illuminated, above all, by reading Cardus, but also other writers on the subject, some disappointing to the imagination, yet imparting knowledge and background to the game. He saw what was good, began to understand it, and he began increasingly to talk to people who knew about it. One day he went to play in a Red Cross match on the Normanton Estate, in the New Forest. There Bert Gibbons, the former Hampshire player and captain of the police team, called him up and asked, 'Ever played here before?'

'No, Skipper.'

'Thought you had played on every bad ground in the county?'

'Yes, so did I, but I didn't even know there was a ground here.'

Enter Lady Normanton. Gibbons said: 'Have you had a ground here long, your Ladyship?'

'Only since yesterday,' she said.

It was a deadly wicket: but Philip Mead, who had retired from the game when war broke out, and whose eyesight was known to be failing, made 33 masterly runs out of a total of 52. The police side were put out for about thirty, but, for Mead, every ball hit the middle of the bat. He struck one through gulley for a bounding four; on the boundary, Sam Pothecary, who was on Mead's side, picked the ball up and as he tossed it back said, 'Look at that old man, playing better from memory than any of us will ever do.' Just two years later a fund was raised for Philip Mead because he was blind. His was mastery of cricket.

In due course this Southampton Police side, one of the strongest club teams in the country, began to play really powerful wartime teams like London Counties and the Empire Eleven; or strong elevens raised from the services, civil defence and so on. The young man, of course, was not good enough to get in the side for those occasions. There was, though, a public address system, primarily to raise funds for charity: he was asked – no, *told* – to take it over, and found himself talking, all too easily, perhaps all too glibly, about the match, but enjoying it.

He wanted, somehow, to extend his reading in order to make a collection of topographical verse. He still did not know enough to realize that this was falling short of the standard of true poetry. He wrote to John Betjeman asking him if he would collaborate with him on a collection of topographical poetry. Incidentally, there was then no general recognition of any possibility that John Betjeman would become the Laureate: indeed, his main output until then consisted of The Shell Guides to Devon and Cornwall, *Mount Zion*, *Continual Dew* and *Old Lights for New Chancels*. Betjeman was kind but he explained that he was already committed to an anthology of landscape poetry with Geoffrey Taylor, which was eventually published by Muller. Still, though, the collection grew.

In plain clothes, out on enquiries, opportunities grew to go to the public library, and Gilbert's secondhand bookshop, with three storeys of books, from the tattily ordinary secondhand to splendid antiquarian books; he ploughed on through, searching. Eventually he was introduced to the Southampton University Library by two friends there: Reg Loader, a lecturer in Classics, and Harry Howell, a physicist. Reg Loader was precluded from any kind of military service by his awful eyesight, but he managed eventually to become radio operator on a Greek tanker through his knowledge of classical Greek. Harry Howell was maintained on the University staff in some distantly high official hope that his knowledge of the spectrum would produce some ray in advance of the one he had already used to stop an internal combustion engine, though he constantly pointed out that he could not even stop that if a fireguard was put in front of it. Interesting they were, though, and became close friends for many years.

Loader and Howell's introduction to the University library enabled him to read books on modern Russian history and military theories, which fascinated him. He studied the subject to such an extent that one day the head of the University's Extra-Mural Department, kind John Parker, a pub acquaintance, engaging him in conversation on the subject, offered the University's assistance – not to be refused – in his studies. Much of the best information came from German sources – surprising in view of subsequent events – but it did give him an insight, available to many who apparently were not interested, into the strength of the Russian army. At length, John Parker suggested that he should give service units lectures on the Russian army and its strategy. Although the University, for its part, gave him all the information it could gather on the subject, it may have been something of a record that, with no qualifications at all, no degree, he was used as a lecturer to extra-mural classes, to services education officers within the University, and was commended to the Workers' Educational Association.

Meanwhile, he remained obsessed by this collection of topographical verse, and eventually, having been impressed by George Rostrevor Hamilton's literary criticism and, above all, his epigrams, he wrote and asked him if he would collaborate on the anthology. Hamilton agreed and off went the young copper to become an anthologist.

About the same time he was summoned to the Chief Constable's office and given two extra duties. One was to compile the fortnightly situation report sent to the Home Office on general affairs, public reaction, thoughts and opinions – a sort of one-man Gallup poll on the 'state of the Union'! This gave him infinite interest and pleasure while, of course, it put him in a position to prowl the town as he wished. He used Messrs Loader and Howell to give what he chose to call intellectual opinion; the rest he picked up in the pubs and at the football and cricket grounds, which were probably as good places as any to assay public feeling. In fortunate confirmation, the Chief Constable received favourable comments on the situation reports from the Home Office. The second new job, rather less pleasant (hard work), was to attend at the Chief Constable's office each morning and take his post from the Home Office. This was, of course, a time of a vast amount of minute Governmental legislation and emergency regulations, at least one every day, if not more. It was J.A.'s job to digest these new 'laws' so that they could be included in the daily orders distributed to the force to keep officers up to date. It seemed simple enough, so long as the constable did not misread the laws. The more diligent poetry researcher, Arlott, was spending a morning in the public reference library researching for his anthology when the Chief Constable, in need of quick knowledge on a piece of new law, rang up the reference librarian – Bumble – and asked, 'Is that Mr Humby?'

'Yes,' said Bumble.

'If you should see my detective Arlott passing your window, will you tell him the Chief Constable wants him?' That must be about the most respectful way any Chief Constable has ever summoned an erring member of his staff.

In retrospect, the young workaholic had shouldered an appalling amount of study: anthology, police duty, air-raid control, reading. Even service lecturing – on days off – took up much time because it involved frequent travel by army lorry which was uncomfortable and slow. It did, though, bring in crucial money – probably the best part of a tenner a week – which, in those days, was complete wealth, and made life very much easier for the young couple. A day completely free of work was virtually unheard of; but, since his wife slept by day after night duty, they did not miss much of one another's company; and, above all, whenever they could get a day and night off together, they made the utmost of it.

At the end of 1942 came an event like a blinding light to him; though to any established writer it would have seemed ordinary enough. He was accepted as a writer – or, at least, a collaborator – to be published. He had suggested to Oxford University Press a collection to be called *The Oxford Book of Topographical Poetry*. To the publishers, the title probably asked too much; at least they rejected it. So George Hamilton took it in hand and, although an Oxonian himself, he sent it to Cambridge University Press, where that good bookman and pretty wit, S.C. – Sydney – Roberts, accepted it. The collection was all but complete when, in the almost uncanny fashion of J.A.'s life-pattern at that time, there was yet another windfall. The collection – arranged in regions and counties – lacked adequate coverage for Worcestershire. An excellent poem by John Masefield seemed to meet the need but when, on behalf of George Hamilton, he wrote respectfully to the poet, there came, after a few days, a reply which began, 'Sir, Please do not address Mr Masefield directly again.' It was a letter from an agent, and no doubt the Laureate was much pestered, but the young man chose to be offended on George's behalf and wrote to him accordingly, observing that he could 'write as good a poem about Worcestershire as that'. A reply from George Hamilton invited him to try it. He hammered out in sweat and uncertainty a piece called 'Cricket at Worcester 1938' and sent a copy off to his mentor who, with characteristic kindliness, corrected some of its elementary errors and said that it was capable – or better than that.

If the young man was not fully convinced, he did not argue. Hamilton had the complete answer: first of all he said it must be included in the collection, but, without telling the young man, he also sent a copy of it to Cyril Connolly, the editor of *Horizon*. To the young man's amazement, a letter of acceptance came from its distinguished editor. For a couple of days his feet barely touched the ground. He despatched other poems, to *The Observer* and *The Fortnightly*, and they were accepted. Some time later he asked Connolly, 'Why on earth did you publish that piece on Worcester?'

'When I was a boy my uncle used to take me to watch county cricket, and it was exactly like that, and that is why I published the poem.'

Then in August 1943, two poems appeared in collections: *The Little Review Anthology* and Reggie Moore's *Modern Reading*. In December, too, occurred by far the greatest event in his life until then: the publication of *Landmarks*, as the collection was titled. It was reviewed extensively in *The Times Literary Supplement*, *The Observer*, *New Statesman* and – by John Betjeman – in *The Daily Herald*. Then came an offer for American publication, and an invitation from Edward Sackville-West to send poems for his BBC poetry programme.

About this time, too, J.A. was, to his delight, recruited as a member of the ENSA Brains Trust, gathered to entertain the forces in fairly large numbers. This was of no little value in terms of the family exchequer, and of his self-esteem; but, above all, for the link it forged with Michael Ayrton. Michael was almost exactly seven years J.A.'s junior, but certainly his intellectual superior, as was reasonable for the son of the poet Gerald Gould and the future Labour Cabinet minister, Barbara Ayrton Gould. The two young men became boon companions from their first meeting. In an odd way, despite the intellectual gap between them, they had it in common that they were both virtually self-educated through reading. Indeed, within a few weeks of meeting they began their collaboration on *Clausentum* – a book of Michael's lithographs with J.A.'s sonnets – which was published in 1946. That friendship opened many portals and engendered much humour.

1943 was the year of domestic establishment. First of all the house in Lodge Road, Southampton, was offered to him to rent or lease: he took a short lease and, on the advice of a solicitor friend, also took out an option to purchase, for which in due course the family was immensely grateful. Then followed a period of driving off to Basingstoke in borrowed, clapped-out vans, begging small items from his parents; buying larger items in sales and junk shops: alas, secondhand furniture was never cheaper than when so many personal tragedies threw it on the market. So, eventually, the couple settled in, knowing themselves to be extemely fortunate; settled in, that is, with the exception of the garden, for which no one contributed any great enthusiasm. Usually though, and with characteristic generosity, Father undertook that responsibility and seemed even to enjoy it. It was a shame to break up the household with the Humbys; it had been companionable and worthwhile. This, though, was a home of their own, and a fresh responsibility even though it involved a certain amount of loneliness. They were not – to their alarm – in a state of complete safety, for now the flying bombs were hurtling over: but at least Dawn could give up night duty and, in an atmosphere of splendid warmth despite the dire conditions outside, there occurred an event of outstanding happiness in the family when James – James Andrew John Arlott – was born, on 4 December 1944. In his short, twenty-year life he gave much happiness, for he was not only handsome but gracious and generous, and his loss left a mark on those, few in number but deep in attachment, who had known him and loved him for the good person that he was.

Now, too, it happened that John Betjeman, talking to Geoffrey Grigson, mentioned that he had come across a policeman who was addicted to poetry. So Grigson, a senior talks producer of the BBC in Bristol, duly wrote and asked J.A. if he would give a broadcast talk on being a policeman who liked poetry. J.A. wrote back to say 'no', that he was not prepared to be regarded as a freak; but that he would be happy to do a broadcast. Grigson simply replied that, if he destroyed his news value, he would need to be a good broadcaster, and would have, first of all, to show how he sounded. So an audition in Bristol was fixed for his day off: it was vital that he keep out of any kind of involvement that might give him a prisoner on the day before, so that he had to attend court the next morning. That was carefully avoided – it could have been a good day for a criminal – and off he went to Bristol. The trip itself was a pleasure (he had never before been to Bristol) and he duly appeared at Broadcasting House in Whiteladies Road, in a mixture of good heart and non-confidence. The selected audition passage from Coleridge's *Biographia Literaria* went on for nearly two and a half pages without a verb or any meaningful punctuation: he felt it his duty to try to put some sense into the reading, and did his best. Once the audition was over, Grigson said, with no enthusiasm, 'That's all right.' It was not until years afterwards that he discovered Grigson had written in his report, 'This man is a natural broadcaster and should be encouraged.' Grigson being Grigson, he did not say anything like that at the time, only, 'Now we have to find out whether you can write a script. What I want,' he added, 'is a kind of lay sermon, for one of those Sunday night postscripts.'

By heaven! that was aiming very high for a completely raw broadcaster. J.A. duly tried to write a script: but he had no experience and all his attempts proved useless. Although he tried again and again, the scripts simply were not good enough and, at last, realizing he was not going to get many more chances, in absolute desperation he wrote a piece called 'The Hampshire Giants' about the eighteenth-century Hambledon Cricket Club, based on direct quotations from Nyren's *Cricketers of my Time*. This time Grigson, thank heaven, liked it. The day was fixed, the talk scheduled in the *Radio Times* and, once again, the difficulty arose of making certain he was absent from police duty on the specific day. He very carefully worked extra hours and built up enough time in the book so that, including his leave day, he could book himself three days off. This meant that, even if on the first day he had to be in court, he still had two days to do the broadcast.

It was to be done in a London studio. He delivered the broadcast and, while he was still there, a telephone call from 'Jack' – Francis – Dillon, producer of 'Country Magazine', asked him to go round to his office. It was almost impossible to bridge in sympathy the difference between Grigson, with his prim, precise, though perceptive literary manner; and Jack Dillon, the husky-voiced former tax inspector, a live wire who had so imaginatively created the format and atmosphere of the 'Country Magazine' programme. Would J.A., he asked, like to compère a 'Country Magazine'? Would he! He hardly knew whether he was on his head or his heels.

All this, it must be realized, was completely unpremeditated, except his marriage and hawking the Anthology for a publisher: everything else had simply happened. What now followed was also sheer luck.

He had been called into the Southampton Police Training School, which was very primitive but helpful to young and war reserve coppers. There he was lecturing on Aliens, Special Branch, and Wartime Emergency Legislation, and on that basis it was decided to send him to Peel House where, already, the Metropolitan Police, on the direction of the Home Office and in anticipation of the end of the war, were setting up a post-war Police Instructors' Training School. While he was there, determined, as one of the juniors, to remain obscure, the head of the school, Commander Legge – a very strange, monocled man – sent for J.A. and barked in his high fallutin' tone, 'What right have you to speak for the police, young man?'

J.A. was bewildered.

'You know what it's all about?' said Legge.

'No, Sir.'

'The BBC have asked for you – you, a junior provincial police-man – to make the broadcast address to the King on behalf of the police on Victory Night.'

J.A. protested his complete ignorance of the matter, but Legge went on, 'What right has any provincial policeman to do that? – only the Metropolitan Police could do it.'

'Yes, Sir,' he said, sensing a position of power. 'I have no wish to do it, and if they ask me, Sir, I shall refuse.'

Legge went red in the face and snarled, 'You have got to do it, go and do it and I am sure you will do it well. Get *out!*'

The police had compromised with the BBC: all right, your man, but our script. J.A. appeared for rehearsal, groped through the script and said, 'But this is unbroadcastable.'

'Absolutely so,' said the producer. 'You had better rewrite it: I shan't notice it and I am sure the police won't.'

So it was done. No one could pretend it was brilliant, but at least it was couched in normal speech forms and rhythms and without the stilted and pretentious manner of the original. Of course, the producer was completely right: it transpired that not one of the 'Met' lordships noticed the alterations.

Victory Night was in theory one of festival: it was the celebration of peace – and an occasion to be celebrated even by the students of the Police School. There was a complete deluge of church bells and, after the blackout, an almost shameful blaze of street lights. Yet oddly it was difficult to feel exultation: relief, yes, but it was all too close for even that to sink in properly. The whole city was slightly hysterical in celebration, but it all seemed so artificial: perhaps incredible was the word. It really was hard to believe.

Solely by coincidence – surely? – after the celebrations in Broad-casting House, on his way back to Peel House, he met three of his colleagues from that establishment. Memory does not recall the details of the evening but it was highly convivial. On their return, Peel House was most officially shut. No doubt its masters had their back entrances or retreats but for their pupils there was merely a bolted door. Presumably the ring of a bell would have brought someone to open it – probably with dire consequences. It is not clear now who had the brilliant idea of climbing the outside fire escape, shinning over the roof, hanging down over the parapet and knocking at his bedroom window to wake a not too delighted inspector of the Birmingham Police. With dire warnings he opened the top sash, they swung down into his room, and triumphantly scuttled along the corridor to their beds.

Next morning, as the hungover revellers paraded, pulling themselves to attention, despite a misting of post-alcoholic sweat, one turned to J.A. and said, 'Look up there, that's where we came in last night.' Three sets of eyes were turned in some awe to the top of the building. And three people realized just how desperately lucky they had been to survive: sober, they would probably have fallen.

A day or so later in another completely unforeseen situation, Campbell Nairn, a *Radio Times* journalist, arrived to write a piece about the constable who had spoken the Police tribute in the address to the King. They got along well; Nairn elicited the information he wanted and suddenly he asked, 'Are you applying for this job of Overseas Literary Producer?'

'What do you mean, Literary Producer?'

'Didn't you know?' said Nairn. 'There is a job going for someone to do poetry and prose programmes for overseas.'

'But they would never look at me,' said J.A.

'Well,' said Nairn, 'You can but apply; though perhaps you had better wait until it is publicly advertised in *The Listener*.'

The course at Peel House ended with no sign of the advertisement, but at Waterloo Station on the day he returned home, there it was, in *The Listener*. He could not get into, and off, the Southampton train quickly enough for his eagerness to type out that application. By dint of sweated care it was completed without observable error and posted off. By all the oaths, he knew how much – how very much – he wanted that job; he had never wanted anything so much.

He was, though, now back to constabulary duties once more and was promoted to acting sergeant – which meant a few extra shillings a week – but ordered back into uniform with a peremptory 'And get your hair cut,' which was far less happy. He was not a boss man, nor even a discipline man, and, by heaven, he did not relish the return to night duty. Time passed – far past reasonable hope for that BBC job. Anyway, it had been too much to hope, and he relaxed into the idleness of patrol sergeant who, at least, could take a bicycle when he wanted and chatter lengthily on their points with the constables he liked best.

Then it came. 'It' was an instruction to attend a BBC interview in London. The new Chief Constable, fortunately, was an accessible man and, told of the situation, affably said 'Good luck.' As an after-thought, he asked, 'What is the salary?'

'£720 a year, Sir.'

'Well, it would take you a very long time to reach that in the police force, wouldn't it?'

'Yes, Sir. But it would be a very difficult day to go.'

'Oh, why?'

'Because it is the day of rehearsal for government inspection.'

'What difference does that make?'

'Well, Sir, the government inspector always asks for the youngest sergeant to drill the parade, and I am not very good at drill.'

'I know that, Sergeant, so you will no doubt find an important enquiry to make out at Portswood.' Not many police chiefs would have been so considerate.

The whole matter, though, had to be most carefully planned. It was the high heat of July. He borrowed Michael Ayrton's flat, which was, most conveniently, only a few yards from the interview room in Cavendish Street. He limited himself to two small beers, with a light lunch; then round to the flat for a cold bath and a change into the clean white shirt he had brought with him. Then, cool if not calm, he went round to the ordeal. It seemed to go well enough; in fact, he had no real expectation of success so he could take it all easily.

It was less officially simple when, to his zanily excited delight, he was offered the job. Again, the visit to the Chief Constable's office and the gabbled breaking of the news.

'Oh, congratulations, Arlott, when will you go?'

'But, Sir, I can't.'

'Oh, and why not?'

'The Home Office instruction, Sir.'

'What does it say?'

'It says I can't go, Sir.'

'The Home Office instruction doesn't mention you at all; what does it say?'

'It says an officer can only leave if he is over the years of service or sick.'

'You are sick, Arlott, aren't you?'

Then with – by disciplinary standards – rather chancy, in fact, still rather hysterical, humour: 'I am sick of police duty, Sir.'

'That has been apparent to me for a very long time, Arlott. You had better go.'

The old man brushed aside the effusive thanks. Happily, several years afterwards, it was possible to do him a good turn that was, in truth, valuable to him in his career. For the moment, though, it was away to a new life.

Chapter 7

TO LONDON

The whole idea of living in London was heady. Until now a visit
there had been an occasion: a holiday, latterly to broadcast or to
seek congenial company. That, under the guidance of the kindly
Daniel George (Bunting) who had a friendly son of J.A.'s age, was
an introduction to so much. Daniel was an in-house adviser to Jon-
athan Cape, a brilliant light versifier and critic in his own right. He
was a guiding light to many young writers in those days and his
humour was splendid – all but wasted on *Tribune*, for which he
wrote book reviews. He it was who in the neighbourhood of the
Pillars of Hercules conjured up a whole cohort of congenial companions – people like Dylan Thomas, Roy Campbell, Laurie Lee
and George Orwell.

Now, though, London was not a day visit but was to be home – to
J.A. then a most exciting prospect. It was to be home for work and
home, domestically, as soon as he could find somewhere to live.
For the few days between the police force and the BBC he had to
make housing arrangements. Most happily and generously,
Michael Ayrton took him into his two floors at the bottom of All
Souls' Place, the cul-de-sac between Broadcasting House and All
Souls' Church. For a budding broadcaster it could hardly have
been more central. His bed was in Michael's studio and his fellow
residents were Michael and his wife and Constant Lambert. For the
newcomer it was all perpetually exciting.

He moved in during that year's season of Promenade Concerts.
After each night's performance, Constant used to celebrate and
then to return, intent on preparing the next night's programme on
his piano. By then, however, after the George, he was modestly but
justly uncertain of his mastery of the instrument. At that point, he

had a specific test-piece which he used to attack until he got it right, before he would embark on his run-through of the performances to come. The other three occupants of the household would lie in their beds, tense and unresting, until at length Constant got it right. When he did, they would roll over and sleep through anything he played, however exciting. Kind, lovable Constant: to dine with him, Margot Fonteyn, Michael and Joan was the beginning of a new life.

The whole atmosphere of what J.A. called work was also changed to a degree which initially he found difficult to grasp. This was escape – escape from the tyranny of the rule-book – to a kind of freedom never truly known before. The title of the appointment was Literary Programmes Producer, Overseas Services. The programmes were syndicated over various sections of the overseas operation but he was attached specifically to the Eastern Service. This was once described as 'The Third Programme before the Third Programme existed'. His work now immersed him in prose and poetry of a high standard. In terms of living it was new, stimulating and compelling of disbelief to such an extent that he had to spell it out to himself day after day, before he could believe it was real.

It would be pointless to pretend that he was an established writer when he took the post. He had published two 'slim volumes' and an anthology. The collection *Landmarks*, made in collaboration with George Rostrevor Hamilton, was of topographical poetry of England and Wales. In compiling it and, specifically, in writing for permission to publish, he had come into touch with a number of established authors and had all the beginner's pride in those contacts. He was up to the ears in books and literary matters but now that ceased to be the eccentricity of a young policeman and became a professional literary operation.

He was shot into an office at 200 Oxford Street, better recognized then as the former Cooperative Store. There he shared a room with Sunday Wilshin – who, as an actress, had understudied Gertrude Lawrence, and was not interested in men – and their two secretaries. All three were new to his experience: Sunday for her general attitude, the two secretaries for just being that splendid type, the BBC secretary – which was, then at least, a quite unique breed of courteous, intelligent, efficient and underpaid young woman.

He had responsibility for three specific programmes, two of which were weekly: 'Book of Verse', a half-hour of criticism and quotations from a specific poet or group of poets, and a similarly shaped quarter-hour prose programme with, usually, a critic and a single reader. Once a month he handled E.M. Forster's book talk to India, which was quite amazingly illuminating. In the first place, the script, written in a readable but ugly hand, was quite masterly in its perception and sensibility; it was invariably delivered clearly, if not particularly excitingly. Forster was held in justifiably high esteem – not entirely derived from *A Passage to India* – in the sub-continent, where his broadcasts were, so far as could be ascer-tained, listened to with something near to reverence.

Forster was a withdrawn-looking little man, with a tiny after-thought of a moustache and small, crookedly perched, metal-framed spectacles. Once he came into the humidly heated studio in the depth of winter, wearing a heavy muffler fastened with a large safety pin which was clearly making him uncomfortably hot. Would he not like to take it off? 'But my mother pinned it on, and I am sure I should not put it back on properly.' Assured that the producer would undertake that motherly duty, he consented to remove it, to his subsequent greater comfort. He was, though, when he left, extemely searching in his questions to make sure that that scarf was exactly as it had been when he arrived. Morgan Forster was always reluctant to sign copies of his books, even for an obviously devoted reader and admirer. Indeed, he once wrote a piece lamenting the fact that people might make money from sell-ing signed copies of his work. He never, though, quite had the firmness to refuse the request from the producer.

If his talk was always illuminating, 'Book of Verse' was quite exciting entertainment. J.A. chose a critic who wrote the back-ground material and selected examples which were read by a team of actors. The latter may have seemed an oddly varied bunch but they had it in common that they felt for poetry and could read it sensibly without exaggeration. Valentine Dyall had what seemed an almost impossibly deep voice – he was 'the Man in Black' – but he was outstandingly good at sensing poetry, probably more likely than any other to get the meanings, stresses and nuances right on the first reading.

Robin Holmes came in one day for an audition as a poetry reader. There was no doubt of his quality – almost delicately perceptive – and it was agreed that he should come into a programme on the first convenient occasion. Then, over a cup of tea in a nearby restaurant, it emerged that, after enthusiastic amateur theatricals at Cambridge, he had volunteered for the Rifle Brigade and had been shot in the head. The crucial effect of the wound was to make it impossible for him to judge distances. Hence, when he returned from the Services and, on the strength of his Cambridge reputation, was taken into the chorus of the Old Vic production of *Oedipus Rex*, he simply bumped into his neighbour. Asked, with all the bluntness of a recent policeman, if he was hard up, he admitted that he was. 'Come on, then,' said J.A., and led him into the office of Aidan Thomson, Head of Overseas Presentations, with the words, 'Here is a superb newsreader for you.' Aidan, like the civilized character he was, gave Robin a courteous but searching test and forthwith – as could be done in those immediately post-war years – offered him a reader's post. Robin accepted uncertainly and ever after humorously cursed J.A. for 'making a newsreader of me'. He became, with that splendidly modulated, sensitive and yet precise, voice, one of the finest of them. So far as the 'Book of Verse' programme was concerned, he was not only a first-class verse reader, but could quite brilliantly take on the reading of a narration that the writer did not care to undertake. A good, understanding friend, he was much missed upon his death.

Dylan Thomas was again quite different – a man with a voice that uttered poetry with the quality of a bugle note. In the introduction to *The Colour of Saying: an anthology of verse spoken by Dylan Thomas*, Professor R. N. Maud and Aneirin Talfan Davies make the point that 'Thomas did over a hundred broadcasts, the great majority of them readings for producer John Arlott in a "Book of Verse" series for the Overseas Service.' He was a delight to work with, provided only that he respected the poetry he was asked to read: when he did not, his scorn was withering, and he could make almost a comic epic out of what he deemed to be an over-serious piece of verse. When he was happy in a reading, though, he seemed to sting out his words, leaving them impressed on the mind and never skimping a single idea. More than one poet felt himself elevated when Dylan read his work. To hear him peal out Blake's 'Tiger! Tiger!' was a profound poetic experience.

He was, too, a most splendid companion, convivial certainly, and sometimes more than that. Yet, however drunk he might become, his taste in many things never wavered; he would be humorous but never crude; he had a distaste for dirty jokes. Twice J.A., greatly daring, asked him why he drank so much. On those two different occasions, he gave two completely different answers. The first was, 'I drink to feel good, and go on drinking to go on feeling good, but then suddenly I am drunk.' Second was, 'I get drunk because every time I get drunk it is different.' However, most of the writers who have wrung out the juice of Dylan's drinking have failed to mention the fact that when he was at work on a poem – which might often last for days – he simply did not drink at all. His respect for his craft was too great for that; anyone who reads his poetry must recognize the immense degree of skill in his poetic technique – certainly far more than anyone could achieve who was not sober. He had humour, humanity and imagination – the latter in the highest and most poetic degree. J.A. loved him and felt constantly a return of affection: and that without affectation.

Less seriously, perhaps, Dylan had an immense appetite for cricket; he would turn up at county matches at Swansea and curl up quietly in a corner of the commentary box, living it all through and then, afterwards, come away to one of the pubs or restaurants of his friends who received him so gladly – the evening invariably ended in sheer contentment, if not utter sobriety. The world was deprived by his death.

Duncan McIntyre had a fine depth of Scottish accent; few could read with greater compassion or more profound tenderness. A good and kindly companion, he seemed never out of voice or temper. Dorothy Smith shared with Duncan McIntyre the Scottish

111

accent and the communication of compassion that made much of his and her work so moving.

Alan Vandyke Price, whose widow, Pamela, writes on wine, was 'discovered' by happy accident in a play at St Mary's Hospital. An imaginative and unforcedly expressive reader, he qualified successfully as a doctor but within a few months of taking up his practice he was dead of an illness which closed in on him quite shockingly.

The scriptwriters were accepted authorities, and frequently experts, on the particular poets they dealt with. Not all of them were competent as broadcasters, which in most cases they accepted; and somebody, usually Robin Holmes or David Jacobs or John Witty, would read the script for them. Most of them liked, in any case, to turn up for the programme. This was invariably a friendly, and often illuminating, occasion which lasted generally through the morning rehearsals and the afternoon recording, with re-takes, from about ten until half past five.

One of the great pleasures of that particular programme was to be able to hire Harry Craig as a scriptwriter. He was indeed a happy discovery, not merely in work, but in life; a friend the memory of whom remains warm and happy. Professionally he eventually became known as H.A.L. Craig, who all too late gained a reputation and, at last, some wealth, for his two films on the Crimean War. Harry was one of the twin sons of a Church of Ireland parson who lived in Eire. From that home deep in the countryside, Harry and his brother Dick won scholarships to Trinity College, where, though on short commons, they lived the splendid life. Harry used to recount how they would pawn the furniture in their rooms to get enough money to eat well before the university sports, confident in the knowledge that they would win enough prizes to reclaim their pledges. Harry was tall, wide-shouldered, slightly balding, cheerfully handsome; an utterly happy creature. J.A. met him when he took an immediately post-war holiday at Malahide, near Dublin. The two hit it off from the moment they met in the office of *The Bell*, presided over by Peadar O'Donnell, who was then the convivial, literary father figure of Dublin. With Paddy Kavanagh those three made a splendid Irish trio. They were part of the new, stimulating and completely fresh atmosphere of Dublin, whether it was captured in talk or drink in the pubs or the cafés, or merely walking the streets and looking over the parapet of O'Connell Bridge. Once, too, there was a crazy, ill-afforded, first-class rail trip to Dublin to see an international football match with, after the recent war, a quite exciting train breakfast, and a match to watch with delight. Harry, though, stood alone: a wonderful creature, whose love-life was utterly spectacular but may not be detailed here for fear the telling might wound some excellent people. He had sensitivity, immense humour and profound humanity; in an odd-seeming combination of nationalism and protestantism, he used to spend much of his limited income on feeding ex-convicts. A whole facet of his character was, though, presumably reserved for the many women he loved, one above all. He spent most of his latter days between London, Dublin and Italy. In London, though, for three or four years after 1946 he gave J.A. a kind of friendship and conviviality neither had ever quite known before. Once J.A. acquired his first London house, in Crouch End, Harry Craig was a regular dinner guest every Sunday, delighting both J.A. and his wife by the generosity of his nature and his humour. Of few people is it ever possible to say that they had not a single enemy; but it is virtually impossible to imagine anyone disliking a man so full of kindness and fun as Harry Craig. His death left a gap in J.A.'s life which no one else has ever filled.

Harry's presence at that time contributed to a general atmosphere of excitement. Merely to be living and working in London was a stimulus, and remained so until years, age – above all, progress – blunted its attractions. There was much to be done, but the energy of a thirty-one-year-old could cope. The house in Crouch End, furnishing it, making fresh friends, all made life quite amazingly and thrillingly full.

Surely that was enough for any man, coming in such concentration. Then, though, another of the accidents occurred. This was, too, a time when he realized increasingly that, if at the time his BBC post had been advertised, any one of a thousand young writers had been available to apply for it, as distinct from being tied to some form of national service, he would simply have been trodden to death in the rush. He was not ungrateful. The new 'accident' occurred at the January meeting of the Eastern Service to plan programmes for the second quarter of the year. He was interested but not worried: his programmes were going to continue as before. Then, all at once, Donald Stevenson, Head of the Service, a quick-witted man who bore a striking resemblance to Lawrence of Arabia, threw in the casual remark which was to change the young man's life once again.

'Isn't there,' he asked, 'an Indian cricket team here this summer?'

'Yes, there is.'

'Ah, yes, I remember from your interview, you are keen on cricket – do you know when they start to play?'

'On the first Saturday in May.'

'How do you know that?'

'I have a copy of the fixture list in my office.'

'Go and fetch it.'

Stevenson read it quickly and then said, 'We must show them we know the side has come. I see the first two matches are at Worcester and Oxford – that Indian Test player for England played for Worcestershire, didn't he?'

'Yes, he did.' (The elder Pataudi.)

'And, of course, a lot of Indians went to Oxford. Can you find any space in the English to India programmes to carry a daily piece on the cricket?'

'Not much, really, we are fairly well packed.'

'Oh, I don't want much – a few minutes will do.'

'We could muster ten minutes at five past four which, of course, would carry up to the tea interval; would that do?'

'Yes, I think so; we ought to cover the first two matches out of sheer courtesy.' Then, thinking aloud, 'We could get a feed from Domestic Services – they would certainly be covering it. No, dammit, they would get the Indian pronunciations wrong. Hamid will be there to do it in Hindi; but his English would not do.' Then, suddenly, 'Have you ever done a cricket broadcast?'

'Yes,' which referred to that early broadcast on Hambledon – nothing like a commentary nor even a match summary.

114

'Would you like to do those two matches? I mean, could you do them without interfering with your programmes?'

'Yes, I could work on the Sunday and take scripts away with me if necessary.'

'Good enough, put yourself down, then, for those two matches – how many days?' Donald was not the brightest man on cricket, neither had he any need to be.

'Six,' and he nodded.

This had opened up yet another glimpse of high pleasure: Worcester had been a place of cricketing delights before the war; it was full of friends and, now, once more, full of promise. It was an almost delirious prospect. To combine producing poetry with watching cricket – without undue work strain – seemed, and continued to be for many years, a combination of happinesses almost beyond his belief. For the moment, though, that was a distant prospect. There were winter months to plough through, a house at Crouch End still to be put in order, but it was all so exciting that even scrubbing out long neglected corners seemed no hardship. The baby was a joy and work no problem – rather an almost drunken excitement.

To change life from one extreme to another: to move from the hard discipline of police life to a world where work was the former hobby was difficult even to believe. That belief never changed: circumstances altered the mechanics of life – after all there are only twelve months in a year – but this was an existence still to be looked back on many years later as without blemish.

Programme narrators were numerous and immensely pleasing. Laurence Whistler was a wartime friend; later to become the finest of all modern glass engravers and still a sensitive poet and prose writer. His appearances to read and to dine afterwards were always fresh and refreshing. James Laver had a most delightful turn of wit and was fine evening company. Edmund Blunden, a tiny, bird-like man, too shy to read his own narration but happy to come and advise – though only when asked – illuminated a vast amount of poetry for a young man who had so much to learn. Ifor Evans was an established scholar with a happy and easy touch in broadcasting. Dylan, on the few occasions when he narrated, was, in truth, a trifle too explosive; but stimulating if used only occasionally. He was another who made the after-programme evening an occasion.

It proved possible, too, to rake in Terry Delaney. He was one of the reliefs in the horror of war and its immediate follow-up years. He used to go up to London – Charing Cross Road and second-hand books – every Thursday during the blackout and catch the midnight train back from Waterloo. He was living at this time on the edge of Eastleigh, and by the time he reached Southampton – on the express which did not stop at Eastleigh – it was a long, long walk home. Once, nodding but not sleeping, towards the end of the journey, he noticed the train slowing on the edge of Eastleigh station. Surely enough, it stopped, momentarily, on the platform: Terry, hardly able to believe his luck, leapt out and slammed the carriage door. The train pulled away and a porter came up, highly indignant: 'You can't get out here, Sir – the train doesn't stop here.'

'You are quite right,' said Terry, 'and I didn't get out.' He departed leaving the porter in a state of disbelief, which he – the porter – related, apparently bewildered, to all who would listen, for many days afterwards. Terry joined Radio Newsreel, where he and Julian Holland made a splendid pair of companions, constantly to be visited when they were busy – but not too busy to chatter or come out for the briefest – as they are the best – of drinks from work.

As nearly as he could be annoying, Harry Craig became annoying about this time. The easiest of guests at Sunday dinner, he was constantly most desperately late for the meal. Pressed on this issue, he protested, 'But you see, in Dublin, we always set off for supper from wherever we are at the time we are due there – and distances in London are so horribly long.' Once he was – even for Harry – impossibly late: hard pressed, he admitted he had met 'one of the loveliest women I have ever seen' on the tube and had continued their courtship on the steps of Russell Square station: 'Ye see, everybody uses the lift there – the stairs must be the safest place in the world.'

So the first quarter of the year went by and the second – which was to include the personal cricket week – began. The whole pattern of life led, despite any wishes to the contrary, to a neglect of family life; of wife and son. Later, that was to become a matter of considerable remorse.

The beginning of May came, and Worcester and cricket. The Nawab of Pataudi – now to be referred to as Pataudi senior – remembered, or at least courteously pretended to remember, the youngster who had acted as twelfth man for Hampshire against Worcestershire before the war. There were introductions to the Indian players, all courteous and interested. There were old Worcester contacts to be renewed – Reggie and Doris Perks, Peter Jackson and many more. A few notes and play going on under the nose made the greatest difficulty of the broadcast the accurate timing of the moment to hand back to the studio. Dick Howorth scored a century for Worcestershire; sharing, in the second innings, an opening stand of 146 in an hour and a half; after which they subsided to 284. Perhaps the most impressive feature of the cricket was the slow left-arm bowling of 'Vinoo' Mankad. The solid, companionable Mankad was, and remains, for J.A., the Indian cricketer nearest to a typical mature English pro. This outstanding, unshowy performer took eight wickets in the match for precisely 100 runs; but Shinde, with his loose-limbed leg-spinners, had 5 for 50 in the second innings. Vijay Merchant, that calm, relentless punisher of the bad ball, made 24 in the first innings, 51 in the second; he was to prove the pillar of the tour batting. Rusi Modi made a quite academic 34 and 84. For all India, batting fourth, could do, and despite a bludgeoning 59 by Shute Banerjee, Worcestershire won by 16 runs. Just to be back at cricket was a huge excitement; and if this book has begun to sound like a parade of excitements, that was the way life was for him in those days.

So on to Oxford, where Martin Donnelly, the young New Zealander, scored a brilliant 61 and 116 not out in a drawn game. Again Mankad (4 for 58) bowled well, but the two leg-spinners – Shinde, 4 for 73 in the first innings, and the younger – C.S. – Nayudu, 3 for 60 in the second – gave promise of results they never, in fact, achieved on that tour. Staying with Dylan Thomas in his house by the river, the most vivid memory of the match is of sitting in a bomb crater on the edge of the Parks with Louis MacNeice, Cecil Day Lewis and Dylan on the second afternoon. They drank and chattered idly – did the other three realize what a wonderful experience it was for him? – until suddenly he looked at his watch. He had precisely three minutes to reach the broadcasting point; no producer – only an engineer in the distant van. He made it, concealed – he hoped – his panting and delivered his due ten minutes.

The next day he was back at 200 Oxford Street with his six days of cricket duly enjoyed when he received a message to report to the Head of the Service. Uppermost in his mind was the probability that there had been a complaint on technical grounds about his short-windedness after that chase back from the poets' bomb crater.

'You should read that,' said Donald Stevenson, tossing a cable to him.

Even at a range of forty-one years, the words of that cable remain sharply in his mind. It was from Jim Pennethorne-Hughes, later to become a close friend, but then a distant figure as the BBC representative in New Delhi. It read: 'Cricket broadcasts greatest success yet East Service. Must be continued all costs, Hughes.' He read it with complete disbelief and looked up for comment.

'Well,' said Stevenson, 'You did it. Do you want to go on with it to the end of the season? And if you did, could you do your programmes? I assume you couldn't?'

The emotion was strange; almost overcoming; invited to take his time and think, he needed the time.

'I should have to miss at least half a dozen matches,' and then, thinking slowly, though as fast as he could, 'but if I worked on Sundays and evenings when the side was playing in London, I could probably do it.'

'Go on then, but take care there is no falling off in the quality of your programmes or you must come back at once and forget the cricket altogether; that may be nice but it is not what you were engaged for.'

'Very good.' He walked away dizzy with disbelief. What was to happen in the coming four and a half months was utter revelation.

He had been up and down Hampshire on his bike, across to Eastbourne, and had spent days and holidays in London. Otherwise he knew nothing at all of Britain; now it was to dawn on him and to make him in consciousness a completely different person. For one who had never been north of Trent, Nottingham, Yorkshire and Lancashire threw open new worlds of perception. Provincial theatres, pubs from the luxurious to the seedy, and a whole range of new friends, mostly, though not all, cricketers or cricket reporters, swam into his gloating knowledge.

It is all too easy not to appreciate Britain in all its variety. Those varieties, too, ranged from the dawning of new knowledge to the utterly ridiculous. Sheffield, for instance, was to seem a haunt of millionaires; of amazing wealth and of champagne drunk for the first time and with awe.

One regret remains from that round of England. It was necessary for him, if he was to record his programmes within the reasonable time limits imposed, to miss the Indian match at Liverpool. So, incredibly enough, Aigburth remained – and remains – the one outstanding first-class ground in England where he never saw a cricket match. So far as the game was concerned, this summer was to be an almost incredible experience; fresh players – and invariably friendly – added to his hunger for knowledge of a game he had never before perceived in its full extent. This was, as it is now all too easy to forget, the first post-war cricket season – in effect, the first time many people in England had consciously watched the game played seriously. For the enthusiasts it was a gloriously nostalgic entertainment.

His literary programmes remained important. Often they involved coming down on the sleeper from Manchester, taking tube and bus across to Crouch End to see the family and snatch breakfast, and down to 200 Oxford Street. He would record 'Book of Verse' until about five; after that the prose programme, a couple of drinks and home again for supper before catching the sleeper back to Manchester. It was a rush, but all was so stimulating that it seemed no hardship. Indeed, on the Saturday after he came back from Oxford he went down to the Oval to watch India v Surrey for pleasure, and saw the beginning of what proved to be a record-breaking stand. India were 205 for 9 when numbers ten and eleven – Chandu Sarwate and Shute Banerjee – both on nought, came together. By Monday afternoon he was watching when they completed the highest partnership ever made for a last wicket in England. There was no previous instance of numbers ten and eleven each scoring centuries, and they put on 249. India's total was 454 and they then bowled Surrey out for 135, made them follow on and, although Bob Gregory made 100 and shared an opening stand of 144 with Laurie Fishlock, bowled them out a second time for 338. They needed only 20 to win. Merchant went in first with Sarwate who, ironically, was out to Bedser for 1 as the touring side won by nine wickets.

Of course it could not all be like that but there were many other pleasures: immediately, a visit to Cambridge for the match with the University. Not great cricket: centuries for Modi and Pataudi, but it was all too easy and the Indians won by an innings and 19. The combination of Hazare's leg-cutters and the mixed spin of Shinde and Sarwate was too much for the University. Vijay Hazare was a captain in the Maharaja of Baroda's army; a Christian, lean, taut and muscular. He was a determined orthodox bat and a useful fast-medium bowler whose oddity was a grotesquely huge leg-cutter – if he could have bowled it to a length, he would have murdered almost any side, but he invariably dropped it short. Cambridge was a delight; the secondhand bookshops made morning arrivals at Fenner's much later than they might have been.

The tourists' next match he undoubtedly should have seen; it was against Leicestershire. There was no play until mid-afternoon on the first day and then a violent thunderstorm broke over the ground and made nothing possible until Monday. It was, too, uncomfortably cold; rain constantly interrupted play, and the game was drawn. It was, though, remarkable for the batting of Vijay Merchant, who made 111 and 57 – both not out – and without detectable error.

Vijay Merchant was a unique batsman. Soft-footed as a cat, firmly built, but giving the impression of gentleness rather than power, he moved easily and purposefully about the crease. Bowl him six bad balls and he would hit every one for four. Bowl him six good balls and he would stop all six. He played in virtually every match of the tour. When asked why, he answered, 'If I don't play, my family in India will think I am ill.' He was the first Indian to score 2000 runs on a tour of England. He was infallibly courteous, soft-voiced but quite decided in his opinions, which he stated gently but firmly.

Instead of the Leicestershire match J.A. nefariously chose to go to the two-day fixture at Edinburgh against Scotland. Edinburgh, seen for the first time, was yet another revelation far more exciting than the cricket. That had its moments. Hazare scored 101, and India won by an innings and 56. In the second afternoon, though, as he was sitting alone in the commentary box, keeping score for himself and with no one to turn to, he recorded the fall of the wickets of Marshall and Clark, and, as Hodge walked out, he asked himself, was a hat-trick 'on' or had there been a ball in between the two wickets? Anyway, Sarwate was hardly likely to knock down a third wicket. But he did; he clean bowled Hodge and the miserable commentator could only say, '90 for 9 and that is a hat-trick – back to the studio.' He raced to the scorebox and there were two very phlegmatic scorers indeed: his spirits fell.

'Was that a hat-trick?'

'Oh, aye,' said the Scots scorer, quite unexcited: J.A. fled to the bar.

The MCC match was only mildly interesting: India beat a side rich in personalities but with only one player – Bill Edrich – likely to play for England. J.A. took three of the touring players – Merchant, Hazare and Mankad – none of whom had had any lunch because they were either batting or waiting to bat – back home to Crouch End to dinner. There it emerged that they did not eat meat – which he had guessed – but that they did not take fish either, nor eggs – nor anything else in the house except potatoes and rice, and strictly no alcohol. Heavens, how they punished the rice – thank heaven there was some – and potatoes; they drank tea copiously and were extremely courteous to him in his embarrassed misery.

Three days in the studio while the touring side rested and had a one-day game with the Indian Gymkhana and then down to Southampton for the Hampshire game. It was a match full of friends – notably Johnny Arnold, Gerry Hill and Neville Rogers; Leo Harrison was still away in the RAF. The Indians won by six wickets, but Charlie Knott took 7 for 36 and 3 for 74 which effectively took him into the second Test trial, at Canterbury, when, with 0 for 60, he did not shine.

Cricket had not fully returned to its former seriousness: it could not, by comparison with the recent war, be taken quite seriously. There was, for instance, some good fun in the Glamorgan-India match. The touring side's batsmen did their best to hit, on a dead wicket and after rain held up the game until mid-afternoon on Saturday. Then Amarnath suddenly found his batting form and hit with immense, wristy power in the score of 376 for 6 declared. Rain again spoilt Tuesday but the Welsh crowd turned up in great numbers with only a draw in prospect. John Clay, the Glamorgan captain, and one of the most urbanely humorous cricketers, was batting with Peter Judge, who was bowled by Sarwate to end the county's first innings. He turned at once to Vijay Merchant who was acting as captain of the Indians in the absence of Pataudi, injured, and said affably, 'I suppose you want us to follow on?'

'Yes, please,' said Vijay.

'No point in going in then with a crowd as big as this waiting, is there?'

'Not if you don't want the roller,' was the answer.

Sarwate picked up the ball and clean bowled Peter Judge again: which must be the first instance of the same player being out twice to the same bowler within a minute in a first-class match. Not according to match regulations, of course, but this was 1946 and there was a huge cricket-hungry crowd to be amused. In fact, John Clay reversed the entire second innings batting order and, when the match was left drawn with Glamorgan 73 for 7, the only two batsmen who had not been used were the two openers, Arnold Dyson and Emrys Davies. It was still a time of shortages and Peter Judge proved a quite invaluable guide to remote country hostelries of the area which had a stock of beer.

The Indians flew from Cardiff to Portsmouth for the Combined Services match; then up to Trent Bridge to play Nottinghamshire. J.A. travelled by train. That, though, was no hardship; Western

Region catered well and, between meals and a couple of books, all was very relaxing. The Services game was drawn. It was good to see Emrys Davies, to meet the thoughtful Jack Davies and, most importantly, Leo Harrison. Though his chief service in the field for Hampshire had always been at cover point, he now kept wicket alertly. Hazare made top score (62 not out) and held the innings together; he followed that by bowling unchanged for 2¼ hours to take 7 for 66, when the worn pitch gave his leg-cutter some purchase.

The tourists' Nottinghamshire match was destroyed by rain: no play on the first day, little on the second. Of the Indians, Merchant (86), Hazare (49) and Pataudi, whose 101 not out cheered him vastly, all took batting practice before the pending First Test. For J.A. it was a fine introduction to Nottingham, and especially to the Trent Bridge Hotel – still 'the TBI' to the locals – where Harry Winrow, Joe Hardstaff and Arthur Jepson provided some happily damaging introductions as the best part of two days was whiled away in the bar.

Then, after a batch of recordings, he was at Lord's, briefly to report a Test match for the first time – to call it a commentary would be too exalted a term. It is all too simple to recall his immense excitement. Some of his colleagues did not disguise their opinion of this down-market interloper. He kept his temper, apart from a threat to throw one of them over the pavilion rails – he could not even have lifted the man. It ended, though, with something better than armed neutrality; by the time the series was over, all was fairly amicable.

The match itself, the first post-war Test in England, was, for that reason alone, an emotional occasion, but absorbing purely on cricketing grounds, too. The selectors had been careful; fearful, possibly, of defeat, they picked their strongest possible side. Pataudi won the toss and took first innings for India. It was, though, Alec Bedser's occasion. Heaving himself up to the wicket and bowling mightily – flinging the ball, it seemed, heavy-handedly into the pitch – he had a rare first Test appearance: 7 for 49 in the first innings; 4 for 96 in the second. It is doubtful if any man has ever bowled better or more effectively in his first Test.

The natural conclusion is that he was fired by the fact that war had kept him back from the chance for too long. Rising twenty-eight, he had been in the services, and this was England's first representative match since 1939. He was hungry for opportunity, and seized it eagerly.

When England batted, Hazare and Amarnath opened the bowling; Gul Mahomed bowled a slingy, bumpy, left-arm-over to allow them to change ends. Then Amarnath demonstrated his threat: to a little extra pace, Len Hutton pushed forward hurriedly and Nayudu caught him at short leg. Denis Compton came in, unhappy and out of form, groped forward at the next ball, was bowled and knew it before it happened. There must have been many present who had never seen a hat-trick in a Test match; and at least as many who did not want to see one now. Wally Hammond walked in; there was a majesty about him, a monumental reassurance – but? He leant calmly forward to his first ball and played it down on the line of the off stump. The next ball he struck mightily straight for an all-run four, ended by Gul Mahomed's explosive throw which shattered the wicket to which Hammond was running – and which he reached barely in time. Together he and Washbrook played England out of trouble before Joe Hardstaff surprised even himself with 205 not out. It was a pure Trent Bridge innings played at Lord's. Paul Gibb plodded patiently beside him but Hardstaff's runs were enough. Mushtaq Ali had been left out and Mankad opened with Merchant, playing soundly and demonstrating his rapid development to a world class all-rounder. Amarnath, Modi and Abdul Hafeez (later A.H. Kardar) batted usefully, but none well enough to threaten England's eventual ten-wicket win; and all accomplished in three days. Doug Wright took two wickets in each innings, but the great triumphs were those of Bedser and Hardstaff. Rusi Modi was a tall, thin, thoughtful, even shy cricketer, with the ability to handle every type of bowling thrown against him. That, though, did not include – for lack of that weapon – genuinely high pace.

Not to dally over the social side of the matter, it was a heady introduction to the Test cricket circus, even if only from its outskirts. The memory remains of Wally Hammond; not simply a good player but one of the few truly great cricketers. He placed his stamp upon any game of cricket, imposing, indeed impelling, respect. He could be a remote man and there was a deep shyness in him. He decided to be kind to J.A., took him to dinners beyond his depth, and, just sometimes, vouchsafed a glimpse of that territory where he resided as a cricketer; where batting at the highest possible level was a simple matter. Soon afterwards he was to suffer failure as England's captain in Australia; but no one who watched him bat in the time of his greatness has any doubt whatever about him. For England, W. G. Grace, Jack Hobbs, Wally Hammond: we await a fourth.

Without labouring it, this was a rebirth: the sudden sight of cricket as those of J.A.'s generation had almost forgotten it. It is all, certainly, an everyday matter now: runs and wickets and wins and losses rolling off radio and the presses unendingly; for some people, almost boringly. Then, though, it was not only refreshing on the pitch but, for many of those coming back from war, a symbol of normality – exhilarating normality. If the recital of it now seems like the ramblings of a bore, it was, nevertheless, at that time, a kind of splendour.

The tour went on and so did the understanding with members of the touring side – men of different races, natures and ideas. Dattu – not a particularly respectful sobriquet – Hindlekar was a natural wicketkeeper and one, rare amongst Indian cricketers of that period, who could laugh at the hard times. By no means all the side could do that and, when there were suggestions about the legality of Sarwate's bowling action, there were many bitternesses in the party. He was left out at the Oval in a most unpleasant atmosphere. The spirit of the side, though, considering the vast diversity of its members, was generally good; and Pataudi himself sometimes succeeded in injecting into the team atmosphere a hint of his own Oxford-induced ironic sense of humour.

They went on to a draw at Northampton and then the sadly missed match against Lancashire at Aigburth. Then came a personal first visit to Yorkshire. It was not inhospitable but it was unusual; and the natives were not disposed to yield superiority to anyone. The game was at Bradford and it was a revival of old time companionship to stay on that rather grotesque hillside with such an old friend as Harry Howell from Southampton University – Geordie, physicist and rich discusser of life. On the field, Yorkshire ran rampant. Arthur Booth, who had spent so many previous years in the shadow of Hedley Verity – killed in the war – emerged, now rising forty-four, as the most successful slow left-arm bowler of the season. Supported by immaculate – even overbearingly hostile – fielding, he took 6 for 33 and 4 for 58: Ellis Robinson 4 for 40 in the second innings. C.S. Nayudu, in one of his rare bursts of form, bowled his leg-spinners well enough to take 5 for 27. He was a lean, taut man, of a cricketing family, who, at his best, bowled the leg-break and the googly with rare fire. Still Len Hutton went in first and batted through for 183 out of 344 for 9 declared. Vic Wilson made 74, but Len, at his best, dominated them all. It was the tourists' heaviest defeat of that tour; by an innings and 82. Notwithstanding the fact that they had the worst of the weather, it was a most chastening result for the Indians. For the visitor from the South it was an extremely impressive demonstration of Yorkshireness.

Every one of these matches was a new experience, a new impression: Lancashire – Manchester – Old Trafford – was another. Cyril Washbrook and Jack Ikin rolled out hundreds; Vijay Merchant came back with 242 not out; nobody else in the Indian side reached fifty but they led by 456 for 8 declared to 406. Then the rains came again. Mankad produced figures of 5 for 62 in 37 overs and Lancashire, in the end, probably were content to make a draw of it. Bob Gibb's bookshop became a port of call for many years to come, and Manchester assumed a character quite unique in Britain for a Basingstoke boy.

Cricket had never been the same before, if only for lack of opportunity. It was never to be the same again because that remarkable immediate post-war atmosphere has never been reproduced. At Chesterfield, the Indians won in the tightest of finishes, with the second ball of the last possible over. Amarnath had helped out by keeping wicket. He came back to bowl at the end of the second innings and took 3 for 33 to decide the game. It was the occasion to start a friendship with Charlie Elliott that has lasted ever since. The first time he touched the ball in a first-class match he caught out Jack Hobbs. He was brought up as a professional footballer by Harry Storer of Derby County and England. He talked, and still talks, cricket and football with true understanding and appreciation. On the field the pace of Bill Copson, the variations of Bert Rhodes and the controlled swing of Cliff Gladwin added to the cricketing education. The Nawab, Rusi Modi and Gul Mahomed – a muscular, lively little left-hander who often fielded effervescently at cover – all scored useful runs in a win by 118 runs.

Then back across the Pennines to Yorkshire again – Sheffield. Once again they piled up runs. Len Hutton did not play; neither did Maurice Leyland – great company after the match – Bill Bowes, or Frank Smailes. The home bowling took a hammering but not until Yorkshire had made 300 for 6 – Paul Gibb, Harry Halliday, Willie Watson and Norman Yardley all making runs. The first three Indians were out for 41 but then Hazare (244 not out), Mankad (132) and Pataudi (51 not out) took their revenge for Bradford. Their 490 put any possibility of a finish far into the distance: India's honour against Yorkshire was at least partly satisfied. An Indian steel magnate appeared to support his country's side. In the best hotel in Sheffield he laid out the kind of meal that never happened in Basingstoke – nor, for that matter, in Southampton. J.A. was suitably awed, overfed and, finally, he thanked his stars, still marginally sober.

The tourists' match with Durham at Sunderland was the kind of extravagance he could not indulge, so almost a week of work in the office saw him off to the Manchester Test in a state of almost improper self-righteousness. The England selectors left out Bill Bowes and Frank Smailes and chose, instead, Bill Voce and the Essex leg-spinner, Peter Smith; but Smith was injured and they called up Dick Pollard, of Lancashire, which was to prove a highly successful move. India left out Gul Mahomed, Sadu Shinde and the younger Nayudu – usually known as 'C.S.' – for Mushtaq Ali, Ranga Sohoni and Chandu Sarwate. The recall of Mushtaq – at Pataudi's insistence – was, at least in part, dictated by his view of cricket psychology. When the two countries had last met here, in

1936, Merchant and Mushtaq Ali, scoring a century apiece, had put on 203 for the first wicket in the second innings.

Now Pataudi won the toss and decided to put England in – a reasonable enough move at the time for there was rain about and it seemed that India were marginally the weaker side.

There was a lot of poor humour about the fact that Manchester rain prevented play until after lunch on the opening day but, once it began, it was full of event. Not only was the cricket full of action and character, but J.A. was learning to appreciate it far beyond his former scope. First of all, there was much talk about Pataudi's decision to field, though most informed opinion was on his side. The first four England batsmen – Hutton, Washbrook, Compton and Hammond – all made runs in their own particular styles. Hutton, hampered by a back injury, was careful and characteristically patient. Washbrook, jaunty and going for his strokes, especially on the on-side, was out oddly and, he may have felt, unluckily: he nicked Mankad to Hindlekar who caught the ball, lost it, juggled it between his pads, and then, still hampered by his injury, scooped up the catch from between his feet. Compton happily, if only temporarily, back in form, was simply himself. Above all, Wally Hammond gave his clearest indication to those 1946 Indians of his greatness. One six over the top of square leg was a mighty blow, executed almost casually. There was a true majesty about his batting – a memory that still lingers. Indeed, England reached 186 with only two wickets down, but then Mankad and Amarnath began to reap the reward for their diligence. After the first four England batsmen, only Paul Gibb, with 24, and Dick Pollard, 10 not out, so much as achieved double figures. On the second morning, the two Indians took between them six wickets for 55.

When India batted, Merchant and Mushtaq Ali put the clock back many years with yet another weighty stand – 124 for the first wicket. They were moving with immense confidence when Mushtaq edged Pollard into his stumps. Pollard went on for some half hour in deadly form – 5 overs, 2 maidens, 7 runs and 4 wickets. India did not recover: only Pataudi of the nine remaining batsmen got into double figures – and he made only 11. Pollard's 5 for 24 was the most striking performance, but Bedser took 4 for 41 to pol-

Nellie and Jack with their fat boy

Nellie and Jack's wedding at Meads Village, Eastbourne, in 1912:
the Clarkes on the left and the Arlotts on the right

The old cemetery lodge, Basingstoke

Basingstoke between the wars: a small, friendly country town far removed from the urban sprawl that it is today *(Arthur Attwood Collection)*

Fairfields School in the early 1920s *(Basingstoke & North Hampshire Gazette)*

Queen Mary's School in the early 1930s, now part of Basingstoke College of Technology *(Basingstoke & North Hampshire Gazette)*

England v Australia, the Oval, 1926: the author's first taste of Test
cricket, still vivid in the imagination sixty-five years later
(Hulton-Deutsch)

Four cricketers who made profound impressions on
the author in the late 1920s and early 1930s
Top left Jack Hobbs, who made the difficulties of the art of batting
seem simple *(Roger Mann Collection)*
Top right Maurice Tate, who looked clumsy and heavy-handed, but
made a cricket ball leave the pitch like an arrow *(Roger Mann Collection)*
Bottom left Learie Constantine (going for the catch): he fielded like the
magical athlete that he was *(Hulton-Deutsch)*
Bottom right Harold Larwood: to a whole generation, he personified
fast bowling *(Hulton-Deutsch)*

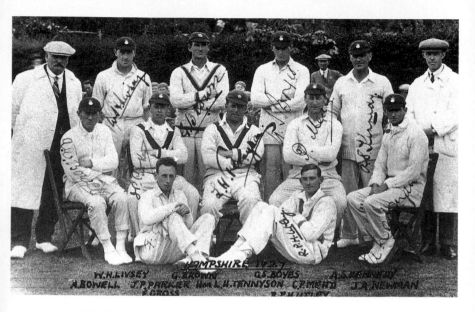

The Hampshire side of 1927, packed with childhood heroes,
many of whom would later become respected friends
(Roger Mann Collection)

The local mental hospital, Park Prewett,
where the job of diet clerk opened the author's eyes
to the real world in the 1930s
(Arthur Attwood Collection)

Above left Police Constable 94, Leslie T. J. Arlott, of the
Southampton County Borough Police Force
Above right Ready to turn out for Queen Mary's Old Boys

Home Office Course for Police Instructors, Peel House, April 1945,
shortly after the 31-year-old J.A. *(back row, extreme left)*
had delivered the broadcast address to the King
on behalf of the police on Victory Night

Aspiring poet *(Hulton-Deutsch)*

ish off the innings, giving England a lead of 124. Hammond's problem now was to frame a declaration. Hutton was out early, but Washbrook hung on, and Compton once more was at his spritely best, with 71 not out when the declaration came at 153 for 5; setting India 278 to win. This time the openers failed: the red-headed Pollard, all muscular but nimble bustling, accounted for both Merchant and Mushtaq for 3. When Bedser bowled the Nawab they were 5 for 3. Hazare set up some resistance; Modi and Abdul Hafeez backed him, but the ninth wicket fell at 138, leaving Sohoni and Hindlekar a quarter of an hour to save the game. In immense tension, Sohoni was twice missed by Paul Gibb behind the wicket and those errors were conclusive. Alec Bedser achieved yet another splendid triumph – 7 for 52 – and now, in the first two Tests of his career, he had taken 22 wickets for 238. Not only were the figures impressive but his rocking power captured the imagination. The thunderous fall of his left foot in the delivery stride seemed to rock his whole body – or was it the earth that moved?

That was the beginning of a month in which cricket truly dawned on J.A. – events, action, people, fresh friends, all these were facets of the new experience. At first, living in hotels was strange; and for a week, so was leaving the company of the touring cricketers for every train journey – the cricketers travelled first class, the BBC only paid for third. He could not afford it, but he knew, in his waking consciousness, that he would never have such a chance again, and he made the most of it: he paid the difference himself – and the family did not go short.

The one-day match with the Club Cricket Conference gave another chance to bring recordings up to date; then he travelled down to one of the most remarkable of cricket matches. It was at Hove, where the atmosphere of peace suddenly seemed stronger than anywhere else in England; although it had been full of servicemen – especially Australian airmen – it now seemed like a peacetime town. The cricket was simply celebratory: Pataudi won the toss and the Indians piled up runs. Merchant (205) and Mankad found batting a simple delight and put on 293 for the first wicket; the Nawab (110 not out) and Amarnath (106) followed them with centuries and, at one amazing point, the scoreboard read 533 for 2. Then Amarnath was out and soon George Cox, to his immense mirth, found himself with bowling figures of 2 for 86, while a couple of his specialist bowling colleagues suffered over one hundred runs without a wicket. Pataudi did not prolong the agony on Monday but declared at 533 for 3. Once again, Amarnath and Mankad – this time backed by Shinde – ran through the batting side. Harry Parks, Robert Stainton, Jim Langridge and Hugh Bartlett set up resistance, but Sussex followed on 280 behind. They then lost their first three wickets for 17, before George Cox settled in to his historic innings: he put on 171 with Jim Langridge, but when the seventh wicket went down they still needed 36 to save the innings defeat. That was soon done – Cox and Jim Hammond made 107 in an hour – and George went on to his 234 not out. The Indians made the 148 they needed for the loss of Mankad: Merchant, the insatiable, scored 63 not out, Rusi Modi 72 not out. One happy side issue of the game was taking Vijay Merchant and Vinoo Mankad to the first ice hockey match they had ever seen, which delighted them immensely. Merchant was indeed entitled to something to cheer him: he would easily have reached his century before lunch but for reflected light off the windscreens of parked cars which the owners, despite loud-speaker appeals, were very slow indeed to mask. Many men might have been angered indeed by such treatment, but Merchant, as ever, accepted it all patiently and quietly.

After all those runs at Hove, the Somerset match at Taunton produced a strikingly different morning: the ball swung in the high-fenced air and moved off the green pitch. An old friend in Bill Andrews, and a new one in Bertie Buse, tore the Indian batting apart. Only two of them – Mushtaq Ali, who boldly cross-batted (20) and the Nawab, using every ounce of his experience (29) – made even as many as five. Andrews took 5 for 36, Buse 5 for 27, and the touring side were all out for 64. The afternoon was like a different cricketing day – even a different match. Frank Lee made a dogged 76, Harold Gimblett a hectic 102, Mickie Walford 141 not out, 'Bunty' Longrigg 74 and Bertie Buse, to cap it all, 59 not out. Longrigg declared at 506 for 6 and India, set to make 442 to avoid the innings defeat, batted steadfastly all the way down; even

Sarwate at number ten made 66 not out and this time they mustered 431 but still lost by an innings and 11 runs.

A first visit to Swansea over the August bank holiday weekend saw a civic occasion. Strikingly, more than 50,000 people – the greatest cricket crowd ever seen in Wales – turned up for the match; and paid over £5000 – unheard of in those parts – for the pleasure. It was a pleasure, too, with C.S. Nayudu's leg-breaks and Mankad's slow left-arm bowling out Glamorgan for 238, but not before John Clay had struck a hectic 24 off a single over from Mankad; the crowd loved it. Once more Merchant (66) dug himself in but Clay, that wise off-spinner, took 7 for 72 to give Glamorgan a lead of 35 on the first innings. In the Glamorgan second innings Maurice Robinson made 79 out of 237 for 8 before the declaration. India batted again and Mushtaq Ali played one of the most surprising innings of the season – strokes which seemed impossible but which, made from a great height and quite fearlessly, brought him 93 and gave the Indians a win by five wickets. That great crowd enjoyed itself in almost every way cricket can give pleasure – and in bright and unbroken sunlight.

On the personal side, it was a happy opportunity to be shown round Swansea by Dylan Thomas, to whom it was a spiritual as well as an actual home. There could have been no better guide on a first visit to West Wales. It was, too, a second and most friendly encounter with that wise, gentle and witty man, John Clay. He had played for Glamorgan in their first Championship season, 1921, as a fast bowler. Now, here he was, forty-eight years old and as subtle and resourceful an off-spinner as any in the world. He plodded rather wearily in, but when he bowled, the spin, the flight and the strategy were all magnificently combined; it was just dawning delight to watch him.

The next match – Warwickshire at Edgbaston – was a further growth of experience. Merchant, acting as captain in the absence of the injured Nawab, won the toss and put Warwickshire in to bat. He would obviously have thought ten times over before doing it again – and then not have done it. The Warwickshire side was full of character. The innings was opened by Eric Houghton, the Aston Villa and England outside-left, with Dick Sale, a tall, raw-boned lefthander. Sale, an Oxford Blue, was not a very prepossessing bat but, given a few lives by the Indians, he made 157. Tom Dollery, an old friend from Reading where he played soccer, was at number four: he was one of the most thoughtful of cricket captains, who would have served England well in that capacity – and a far better bat than his four Test match scores would indicate. Peter Cranmer, England rugby international and most convivial of companions, was at number five.

It was Tom Pritchard's first full county match for Warwickshire; a New Zealander qualifying for the county, he was the fastest bowler in English cricket that year and all too little was seen of him. Eric Hollies went in last; most workmanlike of not-very-quick legspinners, he was a wise and quick-witted cricketer who spun the ball very little, but accurately and shrewdly enough to take 2323 wickets in his first-class career. He had a superb Black Country accent, a delightful sense of humour; he played thirteen times for England and, of course, he turned that googly of his enough to clean bowl Don Bradman on that worthy's last Test appearance two years later, almost certainly robbing him of a representative batting average of 100.

Of the play, Warwickshire, with the benefit of dropped catches, declared, and Merchant was left with the kind of problem that pursues a captain who has put the other side in and seen them make 375 for 9. He bent himself with his usual diligence to the task; he and Mushtaq made a brave start of it but Pritchard, in his second spell, clean bowled Hazare, Mankad and Gul Mahomed in seven balls for no runs. Merchant carried his bat for 86 and, when the tourists followed on, made 14 in his second innings – 100 runs without being out when the game, for time's sake, was left drawn.

So to Cheltenham, where a violent thunderstorm on Saturday morning wrecked marquees and flooded the ground, so there could be no play until after lunch on Monday. Among the old friends when Gloucestershire batted, Charlie Barnett gave a flourish, Andy Wilson jogged along and Hammond made 30 not out, in a vignette of his craftsmanship, before he declared at 132 for 3 in an attempt to make a match of it. In the Indian innings Pataudi, who went in first, was at his best with 71 out of 135 for 8 declared. Tom

Goddard, for his part, took 7 for 81. Tall, saturnine, originally a fast bowler, he wrapped his huge index finger round the ball and tweaked the off-break savagely. Mankad took five wickets and Shinde four, and India needed 185 in about 2½ hours. Goddard and his young understudy, the slow left-arm Sam Cook, kept them just short of it – they were 177 for 9 and the match drawn when time ran out. That game saw the start of a friendship with Colin Scott, who came from, and played for, W.G. Grace's village of Downend, and the infallibly good-natured Sam Cook; not a lucky man: he had a desperately unfortunate only Test match and things did not always go well with him afterwards. Eighteen seasons with Gloucestershire and then a long umpiring stint formed the cricketing life work of one of the game's faithful.

Rain ruined the Third and last Test at Lord's. Surely only the quiet patience of the huge crowd persuaded the umpires to start play at five on Saturday; but nothing could keep it going on the third day. After Gibb's errors of Old Trafford, Godfrey Evans came in for his first Test; he was to play, altogether, in 91. Pataudi won the toss and India batted: once more, Merchant and Mushtaq Ali opened the innings and they put on 94 before Mushtaq Ali was run out; so was Merchant – after he had made 128, then the highest score for India in a Test in England. In fact Merchant, not really hurrying, was run out when Compton, recalling his footballing prowess, kicked the ball into the stumps. Bill Edrich, a slingy fast bowler with the merits of pace and – generally – straightness, took four wickets for 68 in India's 331. There was, though, only time for England to score 95 for 3 – though Hammond's 9 not out made him the first man to score 7000 runs in Tests – before the end of the second day, which also proved the last. So England won the rubber by dint of taking the First Test. It was a subdued end to a nostalgic series.

The Essex match at Southend gave a terrific finish. Once again Vijay Merchant rose to the challenge of the occasion. Banerjee and Shinde had bowled the county out for 303; 'Sonny' Avery made 62, and that friendliest of men, Tom Pearce, 66. In the Indian innings, Ray Smith, great bringer of greengages to cricket matches, took six wickets; Trevor Bailey, then still a relative youngster, got a couple, and India were 165 behind on the first innings. Tom Pearce, though, did not enforce the follow-on; that summer the counties were above all trying to enjoy themselves and to see that the crowds enjoyed themselves also. Southend was a delight for shellfish and good company – Tom Wade, Ray and Peter Smith – and the weekend was enlivened by a slightly zany Sunday cricket match. For Essex in their second innings, Harry Crabtree, who was to become one of the most thoughtful of coaches, made a studious 118, Trevor Bailey 33 not out, and the declaration left India 367 to win. With the help of Modi in a stand of 119 and Mankad in another of 113, Merchant, with the luck to be dropped twice, ploughed on through the innings. He was ninth out – lbw to Ray Smith for 181 – with 13 wanted. That redoubtable number eleven, Dattu Hindlekar, supported by Shinde, just brought it off. Again the Indians produced a holiday occasion – the 10,500 people on the Saturday created a ground record.

The Canterbury game, too, promised well but, in the end, there was only four hours' play: enough for Arthur Fagg to make 109 and Leslie Ames 78 before all was washed out. Against Middlesex India batted first and this time it was Hazare (193 not out) and Mankad (109 not out) who, with Modi (80), carried them to 469 for 5 before they declared and the rain came down. Mankad with eight wickets, and Hazare with seven on the drying pitch, needed only four from Banerjee to win by an innings and 263.

India won a close game at Hastings against the South of England by 10 runs – there were some shrewd declarations on this tour – but the match with Leveson Gower's XI at Scarborough was made a draw by rain. A little thought by Brian Sellers would have given Dick Howorth a century and ten wickets in the match but he bowled him too little in the second innings.

J.A. at the end of the tour was a stunned man. He had received quite unexpected kindness of the highest degree from the touring players and those of the counties. Towards the end, too, he had been asked to do periods of commentary on the counties for the regions – in the absence of any regular commentator, of course. The old BBC formula 'SNF' (standing for 'staff no fee') was very attractive to programme planners. That, though, was no reason for complaint; he had been stimulated, amused and educated and he wanted to be thankful and show it. In fact, he was so broke at the end of it all that, upon advice, he applied to the 'Corp' for £75 on the grounds of laundry expenses – and he got it.

He had, though, become for the second time in little over a year, superficially at least, a different person in experience. First, the policeman had become a radio producer who also broadcast talks and wrote; now he had also become something of a specialist cricket broadcaster. That made him gratefully conscious of the fact that he had been admitted into what Brian Sellers called 'the circus'.

It would be difficult to imagine a warmer or more understanding world than that of the English professional cricketer. The 'bad trot' is not simply one man's run of ill-luck, but it seems often to be felt by an entire team. There was a certain young cricketer – and why dog him by naming him here? – who was recognized while still at university as a sensitively gifted batsman. There was competition among the counties for him and, at first in the Championship, he came off and looked as good as he had promised to be. Then, all of a sudden, it went sour on him. Within a couple of seasons he was gone completely from the county scene. It happened similarly to a young pace bowler; in his case he did actually produce the figures over a single season: then he lost it all. The closeness of professional cricketers' lives in England – breakfast together, talking themselves into close personal knowledge in the pavilion waiting to bat, a common table at lunch, drinks and supper together afterwards – builds up an intimacy almost unique among games players. It is a world of friendship, sympathy, humour – often wry humour – and when the time comes that form is lost, a world of tragedy. To see it dawn on a good professional that he has lost that blend of luck with skill that makes for acceptable form, is almost as painful for those who watch it as for the sufferer himself. The world of professional cricket is so small, essentially and almost solely English and numbering some 220-odd on the inside, another hundred on the edges of the game who may never make it. Gradually over that summer of 1946, and increasingly afterwards, understanding of that world grew in J.A. He has never lost it. That is why, he can only assume, in 1967 he was made President of The Cricketers' Association – in effect their trade union, and confined, with the single exceptions of himself and the professional Secretary, Jack Bannister, to active county players – which seemed to him, and still does, the greatest honour any of his fellow men ever bestowed upon him.

So, by September 1946, he had been granted that very human view of another world, and he went back – not discontentedly, of course, for radio and poetry still drew him – with what seemed an extra dimension of consciousness. He had had his summer of cricket and, whatever wild thoughts might race through his mind, he did not believe he dared ask for more in that direction. It had been, as it seemed, a separate chapter of pleasure and vision. So it was some kind of cliché of life to be sent for by 'Lobby' – S.J. de Lotbinière, Head of Outside Broadcasts and a lofty figure to a mere Overseas producer – with the most amazing suggestion. 'I listened to your broadcasts last summer,' he said, 'and while I think you have a vulgar voice, I think you have a compensatingly interesting mind – would you like to broadcast on next summer's South African tour?'

Once more, life had come up with an incomprehensible surprise. He spluttered; he explained that he could not leave his poetry: could – and would – he once more combine the two? It was agreed that he could. There was not at that time any absolutely legal apartheid, and he had no hesitation about his eagerness to agree.

That, though, lay six months – in those days for him a long time indeed – into the future. It was an autumn and winter of mixing with the professionals of broadcasting; and rather awe-inspiring they seemed; so different from man to man as to be of no fixed kind. Many were coming back from the war with mixed experiences and reactions. As he perceived their abilities, he recognized his amazing good fortune in having captured that job while the going was good. Home life, too, was delightful: no more bending to early turn or night duty, but a lazy breakfast, a late finish and then home in the evening with, invariably, friends to receive or visit. Reading was still a bug; writing still an obsession. It was then that he learnt a simple but difficult lesson. The BBC was surrounded by the most convivial of pubs frequented by the most interesting and, to him, desirable companions. One afternoon he came back to his desk, looked at a corrected script and realized that he was too drunk to do anything about it. He had, though, the sense to recognize his condition – old police experience ensured that – get out, go to a coffee shop and sober up. How dull he must have seemed to the men who could have their ideas, write their pieces and get out at lunchtime not to return until their seniors were thoroughly departed. He was, of course, still quite comically grateful for the job in which he found himself; that was a condition he never lost.

He must have seemed a very strange character to the other three in the office: Sunday Wilshin, with her own clear, determined view of the world; her secretary, a misty figure now only dimly recalled; and Barbara Forrester, most reliable of secretaries, that rare combination of efficiency, attractive appearance and modesty. She lived in a female household of mother, aunt and sister; the father had died many years before, and to visit them was to find a quite charming aura of femininity and innocence. Above all, she was reliable, covering up with infinite tact for his aberrations and worse; having the good sense to hide some letters he had signed until he could examine them next day with a clearer mind and calmer temper. She remains a friend, though hardly ever seen, far out in Essex with her husband and children, but one to whom he will always be grateful.

The byproduct of that cricket summer was his first prose book. Eric Gillett, that most artful 'man of letters', came along with the suggestion on behalf of Longmans the publishers for a book on the Indian tour by J.A. Acceptance was not simply eager but excited. Then, though, he did nothing at all about it as the season ran out. With Eric Gillett pressing, he turned at last to the book which he had, in truth, always been keen to write – if only life had not been so full. No sooner was the cricket season over than he adopted a schedule which, in later years, would have filled him with dread. Home from work without undue hurry, play with young James, natter with Dawn, dinner, general chatter, often with guests, and then, about ten o'clock, he settled to his typewriter. He was, by good fortune, a very fast – if not particularly accurate – typist, and he wrote the book – some 60,000 words – in ten nights. To look back at it now is to be amazed by his naïveté on the one hand, his industry on the other. The practicalities of life were still not simple in England, so the book was printed and bound in Calcutta. The dust-jacket, too, was produced in India and the blurb began, 'John Arlott, an experienced cricketer, a reputed radio producer . . .' Thank heaven that was deleted from the British edition. The book had some most friendly reviews and if he could have purred, he would have.

In 1946, too, *Clausentum* appeared. Its subject was the old Roman landing site on Southampton Water; the content a sonnet sequence by J.A. and a series of lithographs by Michael Ayrton. The place had fascinated both of them and, one night, to the ribald scorn and mirth of their wives, the two spent the night covered in waterproof sheets on the river's edge. The lithographs were splendid: it was J.A.'s last book of verse. Everything seemed rather deliriously joyous. Recordings were built up far in advance against that cricket tour with the South Africans. Meanwhile, there was any amount of broadcasting in several departments. All 'staff no fee' of course, but that was not strictly accurate for some sum was paid – was it £300 or £600 for the year? It does not matter, and he would gladly have done it all for nothing.

The work, its material success, and such reputation as it made was, of course, immensely rewarding; but the greatest delight of all lay in the new friendships and company of that period. There lay ultimately the greatest difference from police duty, and it made him, mentally, a completely different man.

Chapter 8

THE SUMMER OF 1947

At the end of 1946, J.A. began to plan his work for the next year. Settled into the BBC and the world of cricket, the whole of life seemed more expansive. 1947 was to be effectively the first truly post-war year. In 1946, so many had been pinned down by the aftermath of war away from normal life. They were now flooding back into England, wealthy with a kind of holiday spirit about ordinary life. That summer, too, echoed their feelings; the sun was high day after day and, in terms of cricket, it was to be remembered as 'the Compton-Edrich Year'.

Those two, for Middlesex and England, kept high carnival – and broke records right, left and centre. Not only did Compton beat all records with eighteen centuries in the season and an aggregate of 3816 (average 90.85) but Edrich, too, beat the previous record – Tom Hayward's – with 3539 (average 80.43). Compton made four of his centuries against the touring South Africans and Edrich weighed in with two more. The statistics, though, give only part of the picture. It used to be said – or so Neville Cardus wrote – that, when W.G. Grace was not out at lunchtime at Lord's, the hansom cabs tinkled up from the City and West End and along St John's Wood Road so that London could watch the great man. Now, that situation was repeated and with a rare and even wider pleasure. It was sheer delight to be at Lord's on those days; to be paid for going and babbling about it was an almost incredible bonus.

After 1946, he felt he knew the cricketing ropes for a broadcaster, and now there was the added delight of a motor car. He could not afford it, that grey AC, but it was of infinite convenience – especially in rapid dashes back from cricket to poetry recordings – and it gave him immense, rather cocky pleasure.

The touring South Africans were a happy bunch. There was no official apartheid then and no protests; though, with hindsight, it would be difficult to pretend that something very like it did not exist. For the moment, however, ignorance kept the picture, perhaps artificially, clear.

The touring side was captained by Alan Melville, remembered from his Sussex days. Tall, slim – in fact so short of flesh that he had to pad his bat handle to cushion the jolt of the ball against his highly bruisable fingers – he was a man of good wit and easy laughter who never made the mistake of thinking that cricket was the be-all and end-all of life.

Dudley Nourse was the resistant, old sweat vice-captain; fearless against pace, intuitive against spin, which he played so immaculately well as to force England's spinners on to the defensive, even on a turning wicket at Old Trafford. Bruce Mitchell was the calm, patient, thoughtful, quiet run-maker all the way through. 'Ossie' Dawson was a good-looking stylish bat and a bowler of outswing who, with more pace – appreciably more pace – might have been extremely difficult to play. Athol Rowan, who became a close friend, was the tall, K-legged (from a war injury) off-spinner who could also bat a bit. His bowling was intriguing and delightful to watch. Jack Plimsoll was left-arm quickish and another good companion at the drinking table. Lindsay Tuckett was the placid, hard-working, uncomplaining, main pace bowler. The chief burden, though, was carried by the spinners. 'Tufty' Mann, who delivered more overs than he could have dreamt existed on the tour, grew a completely new muscle in his left shoulder from his hours of left-arm slow bowling; he was a charming man, who came through the war as an escaped prisoner of war in Italy and died tragically early at thirty-one.

Dennis Dyer of Natal had a disappointing tour as an opening batsman, largely because he was never truly well; nevertheless he contrived to enjoy the cricket and the company. Ken Viljoen was a batsman who worked hard at his cricket and was constantly making useful runs; quite freakishly, he finished top of the bowling for the tour with one wicket for 11 runs. Tony Harris, a rugby player of some distinction, fielded well and scored usefully. Johnnie

Lindsay kept wicket well and batted gamely. George Fullerton, Denis Begbie and Douglas Ovenstone batted earnestly without making any deep impression. Ian Smith was the young leg-spinner with, alas, no googly, but an occasional unpremeditated top-spinner, who did enough to establish his promise; Les Payn, a farmer from Natal, and most admirable company, was simply over-shadowed as a slow left-arm bowler by Tufty Mann.

The whole party was a pleasure to be with. The tone was set by Alan Melville who was determined to enjoy himself and did his best to ensure that every other member of the side did so, too. The tour began, as usual, at Worcester – starting on 30 April, it was played in quite diabolical cold after the ground had recovered from one of the worst Severn floods ever recorded there. Worcestershire, batting first, lost early wickets to Athol Rowan but Alan White and Ronnie Bird engineered some kind of recovery; 'Hugo' Yarnold and Roly Jenkins weighed in, and the County fin-ished with 202. The South Africans fared even worse against the pace of Reggie Perks and the off-spin of Peter Jackson; only Dyer, Viljoen and Rowan so much as reached the twenties when they were put out for 167. At least, though, when they were out, they could go in and sit over the pavilion fire, which was more than they could do when they were fielding. Worcestershire mustered only 111 and again the South African spinners were responsible for the damage. Rowan's figures were 5 for 59 and 5 for 34; Mann's 3 for 40 and 5 for 36. The South Africans needed 147 to win but the pitch, a turner from the start, was too much for them: Jackson (4 for 53) and Howorth (6 for 38) dealt with them; they were all out for 107 and Worcestershire had won by 39 runs.

The evening of Thursday set the pattern for much of the tour. The tourists were scattered between several hotels; the county players, of course, came from their homes, to gather, both sides together, for an easy, relaxed dinner and to talk far into the night.

The games of the tour were of constant event and variety. In the second match, the tourists – thanks to a century by Melville and the bowling of Tuckett – 9 for 59 in the match – beat Leicestershire. They went on to beat Cambridge University and, with the help of another century by Melville, the bowling of Tuckett and Mann, and despite eight wickets by Alec Bedser, they beat Surrey by 115 runs. Hampshire, with a jaunty 138 from John Arnold, contrived a draw, but they were lucky in the second innings when Plimsoll and Rowan reduced them to 79 for 7 by the end. In spite of Mitchell carrying his bat for 103, they lost to MCC through the bowling of Jack Martin and Tony Mallett – fast-medium and medium of Kent – and the left-arm spin of Sam Cook of Gloucestershire. They scored too many runs against Oxford University – 510 for 6 – to get the other side out twice. Nourse and Viljoen made centuries, Harris, Mitchell and the run-hungry Melville all made useful scores.

Glamorgan were beaten by an innings – centuries by Mitchell and Rowan, seven wickets by Tuckett. They beat the Combined Services, too – another century by Mitchell. Then came the Middlesex match when Edrich (67 and 133 not out) and Compton (154 and 34) first set out their stalls. They were to score in quite unprecedented fashion – over 2000 runs between them (Compton 1187, Edrich 869) – against the touring side. That match was drawn but it was a measure of things to come. As preparation for the First Test they beat Northamptonshire – despite the likeable West Indian, Bertie Clarke, bowling his leg-breaks so well – by an innings, thanks to the bowling of Plimsoll (11 for 130) and Dawson (8 for 108).

It is difficult now, forty-three years afterwards, and with cricket changed to an everyday affair, to recall the atmosphere of that 1947 season. For players all round the country and, most of all, perhaps, in the touring side, this was a return to a normality which seemed quite heady. Of course winning mattered, but it is hard to remember a time when it mattered less.

That is not to say that the First Test was played any less than seriously – indeed, it was dramatic and, for the South Africans, tragic. They made 533, with centuries by Melville (189) and Nourse (149). Poor Sam Cook in his only Test match, straight from Gloucestershire, missing the sergeant-majorish advice of Tom Goddard, and quite out of his depth, found it hard indeed to bowl to Melville with 300 on the board and only two men out. At one stage he sought to produce surprise by bowling Melville a quickish full toss. That was promptly despatched for six to square leg; Cook visibly wilted. In that match he took none for 127. He was to become a much more resilient and resistant bowler but that lay in the future; like his steady, philosophic umpiring. It can rarely be said that a cricketer's chance came too soon, but it was certainly true of Sam.

Tuckett and Smith bowled England out for 208 and Melville enforced the follow-on. Edrich and Compton had made 57 and 65 respectively in the first innings. Now, they scored 50 and 163; Edrich was bowled by the leg-spinner Smith in both innings, while Compton can hardly ever have batted better. Certainly it was a Test match, certainly England had followed on – and lost their first wicket at 20 – but Compton patently, almost boyishly, enjoyed himself. It was a good Trent Bridge wicket and he proved that England's first-innings failure was a freak. His ease and command were at times quite amazing; it was an innings of joy, brilliant improvisation, mixed with happy orthodoxy, and everyone on the ground must have shared in its immense pleasure. Yardley made 99, Evans a sparkling 74, but the match was probably decided a quarter of an hour into the day when, at 298 for 4, Yardley snicked the patient Tuckett to slip and was dropped. That seemed fairly unimportant at the time and still did just after half past three when, with England 500 for 9 and 3 hours 7 minutes remaining for play, Martin and Hollies came together. Someone had already described this England side as having three number elevens; and few can have expected that these two would hang on for an almost impossible 49 minutes before a laughingly incredulous crowd and score 51 runs in the process. Jack Martin made 26; Eric Hollies, whose highest score in 41 county innings that season was 5 not out, made 18. The game had been tilted.

South Africa needed 227 in 138 minutes, nearly 100 an hour. Even on that lovely pitch it was not possible against the pace of Martin, Bedser and Edrich. Mitchell was out early but Melville made his second century of the match, but, even at 166 for 1, South Africa failed to win the match they had so completely deserved to take – missing out by just about the time of that freakish and, for them, feverish Martin-Hollies stand.

It is not the purpose of this book to give a running account of cricket tours. The summers of 1946, 1947 and 1948, though, were exceptional, not solely for this writer. To many people the return of cricket was the great symbol of peace and normality. The South Africans, above all, enjoyed themselves; several of their wives came over to join them, and the whole season was for them, and for many of their hosts, a social occasion.

In the ten days between the First and Second Tests, Somerset were beaten by an innings when Plimsoll, with eight wickets, and Dawson, with seven, twice skittled them out. The young Maurice Tremlett had a bad match. He batted at number nine, scoring 0 and 7, but he took two good wickets, had two important catches dropped, and already had the air of a fine player.

So to the Lord's Test, to be fairly described as the finest cricket match of the season, with crowds to match the occasion. South Africa kept the same side as had played at Trent Bridge, but England dropped Sam Cook, Jack Martin and the rather unlucky Tom Dollery in favour of Charlie Barnett, George Pope and Doug Wright. Indeed, at this time, Wright ought never to have been left out of an England side; he had his technical flaws but, more than any bowler then within the game, he had the ability to deliver the unplayable ball.

Much lay in the toss, and Norman Yardley won it. Len Hutton and Cyril Washbrook saw away the shine on the new ball and the early life in the wicket. Hutton went for 18 – more valuable than it sounds – Washbrook soon afterwards for a somewhat more belligerent 65, and there, to the South Africans' undoubted dismay, Edrich and Compton were together again. So different in manner – Edrich crouched, tense and quick on his feet, Compton apparently casual but, in fact, placing the ball through gaps in the field with absolute mastery.

So England began the second day at 312 for 2: Melville set defensive fields and, no doubt, prayed. Athol Rowan and Tufty Mann bowled to a length and spun but the batsmen were on top, felt it and knew it. When Ian Smith was brought on, Edrich, whom he had twice bowled out at Nottingham, struck him for four fours from consecutive balls. The score was 443 for 2 at lunch. Soon afterwards Edrich, trying to hit Mann, lifted his head and was bowled: they had put on 370 for the third wicket. Tuckett had Compton and Yardley caught by Rowan, and bowled Barnett, Evans and Bedser before Yardley declared at an awe-inspiring 554 for 8. The wicket was still good but, before the close, Compton had had Mitchell stumped, and Wright bowled Viljoen with his, always surprising, faster ball. Melville and Nourse, though, stayed to 167 for 2.

Next morning, Melville went on to his third century of the series – in fact, his fourth in consecutive Test innings, for he had scored 103 against England at Durban in 1939 and had not played in a Test since. Wright took five wickets, Hollies and Compton two each, and even South Africa's 327 did not save them from the follow-on, when Edrich, bowling at his usual furious pace, put out Melville and Viljoen for 8 and 6 respectively. Next day, Mitchell and Nourse, both for the second time, put up game resistance, and Rowan and Tuckett bravely saved the innings defeat. None of them, though, had adequate defence against Wright – 5 for 80. Hutton and Washbrook carefully made the 26 England needed to win by ten wickets.

There were only ten days between the Second Test and the Third. In that time Douglas Ovenstone broke a finger keeping wicket and George Fullerton took his place against Nottinghamshire; an advantage of carrying three wicketkeepers. The tourists made two changes, bringing in Dennis Dyer and Jack Plimsoll in place of Tony Harris and Ian Smith. England surprisingly included Ken Cranston, the new Lancashire captain and all-rounder, who had played a bare dozen county matches, and Cliff Gladwin in place of Alec Bedser and George Pope. The time was soon to come when to leave out Alec Bedser would have seemed cricketing madness, but he was beginning to show signs of tiredness; though losing his place spurred him to considerable effort in Surrey's defeat of Yorkshire while the Test match was being played.

The game took place in appalling Manchester weather – a raging north-west wind so strong that it several times blew off the bails and once brought down a sightscreen. A spartan crowd watched with sustained interest despite some extremely slow going by the tourists' batsmen. These were no sort of conditions for South Africans and this was to prove another Edrich-Compton triumph. Bill Edrich, who slung the ball down extremely fast but quite straight, took four wickets in each innings. He scored 191 and 22 not out, Compton 115 and 6; this meant that, in seven consecutive innings – of three Tests and the one match for Middlesex – Edrich had scored 708 and Compton 745 runs against South Africa.

Melville won the toss and South Africa ground their way cautiously – at about 46 runs an hour – on the placid wicket, and mustered only 278 for 6 in the full day's play. Hutton caught Melville brilliantly at short leg and Nourse became Cranston's first Test wicket. That left the main burden of the batting with three slow scorers in Dyer, Mitchell and Viljoen. They might, nevertheless, have built something of a stand if Hutton had not quick-thinkingly run out Mitchell. There was rain in the night and, next morning, the lifting ball battered Viljoen about the hands; but he seemed sure to make a hundred when Compton, leaping high to his left, caught him at slip. Once the fourth wicket fell, at 214, the England bowlers, without rising to any great heights, nibbled their way through to finish the innings for 339.

England's reply was founded on Edrich and Compton's third-wicket stand of 228. Plimsoll, in his first Test, took 3 for 128 but suffered violently at the hands of Edrich who, when he took the second new ball, three times pull-drove him for six; to be regarded as disrespect by any pace-bowler. These two batsmen, though, were now in the fullness of form. There were useful contributions from Yardley, Cranston and Evans and England finished with 478. This lead of 139 seemed largely to dishearten the South Africans and on a drying wicket only Melville (59) and Nourse (115) put up any measurable resistance, with 174 out of a total of 267. That left England no simple task to win on that pitch, but they achieved it for the loss of only three wickets. In making 22 not out, Bill Edrich became only the third player (George Giffen and Aubrey Faulkner were the others) to score 200 runs and take eight wickets in a Test. It was, incidentally, the first time a positive result had been reached in an Old Trafford Test for ten years (statistical joke). As a more cheerful, if not statistical matter, Dudley Nourse thought this – his fifth

Test century – the finest innings he had played for South Africa.

The touring side went off to Ireland for two official matches and one fill-in for the next week. For J.A. it was recordings of immense interest – indeed, he found it hard to decide which of these aspects of his life he enjoyed best. Then to Derby, where the touring side won narrowly by three wickets and there were two magnificent parties. Charlie Elliott opened the first innings for Derbyshire and made 56; in the second, when they were put out for 32, he was the only man to score double figures (18). It was in an evening of the match that he told his much relished story that, the first time he ever touched a ball in a county match, he caught Jack Hobbs. In due course he became an honoured member of the Master's Club. Even at that, the South Africans, who had been 52 behind on the first innings, were hard pushed to win against the bowling of George Pope, 5 for 36. After his 5 for 60 in the first innings, it looked possible that that might win his Test place back for Leeds but it did not. On to Sheffield where Len Hutton, to the delight of the local crowd, made a century. Bill Bowes took 4 for 36 in the tourists' 279; Ian Smith, for the tourists, a hard-working 5 for 105 in 48 overs. The South Africans went on to Scotland but cricketing Yorkshire simply waited for the Fourth Test at Headingley at the end of July. England had brought in Harold Butler, the Nottinghamshire fast bowler – he hammered the ball into the pitch from mighty shoulders – and Jack Young, slow left-arm of Middlesex, in place of Gladwin and Hollies. For South Africa, Lindsay was unfit and, with Plimsoll, was left out for Fullerton and Smith.

South Africa were in trouble from the start. Bill Edrich, who seemed to coil himself into a ball and then to explode into delivery, took another early wicket – that of Alan Melville for nought – with a ball which, unusually from Edrich, bit back off the pitch. Bruce Mitchell (53) and Dudley Nourse (51) threatened a stand but Butler was too good for the middle of their batting and they were out for 175, while England managed to finish the day at 53 for no wicket.

Monday was the Yorkshiremen's day. There were vast crowds outside, for there had been no Test in Yorkshire in 1946. A savage thunderstorm in the morning took an hour off the start and made some of the thousands locked out wonder if perhaps they had been lucky. There was play, though, on a turning wicket, but against the highly capable spin of Mann and Rowan, Hutton and Washbrook played, probably, as well as they ever did. In the way that south country folk associate with northerners, they dealt with the turning ball in quite masterly fashion. They had 141 on the board before Washbrook was bowled by Mann. That, though, did not worry a Yorkshire crowd: they cheered Hutton run by run – and they were not easy runs against that bowling. When he reached his century, he had a rapturous reception. Immediately afterwards, going for a quick run to cover, he slipped and fell and was run out. For once Edrich and Compton only scored 43 and 30 respectively, but Yardley could declare with a lead of 142 on a pitch which still gave the spinners more than a reasonable chance. Again Edrich took his early wicket; only Nourse, lbw to Butler for 57, scored more than 30. Again Butler cut away the middle of the batting; Cranston polished it off with 4 for 12 and Hutton and Washbrook could potter to 47 to win without real trouble. Yorkshire was in joyous mood; most happily it had come about in the right way with Hutton's hundred, and they celebrated when he made the winning hit – a six off Mann. In fact, the gate receipts – £16,000 – were a record for Headingley; and England had taken the rubber.

The touring side's match against Glamorgan was not, of course, an official Test match but it was, certainly so far as the Welsh people were concerned, an international. Their two off-spiners, John Clay and Len Muncer, put out the South Africans for 260, in which Tony Harris made a highly capable and cheerful 100. Athol Rowan took 6 for 53 – including the first four – to give the tourists a first-innings lead of 63. That delightfully drily witty man, John Clay, took 6 for 86 to go with his first-innings 5 for 76 and, needing 252 to win, the county lost their first six wickets for 39 runs. Then, though, Allan Watkins (75) and Maurice Robinson (32) made 89 together and, following them, George Lavis and Haydn Davies another and very fast 59. The delighted crowd – 50,000 for the three days – cheered them on, but Dawson finished off the innings and Glamorgan lost, gamely, by 40 runs.

Beating Warwickshire by an innings, drawing against Lancashire and winning easily against Gloucestershire, despite a reminder by Cook that he remained a capable spinner, the South Africans went on to the last Test at the Oval. Both sides seemed to find the immense heat enervating. Precisely when there should have been match-winning cricket, both of them seemed to flag. All, that is, except Bruce Mitchell who made 120 in the first innings, 189 not out in the second. Once, when South Africa needed only some 40 to win, Mitchell pulled up in the middle of the pitch, after his stroke had gone for four, looked at his partner, Tufty Mann, with a puzzled air and said, 'Tufty – but where is George?' George Fullerton had been out half an hour earlier, but such was Mitchell's concentration that he had forgotten whom his batting partner was. In emulating Melville's performance of the First Test, Mitchell was on the field for all but eight minutes of the entire four-day game. Dick Howorth, to his quiet delight, took Dyer's wicket with his first ball in Test cricket. The game, which either side might have won, ended in a draw with huge crowds somnolent under a blazing sun.

It is not often that a side produces three batsmen with averages of over 60 and yet loses a rubber by three to nil. Neither let it be thought that the South Africans played that series less than hard. On the other hand, the figures show that Edrich averaged 110.40, Compton 94.12, and Washbrook, Hutton and Evans all over 40. Cranston's 11 wickets at 16.90 represented slightly freak figures but Edrich – soon rarely to bowl at all – took 16 at 23.12, Doug Wright 19 at 25.47.

The South Africans enjoyed it down to the end. Begbie scored his solitary century in the win against Essex. Viljoen made 104 and 35, while Mann took thirteen wickets, when they beat Kent in extra time. Lashings of runs were scored in the Sussex match when bowlers suffered quite alarmingly in the first innings. Then to Hastings where Denis Compton scored his seventeenth hundred of the season to beat Jack Hobbs's long-standing record, although the touring side won the match against the South of England by nine wickets. There was only time for a one-day game against the Club Cricket Conference, in which Tony Harris nevertheless made 229 not out, before, because of difficulties with the shipping companies, the touring side had to miss the Leveson Gower XI fixture at Scarborough. The highly gifted off-spinner, Athol Rowan – who used a little finger turned in the ear as a conversational gambit – was their only bowler to take a hundred wickets in the entire tour (102 at 24.97); but Tufty Mann, Ian Smith, Jack Plimsoll, Lindsay Tuckett and Ossie Dawson all had good bowling figures. Bruce Mitchell had the highest aggregate (2014, with eight centuries at 61.03); Ken Viljoen, Dudley Nourse, Alan Melville and Ossie Dawson all scored over a thousand runs. This had been as hospitable and as hospitality-prone as any touring side that ever came to England; popular, sporting in the best sense and a credit to the cricket that produced them. We can only regret that so soon politics were to cast such a shadow over their world.

There was so much more to life than cricket, but broadcasting led to one of the most warming experiences of his life. He had written to Dylan Thomas asking him for a poem for an anthology – later published as *First Time in America* (1948) – to which Dylan eventually contributed two poems. At that time Dylan was staying at the Sitwells' villa in Italy and this was his letter:

June 11th 1947
Villa del Beccaro Mosciano Scandicci Florence

My dear John,

Thank you for writing. It was very good to hear from you. Though I hear your voice every day: from Trent Bridge, at the moment. You're not only the best cricket commentator – far and away that; but the best sports commentator I've heard, ever; exact, enthusiastic, prejudiced, amazingly visual, authoritative, and friendly. A great pleasure to listen to you: I do look forward to it. Here, in the hills above Florence, I lead the quietest life I ever remember leading: it is sizzling hot, the hill to the nearest village is a spinebreaker, I am far too limp and lazy to go often to Florence, and I can work only in the early mornings and evenings: never my best time: I'm used to working from after lunch until pub-time, which in the country used to be about seven. Here I drink in the garden, alone or with Caitlin: we have no

social life: I am a sun vegetable: I live on red wine, cheese, aspar-
agus, artichokes, strawberries, etc. The etc. is usually more red
wine. We have our own vineyard. The villa is enormous. So,
probably, am I, after two months. I'm coming back in August: if
the lire last till then. I was given some travelling money by the
Authors' Society; otherwise I'd have been back long ago. And I'll
be broke when I return, so any bits of booming – I heard Rape of
Lucrece today; is Shakespeare over? and what is the next series?
– narrating, etc., will be very welcome. Also, I'd love to write any
programme you think I could do: and, scrupulously, on time.

Yes, of course I'd love some dollars, but I have so far, no poem.
It would be useless giving you a chunk of the long one I'm twist-
ing and gnarling: it's got to be read as a whole. If I do manage to
write any short ones in between, I'll send them to you straight-
away.

I can't afford to go to Venice. I've spent some time in Rome, in
Genoa, in Siena, and on the Riviera. But now I can just afford to
stay here on my sunburnt behind. I would like to go to Venice
though. Perhaps I can seduce your girl: or am I the wrong shape?

I'll be ringing you in August. Love to you & your family.
Remember me to Val, when you see him. My daughter has fallen
in a cactus bush.

Yours,
Dylan

That book was only part of a year of immense variety that opened a
world of an extent he had never so much as contemplated; probably the richest of his life. First of all came the lecture tour to the
Forces in Austria and Italy; in effect Vienna and Venice. On his
arrival by services aircraft in Vienna he was introduced to the
Army Education Corps officer who was to conduct him through
the month's tour. His predecessors had been senior or even retired
educationalists; sixty years old at least. Now, when this quite
beautiful young woman was brought in, the AEC officers in charge
suddenly put two and two – or even more – together and realized
they were sending a young man in his thirties across much of

Europe with a beautiful girl in her middle twenties. He refrained from laughing only with the utmost difficulty. Their embarrassment was patent and painful. There was, though, nothing they could do without obvious offence to both the people concerned. The two set off in what had been one of Goering's Mercedes Benz, driven by a serviceman who did not long survive idleness in Venice. He was replaced; the cause was never given but he did confide in his brief farewells that 'it was worth it'.

This was an experience of quite mountainous quality. Venice is, surely, a city without comparison in the world; and Vienna is not far behind it. This was a new realm of beauty which had never been swept into his consciousness. Everything – literally everything – architecture, art, food, the people, their generous attitude, the drink, all were ingredients of a new world. The young woman not only spoke good Italian and fair German but was capable of teaching, most essentially, Italian.

For J.A. it was glorious to accept but difficult to digest. It is hard to believe that anyone could take quite such imaginative inflow in days. The *heurigen*, the local taverns, and the *buschenschenken* of the Austrian visit added new dimensions to a glass of wine.

Above all, the cafés of Venice were places of a new civilization – old as civilization, of course, but staggeringly new to one raised on English pubs. Then the buildings of Vienna and, above all, those of Venice: he felt almost drunk on their splendour. Fortunately the progress was reasonable; from the churches and the Brueghel exhibition so difficult to assimilate in Vienna, to the unending wealth of Venetian palaces and paintings. It was an experience which has never faded. Much has happened to him since but nothing so staggering nor, still, anything more deeply reaching the soul than the art of Venice.

He came back a different person yet again; feeling like one who has suddenly come from poverty into immense but fully enjoyable wealth. Did he understand it? Probably not, though he groped desperately to do so through his amazement. Over subsequent years and renewed visits perhaps he came near to appreciating what had happened to him.

Chapter 9

LIFE IN LONDON

Most people who live in London seem by definite choice to make their homes, or series of homes, either north or south of the Thames. His family went north: first to Crouch End – reached by way of Finsbury Park tube and a bus – but then, with a glimpse of solvency, up the hill to Highgate. Finally, so long as he lived in London, he had two floors in George Street, off Baker Street.

Dawn settled easily into the suburbs, maintained a highly efficient household and brought up the little boy with all her nurse's skill. Fortunate in their next-door neighbours, the Dallings, they could leave the child without anxiety to go out for an evening.

Here, now, was a young man in his early thirties learning London like a boy in his teens. Soho and the National Liberal Club seemed to him the height of sophistication; to entertain was, as it still is, a major pleasure of life. Boon companions made the after-work hour or so the kind of joy the police force had never permitted. That, though, had to be kept within bounds for there was work to do, quite apart from broadcasting. There was much writing – always done at home – to earn enough for the household to grow in creature comfort; they acquired fresh furniture and a general look of grown-upness; and there was the continuing responsibility for a son.

Broadcasting suddenly assumed a fresh importance and presented a fresh challenge. In the earliest days, the production of a poetry programme had seemed a simple pleasure. Now, though, production began to assume a fresh significance. He adopted in the back of his mind, though never voiced, an intent to 'rowel for meaning'. No doubt the phrase sounds meaningless but to him it meant driving himself, and those who worked for him, to give every phrase of every poem its true clarity of meaning. He was, of course, broadcasting to India, where speech qualities, even in the use of English, were, as they still are, different from those in England. He had, though, the good fortune to be working constantly with Indians, and he never failed to try out his ideas on people like Aslam Malik and Abdul Hamid Sheikh. The key to it all was stress, with inflections a close second: in a word, sense. Almost any poem worthy of the name could be reduced to natural English speech-rhythms and emphases; so at least he believed then – and does still. If poetry is to be read in the English language it must subscribe to those values; it must be intelligible to the English speaker and, essentially, without affectation. Preciosity is poison. It was here that people like Valentine Dyall, Robin Holmes and Alan Vandyke Price, for all the contrasts in their voices, met all demands. If they could not make a poem sound like sense, it simply was not sense.

After a little more than a year, Donald Stevenson moved on and up, and Jim Pennethorne-Hughes came from New Delhi to take his place. He and J.A. instantly became friends and remained so until 'Penny's' death as a widower, when he left J.A. the contents of his cottage in Keevil, Wiltshire. That, which gallops far ahead of the story, was a strange experience.

J.A. was, and is, a serious book collector, concerned with not only – and primarily – their content, but also their condition, their look and their standing, with a respect for first editions. Nice, kind, Jim Hughes was a book amasser. Vast shelves of his cottage held books three lines deep, many of them dog-eared. In fact, he had kept every book he had ever owned: from infant rag-books with his name written in his mother's hand. He kept, too, every letter his mother had ever written him, and every one from his wife, who had died after a short marriage.

He had, though, two immaculate collections; one of books on witchcraft, and one on names. One day he asked J.A., 'What would you, as a book collector, do with another man's book collection?'

There was only one possible answer from an ingrained book collector: 'Preserve it.'

That, no doubt, though J.A. did not realize it at the time, was the reason for the bequest. It was a fantastic deposit: for instance, there were ten bowler hats in various stages of mildewed greenness, some eight overcoats and a general hoard of the unusable. There were about a dozen chairs, all with upholstery ripped and out of service. J.A. dutifully had them all restored at what then seemed a fantastic price. They still look healthy and handsome about the house. There was a one-man four-poster bed and various odd- ments duly preserved despite their apparent worthlessness, solely, really, because so nice a man as Jim Hughes had treasured them. The bowlers and the overcoats, though, had to go; likewise the umbrellas and the raggle-taggle secondhand and childhood books; three-deep on Jim's shelves, they would have crowded out J.A.'s house. Much of the rest, though, remains to be left to the chil- dren of another family, for Jim had no children of his own and no close descendants. His wife was Belgian, daughter, if memory serves, of the man who founded the tram service in Cairo, where Jim met her in the short period when he was BBC representative there.

His was a civilizing influence. There was a manner about the man, yet he got a tragic number of things wrong. He was in love with his BBC secretary, yet there was enough of the snob in him to deny the possibility of marriage – despite J.A.'s vehement argu- ments in favour of it. He remains a happy memory, though in ret- rospect his was not a happy life. He dearly loved his mother; deeply respected his Yorkshire parson ancestors and, having lost his father early, referred to him like a work of fiction. He wrote a fine history of witchcraft with that delicate and witty touch which was characteristic of the man and which is indicated by the title of his other book *While Shepherds Watched*, about wartime Cairo. He was without apparent conceit; convivial but inclined to become a little tight under the combined influences of alcohol and nostalgia. His memorial ought to have been the BBC Training School, of which he was a magnificent and sympathetic Head, yet few remember him for that and he must stand now by his two books – of which any man might be proud. Let us not categorize as impor- tant the extremely comic pen drawings with which he used to embellish his correspondence; he had a pretty wit and wit, alas, is extremely transient when it is communicated, at its best, in conversation.

The work as a radio producer formed an entirely separate section of J.A.'s life. Most of a writer's and broadcaster's activities can be continued throughout his life but production cannot. Within the BBC at least, that is a staff job and, so far as he was concerned, it ended in 1950 when he followed Jim Pennethorne-Hughes to the Staff Training School, where he became General Instructor. That in itself was a considerable experience and one he would not have missed, but he did miss, and it would be stupid to pretend he did not, the period of producing 'Book of Verse'.

It is easy to say that that activity consisted of producing speakers – some amateurs, some professional – and ensuring as fully as possible that they spoke their scripts as distinct from reading them. In that respect he would claim credit for endowing more than one actor with the ability to sound conversational – a rarer gift than it may seem. It is also true to say that J.A. learnt as much as his victims in the process. At first it was all somewhat hit or miss – a programme on comic verse up to 1850 presented by Michael Roberts, followed closely by one on the English hymn by V.C. Clinton-Baddeley and one on Lewis Carroll and Edward Lear by Daniel George. The major undertaking of it all, however, consisted of thirty-nine weeks – all BBC programme series used to be reckoned in thirteen-week units – on Shakespeare and his works. There was at least one programme on every play, others on Shakespeare's life, the Sonnets and criticism of his work. The well known plays were obviously satisfying to work on but the programmes on *The Rape of Lucrece*, *Coriolanus*, *Timon of Athens*, *Pericles*, *Cymbeline* and *Henry VIII* were altogether different matters. There was no opportunity to see a performance of them and not only the producer but also the more conscientious among his actors found themselves reading and, in their way, coming to understand those plays and, as one of them pointed out, discovering in the process why they are not often produced. An important aspect of it all lay in meeting the writers chosen to present each programme. Each half hour consisted of explanation, indication of continuity and readings – in effect, acting – of significant passages. The scriptwriters and readers included P.H. Newby, Ruth Pitter, Maurice Willson Disher, Ralph Currey, Clifford Bax, Philip Tomlinson, Ifor Evans, J.C. Trewin, Professor C.J. Sisson, Allardyce Nicholl, Andrew Young, Laurence Whistler, Victor Pritchett, Richard Aldington, Ivor Brown and Daniel George.

Apart from the illumination of reading, absolutely thoroughly, the entire works of Shakespeare in something more than half a year, there was constant discussion with the programme writers, all of which added up to a valuably educative phase.

Most of the contributors were happy enough to read their pieces. Strangely enough, Andrew Young was not: he was a fine preacher but his was essentially the manner of the pulpit and he was probably conscious of this. It might well have been effective but his refusal to do it was very firm indeed; and anyone who knew Andrew knows just how determined he could be.

The programmes resulted in some good and enduring friendships; they also helped considerably with the anthology *First Time in America* which was, as its name implies, a collection of the first American appearances of some English poems, though not necessarily the poets.

It was all so different from the cricket scene, and yet so sympathetic to it, that this may have been the best balanced period of J.A.'s life. Essentially the friendships were important: those with cricketers were very obvious: with writers less so but nevertheless genuine.

There was always the danger of working too much from textbooks and established anthologies so, immediately after the Shakespearian series, J.A. moved on to modern verse chosen in a long series of programmes by Philip Tomlinson, Michael Goodwin, Cyril Connolly, David Gascoyne, Louis MacNeice, Stephen Spender, Christopher Hassall, Robert Herring, John Lehmann, Cecil Day-Lewis, Leonard Strong, George Stonier, that good old friend Terry Delaney and, finally, to fill in what he conceived to be the gaps, J.A. himself. 'Book of Verse' was a wonderful phase, complete in less than five years (cricket matches excepted), for him never to be forgotten and never to be written off in its immense impact on his mind and his way of thought. It created a fresh kind of training in scriptwriting.

Writing for radio needs a special technique: it can be too tight or too slack. There is no standard of perfection because the whole method depends upon the voice and manner of the person who will deliver it; and that in its turn is dictated by the matter of the broadcast and the language used. Some writers can be stilted yet acceptable, others familiar yet unnatural: essentially, the style is the man; but it must be the true man, for the medium exposes insincerity with no mercy whatever.

Any amount of unplanned work continued to be offered. A female voice one day announced itself from another department of the BBC to ask, 'Can you write hymns?'

'I expect so but I have never tried.'

She then went on to explain – not particularly flatteringly – that she had approached 'some of the best poets' but that their efforts had not pleased the editors. She said she wanted three hymns; how soon might she have them? On being told, probably the next day, she undoubtedly took umbrage. So much umbrage indeed that J.A. dived into the exercise at home that night: found it harder than he had thought and worked into the small hours. Nevertheless, the hymns were written and duly delivered next day. They were to be on the subjects of Harvest Festival, Rogation and Plough Sunday. Oddly enough, one of them – the Harvest hymn – caught on. It was simple enough in all conscience. The chairman of the editorial board – who was a bishop – objected to the Almighty being referred to as 'you'. The amused author pointed out that he did not wish to sound deliberately archaic, so the matter was resolved when the bishop agreed to such use, provided the initial letter was a capital. Although J.A. sang the lines to himself, in his utterly tuneless voice, as he wrote, he did not dare to make any suggestion as to music. It was the editorial board who decided on the use of the English traditional melody 'Shipston', though congregations all over the place seem to use any sort of music that occurs to them.

He never hawked it – not once – but demands for it came in from almost every Christian denomination and from all over the world.

It made him several hundred times more per word than anything else he ever wrote. The Americans in particular were generous in their payment. Of the three hymns, that was the one that gave the least trouble – first written, it prompted the idea that hymn-writing was simple; the next two, stretching far into the night, convinced him that it was not. This is the Harvest hymn:

1   God, whose farm is all creation,
    Take the gratitude we give;
    Take the finest of our harvest,
    Crops we grow that men may live.

2   Take our ploughing, seeding, reaping,
    Hopes and fears of sun and rain,
    All our thinking, planning, waiting,
    Ripened in this fruit and grain.

3   All our labour, all our watching,
    All our calendar of care,
    In these crops of Your creation,
    Take, O God; they are our prayer.

Despite its apparent popularity, nobody ever asked him to write another hymn, which was fortunate because he probably could not have done so. The young man's confidence soon faded into humility. It is, though, it must be admitted, deeply stirring to hear one's own words sung, not necessarily by a master choir, but by ordinary people who, unlike the writer, can sing in tune. Less comfortable is the feeling when one of those students, who call themselves 'hymnologists', writes with earnest questions about his spiritual experience or something even more elaborate. It remains, nevertheless, seriously and, quite apart from its continuing contribution to income, a rewarding experience, humbly accepted.

So the winter of 1947 passed absorbingly and happily with no suggestion of monotony since, in any case, it was all so varied and, also, another cricket season lay ahead. That was to be the finest season of J.A.'s experience. 1946 had been a summer almost of novelty with the return of cricket; 1947 one of cheer, variety and an even fuller return of the game in that it involved steadily more people returning from war service. 1948, though, was a great season by any standards; it was the year when Bradman in his last tour and season brought over a mighty Australian side. They achieved a record four-nil result in the Tests but England were not completely outclassed. Indeed, in two of the Tests – the Third and Fourth at Old Trafford and Headingley – they seized such advantage as made it seem possible – indeed at Headingley probable – that they might win. Ultimately, though, the Australians were a great side and once more, as in 1921, they were bowling at England sides starved of practice against true pace. So, while their batting was massive, it was the Australian bowling that ultimately took them unbeaten through the tour – also a record.

Thus, in Tests, Ray Lindwall took 27 wickets at 19.62 and Keith Miller 13 at 23.15 as those two became a virtually legendary pair of pace bowlers in the minds of English cricket followers. Meanwhile there was also the splendid Bill Johnston, bowling left-arm at various paces but basically, after changing his mind several times, fast-medium, who took 27 at 23.33. Even their 'defensive' Ernie Toshack – brought on to fill the experimental 55 overs between new balls – achieved 11 at 33.09 in Tests. Meanwhile, in all matches, five men – Lindwall, Miller, Johnston, McCool and Johnson – had over 50 at less than 20 apiece; Toshack, 50 at 21.12, and the leg-spinner, Doug Ring, 60 at 21.81. Against such a bowling background it was small wonder that ten of their batsmen achieved between them 47 centuries in all matches, eight in Tests spread over six players. Against that, Denis Compton and Cyril Washbrook both averaged more than 50, Len Hutton 42.75 in the Tests. Yardley, predominantly a change bowler, was easily top of the English bowling averages, with 9 at 22.66; but the main burden fell upon Alec Bedser – 18 at 38.22. So much for the figures, which are so impressive they could not be ignored, but the crowds flocked to see Bradman on his last tour, and were pleasurably chilled by the fast bowling of Lindwall and Miller; delighted in the batting and fielding of the young Harvey, and were much impressed by Arthur Morris, who topped their Test batting with 696 runs at 87.00; while Barnes had 329 at 82.25, Bradman 508 at 72.57; two more averaged better than 50, another two more than 40.

Wherever they went the crowds swarmed in; they had been titillated by the advent of the Indians, had relished the South Africans; but this was genuinely heavyweight cricket, and even the supporters of the beaten country could not withhold their admiration. It was, too, a happy side, with none of the dissensions that had marred some previous Australian tours.

It all got under way at Worcester in appalling weather, cold and wet. Ray Lindwall took a wicket with his second ball, having Don Kenyon lbw, but then Eddie Cooper and Charlie Palmer put on 137 before the Australian weapons of destruction in an assorted hand of bowlers put them out for 233. It was a first sight of Ray Lindwall. It was later to become clear that he was simply loosening up but, despite his low arm, he made the occasional ball lift alarmingly and swung it both ways in the air. Miller, too, took it easily, with only an occasional hint of his potential pace. Five bowlers shared the wickets. Then came the steamroller tactic; a century for Bradman – the repeat curtain performance which was what the crowd had come to see – but one also for Arthur Morris, and a violent 50 for Keith Miller coming in as low as number nine. They reached 462 for 8 before Bradman declared and, of course, enforced the follow-on. In the second Worcestershire innings, Bob Wyatt, that good, wise cricket talker, was absent hurt and his company could be enjoyed on only one evening. Laddie Outschoorn made 54, but this time Colin McCool, with his leg-breaks and googlies, took 4 for 29 and, despite another useful innings by Charlie Palmer, the county lost by an innings and 17 runs.

On to Leicester and there the tourists achieved another innings (and 171) win; in fact, of their 34 matches, exactly half were won by an innings. This time it was Miller's turn to make the highest score – 202 not out – at number three, while Bradman scored 81 and their 448 was more than enough. Of Leicestershire's two companionable Australians, Vic Jackson took 5 for 91 and scored 17 out of their 130 in the first innings and 31 not out in their 147 in the last; while Jack Walsh made 33, to his surprise top score of the first innings; but his wrist-spin was played with greater ease than English batsmen usually showed. Ian Johnson, the off-spinner, took two wickets in the first innings, 7 for 42 in the second; Doug Ring, the burly leg-spinner, 5 for 45 in the first.

It was a shame to have to miss the Yorkshire match at Bradford when the county threatened to win a low-scoring match. They scored only 71 and 89 but Frank Smailes and Johnny Wardle, with thirteen wickets between them, made it a close-run thing – the tourists' scores were 101 and 63 for six wickets. The Surrey match was a different matter, a massive innings – Sid Barnes 176, Don Bradman 146, Lindsay Hassett 110, Arthur Morris 65 and Don – 'Deafy' – Tallon weighing in at the end with 50 not out for a total of 632. Bill Johnston, ducking and weaving his way in, bowled well, as did Ian Johnson with eight wickets.

English comfort in that match lay in a bold 81 by the lefthander Laurie Fishlock, footballer and cricketer, with immense courage against pace, who carried his bat through the innings. Only two others so much as reached double figures – Tom Barling made 10 and Stuart Surridge, to his immense mirth, 15. When they followed on there were several brave little innings before Johnson and Johnston mopped up.

Cambridge University, like so many others, not surprisingly went down by an innings: their bowling was butchered in a score of 414 for 4 declared. At the second attempt Trevor Bailey made 66 not out and the patient lefthander John Dewes 40 which, as it proved, won him a place in the final Test.

The Essex match could hardly be taken seriously. The Australians made 721 on the Saturday: and Tom Pearce was made a member of the Purchasers for being the first captain to bowl them out in a day! Sid Barnes made 79, Bill Brown 153, Bradman 187, Sam Loxton 120 and Ron Saggers 104. A moment of relief for Essex came after the stand of 219 in 90 minutes between Brown and Bradman for the second wicket: Keith Miller came in and simply removed his bat from the line of his first ball – from Bailey – and allowed it to bowl him for nought. On the Monday, Tom Pearce, by a rather primitive system of play and miss or hit, mustered 71 and Peter Smith 54, but Essex were bowled out twice in the day to lose by an innings and 451 runs. So to another innings win – over

Oxford University – when Tony Pawson twice batted bravely but the University bowling buckled at the knees.

Surely a strong MCC side with seven England probables and the gifted New Zealander, Martin Donnelly, would make a better show of things. In the event, they, too, lost by an innings – and 158 runs. Toshack took six first-innings wickets, Johnson three and McCool four in the second. Len Hutton, with 52 and 64, put up the resistance of a class player but, for the rest, the best anyone did was look like being in and then get out.

Missing the Lancashire match, J.A. went on to Trent Bridge for the Nottinghamshire game and thereby hangs one of the better tales of the summer. On the boat back from the West Indies, one of the powers in the cricketing land had said to Joe Hardstaff, 'You shall never play for England again.'

'Want a hundred quid on it?' asked Joe. The bet was taken. Now, against Lindwall – limbering up with 6 for 14 – Miller, Johnson and the fairly pacey Loxton, Joe proceeded to score 48 and 107 – and centuries against that side were rare indeed. When the team was announced for the First – Trent Bridge – Test, he was chosen, and received an envelope containing a cheque for £100, with no comment.

The next county game was against Hampshire who, in 1912, had been the last county side to beat an Australian touring team. Now they threatened to do it again. Put in to bat on a 'turner' they were bowled out, largely by Bill Johnston (6 for 74), but Charlie Knott with his off-breaks, and Jim Bailey with his slow left-arm, in their turn, shot them out for 117 and gave Hampshire a first-innings lead of 78. Then, though, for all Johnny Arnold's belligerent 42 (after 48 in the first innings), Miller and Johnston, with five wickets apiece, cut them down to 103 all out. Still the Australians wanted 182 to win, and before they had scored, Knott had Barnes lbw. At least one commentator was at this point slightly delirious, but Bill Brown, Lindsay Hassett and Ian Johnson made the runs they needed for an eight-wicket win: nevertheless it was much nearer than most sides came to making it a game against the Australians.

Then at Hove Sussex were bowled out for 86 and 138 in

response to the Australians' 549 for 5: Morris, Bradman and Harvey made hundreds. Most significant of all, though, Ray Lindwall 'slipped' himself, bowling faster in the first innings than he had done so far on the tour; and faster still in the second, to take 6 for 34 and 5 for 25. Harry Parks made a gutsy 61 out of 134 as Sussex went down to defeat by an innings and 325.

1948 was for J.A. the peak of his cricketing experience. The Australian performance was so outstanding in virtually every department, excepting only finger-spin, as to give him the yardstick against which forever after he judged all cricket. He was not alone in being impressed; the British public, as if determined to suffer, turned up in vast numbers to watch a process of destruction which twice their team threatened to reverse but could not. In addition, of course, the tourists had the great crowd-puller in Don Bradman as well as the more than life-sized pair of fast bowlers, Lindwall and Miller, who became as legendary as Gregory and McDonald in 1921.

Reverting to the First Test, Lindwall's performance was almost awe-inspiring. His action was not impressive. He had a low-arm, slingy delivery, but he commanded movement through the air and off the pitch with near-perfect control of length which included the ability to bowl his bouncer without telegraphing it. Indeed, at times he would give every indication that he was about to bowl one, only to deliver a yorker or a slower ball. He was, surely, the most complete fast bowler of the modern age; terrifying at times by virtue of his pace but in normal behaviour a friendly, amiable, relaxed man. He had obviously built up to the First Test; using his pace sparingly, though even such careful planning largely failed in the Test when he damaged a groin muscle and was unable to bowl in the second innings.

For the moment, however, he was able to start an English decline. When, following Miller's clean bowling of Hutton, he had Washbrook taken at long leg hooking, and when the eighth wicket fell at 74, it had every appearance of complete collapse. Laker (63) and Bedser (22), though, steered England to 165 – bad, but not as bad as it might have been. It was put in perspective, however, when Australia proceeded to build a vast total. Bradman, who in the course of his 138 became the first player of the season to reach 1000 runs, and Lindsay Hassett, determinedly defensive, carried them to 305 before the fifth wicket fell; and their final 509 gave them a lead of 344.

When England in their second innings were 39 for 2 with Washbrook and Edrich gone, another disaster threatened but, in appalling light, Hutton made a patient 74 and Compton 184, full of his own character, before he tried to duck under a bouncer from Miller, slipped and fell on his stumps. Joe Hardstaff made 43, which ought to have been enough to have kept his place for the next Test, and Godfrey Evans 50 in their 441, but in the end Miller's seven wickets and Johnston's nine in the two innings meant that Australia needed only 95 to win. Bedser bowled Arthur Morris and, for the second time in the match, he had Bradman caught at short fine-leg by Hutton – this time for nought. Barnes (64) and Hassett (21) ensured that there were no accidents, though at the end Barnes hit a four which he thought had won the match, grabbed a stump and was halfway up the pavilion steps before he was called back and informed that the scores were level. Hassett, in fact, made the winning stroke – and in that scramble, Barnes did not get a stump at all. The atrocious conditions and awful light made Compton's highest score against Australia memorable. There was, though, some unfortunate barracking of Miller for bowling bouncers in front of Nottinghamshire people who recalled the Australian treatment of Larwood in 1932–33. Miller, never one to knuckle under to anything or anybody, merely tossed back his spectacularly uncontrollable mane of hair and did whatever he wanted. Up to this point Australia had had a relatively easy run against mainly county sides, but this Test performance showed just how good they were when, although lacking Lindwall in the second innings, they won by eight wickets. In fact, after the initial England collapse they were always winning.

Northamptonshire gave the tourists another innings win – a century for Hassett – but Yorkshire made a tight-run thing of it, which would have been tighter still if the county had not dropped half a dozen catches.

So again England dared to hope as they went to the Lord's Test.

Tom Dollery, Alec Coxon and Doug Wright came in for Barnett, Hardstaff and Young. England made a good start when Coxon celebrated his first Test experience by having Barnes caught by Hutton at short fine-leg for nought. Once again, too, Bradman was caught in the same position – for the third time in consecutive Test innings – off Bedser. This time, though, it was Arthur Morris – a gentle person but a firm, accomplished batsman, indeed, the discovery of the tour, who made a century in a total of 350 – Bedser 4 for 100. Compton (53) and Norman Yardley (44) were the most successful English batsmen and, although Miller was not fit to bowl, England were put out for 215 (Lindwall 5 for 70). In the second Australian innings Barnes got a hundred, Morris 62, Bradman 89 and Miller 74 out of 460 for 7 declared. So England needed 596, rain enlivened the pitch and now it was the droll Ernie Toshack – with 5 for 40 – who did the damage, and England – 186 all out – lost by 409 runs.

The English spectators continued to revel in their suffering and the attendance of 132,000 (£43,000) was a record for a Test in England. It was now clear that Australia were superior in every direction and they were, too, quite wonderful to watch. The wicketkeeping of Tallon, the slip-fielding of Miller and the general work of Hassett decorated their outcricket. It is tempting to go through that tour in detail for it was utterly compelling, at times almost shattering, and inspires deep nostalgia. For instance, in the following week, against Gloucestershire, when Morris made 290 and Sam Loxton 159 not out, they scored 774 for 7 declared: their highest total of the season, the best by any Australian team against an English county and the highest total but one of any Australian side in a match in England. Jack Crapp, however, exacted a little revenge with 100 not out which took him into the side for the Third Test.

Then, at Manchester, England briefly threatened to win – only to be robbed by the weather. Denis Compton (145 not out in the first innings) and Cyril Washbrook (85 not out in the second) seemed to have given them a chance but the rain had the last word and washed out all hope of a finish on the Tuesday.

For those who followed England, the Fourth – Headingley – Test was the cruellest blow of all. Once again it had all the ingredients of cricket drama. England batted – indeed Bradman only won the toss once in the entire series – and made a splendid start of it. On a perfect batting pitch the recalled Hutton (81), Washbrook (143), Edrich (111), and nightwatchman Bedser (79) played major roles in England's 496 and for once the Australians' long bowling list really suffered. Barnes and Tallon were injured and, for Englishmen, nothing was more ironic than the fact that, of their two replacements, Neil Harvey made a century in his first Test in England and Ron Saggers kept wicket beautifully.

The charmingly boyish Harvey's 112 was the highest score of Australia's 458 but England led on the first innings by 38. Sam Loxton made 93, Ray Lindwall 77 (it seemed that all their bowlers could bat) and Miller 58, but the effective work was done at the end when their last two wickets put on 103 tactically valuable runs; quite how valuable nobody realized at the time. It was, though, apparent that England had made a mistake in leaving out Jack Young, the slow left-arm spinner.

For the second time in the match Hutton and Washbrook put on a hundred for the first wicket. In fact all the recognized batsmen made runs, towards the end of the innings quite quickly, though nobody scored more than 66. Yardley batted on for five minutes into the last day so that he could use the heavy roller in the hope of breaking up the wicket before he declared at 365 for 8, leaving Australia 404 to win. Not for seventy years had a side won a Test match against a declaration. A wrist-spinner could have worked havoc. Indeed, Compton, bowling his left-arm Chinaman, made the ball both turn and lift, and even Hutton set problems with his right-arm leg-breaks, but unhappily Evans missed chances off both of them. Compton showed what might be done quite early when he took the wicket of Hassett, caught and bowled off one that turned and jumped. Then, though, dishearteningly for English supporters, Morris (182) and Bradman (173 not out) put on 301 for the second wicket. There was some slack fielding, dropped catches and dispirited bowling, as well as some terrific effort – especially by Alec Bedser and Dick Pollard of Lancashire at pace, and Jim Laker with finger-spin. On that single stand, however, Australia could relax and they duly won by seven wickets, hitting sixty-six fours in the process – with a quarter of an hour to spare. Selectors and England bowlers were blamed for the 'failure' but the fact remained that Australia were overwhelmingly the stronger side.

That correct batsman and pleasant, wise human being, Bill Brown, who had previously been an Australian opening bat, did not even manage a place in the Test side, but he gained some compensation with 140 in the next match – a win over Derbyshire by an innings. Colin McCool took 6 for 77 in the second Derbyshire innings.

Still the crowds swarmed in; for the Glamorgan bank holiday match at Swansea there was no play at all because of heavy rain until three o'clock on the second day; yet over 50,000 people watched, and they were rewarded by a spectacular hitting innings of 84 – five sixes and seven fours – by Keith Miller.

Eric Hollies played himself into the England side for the last Test with 8 for 107 in the first innings of the Warwickshire match – he took the only wicket to fall in the second innings, too, as the county lost by nine wickets. At Manchester, most unusually, the game against the Australians was given as a benefit – to Cyril Washbrook – who made top score of 38 in their first innings of 130. Bradman did not enforce the follow-on but in the second innings scored 133 not out as the game went down as a draw. Even on the single day when play was possible between the tourists and Durham at Sunderland, there was an attendance of 17,000.

For the final Test Washbrook was injured and replaced by John Dewes (Cambridge University and Middlesex). Allan Watkins of Glamorgan, another lefthander, was brought in, while Ken Cranston was left out. There was much public criticism of the changes and, after Yardley won the toss for England, it proved to be justified. There had been such heavy rain earlier in the week that no play was possible until midday on the first day, and the whole ground was an ugly sight with its huge sawdust patches. It proved the background to a dismal English innings. Lindwall, Miller and Johnston bowled England out for 52. The whole crowd sat hushed, dismayed, depressed, amazed. Only Hutton stood above the shambles. He made a resolute 30 before he was last man out, brilliantly caught wide down the leg side by Tallon. No one else scored double figures and, after lunch, Lindwall, at his finest – varying length, pace and movement – took 5 wickets for 8 runs in 8.1 overs (altogether 6 for 20).

The English depression deepened when, immediately after that rout, Barnes and Morris, batting with complete freedom, put on 117 for the first wicket before Barnes was caught at the wicket by Evans off Hollies. At that point – nearly six o'clock – Bradman walked out to play his last Test innings in England. Yardley moved over to shake his hand and called on the England side to salute him with three cheers. It was a moving occasion: enough, though Jack Fingleton discounted the possibility, to have brought tears to Bradman's eyes. In any event, he played his first ball from Hollies but the second was a googly and it bowled him. He did not need to bat again, wherefore his batting average in Tests still stands at a mere 99.94.

That was enough of emotion for that day. On the Monday, Morris went on to 196, missing his double-hundred through a good run-out from third man by Simpson (substitute for the injured Watkins). England batted again 337 behind, lost Dewes early, before Edrich and Hutton contributed a gritty little stand of 44, and then Hutton and Compton, the two English hero figures of the season, put together 61. After that the innings fell to pieces and play continued into Wednesday only because of stoppages for bad light. Australia's eventual winning margin was an innings and 149 runs and that gave them the rubber by four matches to none.

The tourists went on virtually to annihilate opposition. They beat Kent, the Gentlemen – despite a second innings of 128 by Edrich – and Somerset each by an innings. They scored 522 for 7 declared and 489 for 8 declared in rain-ruined draws with the South of England and Leveson Gower's XI. Record crowds in Scotland saw Bradman make a century in his last innings in Britain.

All this reduced the two previous seasons of England's wins against India and South Africa to trifling matters. For many who either played or watched, it was the most towering cricket performance of their lives. This was not only a great side capable of steam-roller batting (Bill Brown, who could only gain a place in two Tests, averaged 57.92 in all first-class matches for the tourists);

but, above all, the bowling of Lindwall, Miller and Johnston was probably as sharp as any ever seen in England.

For J.A. it was a most impressive journey round England and one which he has still not forgotten. Nothing else in cricket ever really matched it for him. It was, too, the time when distant, Olympian cricketers became friendly creatures. In performance these Australians were more than life-sized, yet they proved so companionable as to be remembered for their pleasing personalities as much as their playing ability. The blow to his, as to many others', English cricketing pride was immense. The old enemy, as in 1921, yet even more spectacularly, had trampled on English aspirations and he had shared in the cold chill of the crowds as disaster befell. When the season started he was halfway between awe and companionship with the great men of the game. This tour with its divergent influences threw him forever into the camp of the English professionals. In 1948 his sympathy went out to the English players as never before, while he found himself admiring, fraternizing with the Australians and coming to know them as cricketers and men. Perhaps the hardest of them all to know was Bradman. He was often positively friendly and understandable, yet it was impossible to watch his general public relations without realizing that they were bad because he was pained by contact with strangers, however admiring they might be. Miller became a good and enduring friend. A fine leader of men, with an infallible sense of humour, he was unlucky never to captain Australia. One can but wonder who on earth made Ian Johnson captain in preference to Keith in 1954–55 and 1956.

It was a season of immense satisfaction, excitement, understanding and development for the young – or relatively young – commentator. In fact it was, in its effect on him, a mixture of many influences: the still growing appreciation of his freedom, an increasing understanding of broadcasting, the enjoyment and perception of cricket and general acceptance by editors and publishers. There was, too, an important background ingredient of increasing financial prosperity; the family was solvent and able to enjoy many of the pleasures that had previously been out of reach.

There came, too, towards the end of the season, quite out of the blue, a suggestion that he should go to South Africa to cover the forthcoming tour there by an England side for the BBC, and also do such commentary as the South African broadcasting authority might request. The fact was that the South Africans had asked for him because he was virtually the only English commentator they knew – he had broadcast their tour of 1947 and such public as there was for cricket there knew him. So the interview with Lobby was a comfortable one and ended with the injunction to enjoy it.

The practical fact was that he needed to pre-record best part of a winter's programme: at the same time he was writing a book on Bradman's tour as well as sundry articles. He was flattered by all this attention but, above all, he was looking forward to the tour of South Africa. Everything became an adjustment in order to make it; nevertheless he went in almost complete ignorance of what he would find there.

At the end of the season a totally unexpected three-day period made a specific change to his commentating life. Glamorgan had only entered the County Championship in 1921. Since then they had been twelve times in the bottom three of the table and, prior to the war, only twice in the top half – eighth in 1926 and seventh in 1937. The post-war years had shown an improvement – sixth in 1946 and ninth in 1947. They were certainly not, however, among the strongest batting or bowling sides in the Championship. They were, though, an outstanding fielding combination, captained by Wilfred Wooller who set great store by that aspect of the game.

Now, to the incredulity of the cricket world in general, they were in a position to win the Championship if they could beat Hampshire, and so long as Yorkshire, their closest rivals, did not beat Somerset in their match taking place at the same time. It was a complete somersault of cricket history.

It was hard in close contact with the players – who were staying in the same Christchurch hotel – not to react to their well controlled excitement. They were, which was a serious matter, without Phil Clift, their opening batsman, and Allan Watkins, their most considerable all-rounder and great fieldsman. In their places came Arnold Dyson, back from coaching at Stowe; and J.C. Clay, who twenty-seven years before had played in their second match in the Championship. Then he had been a fast bowler; he had matured to one of the wisest off-spinners in the game. He was, moreover, one of the game's great gentlemen; courteous, dry-witted, shrewd and, though he gave little outward sign of it, quite passionately devoted to Glamorgan.

Surely enough, on Saturday 21 August, Wilfred Wooller won the toss and decided to bat. It was a brief enough affair; Emrys Davies and Arnold Dyson walked out, faced three overs and two balls, and then were driven in for the rest of the day by rain.

So it became virtually a two-day match – Monday 11 to 7, Tuesday 11 to 4 – or 4.30 for a finish; 11¼ hours to get Hampshire out twice and score enough runs to beat them. A tall order: it seemed that time was bound to win; the Bournemouth pitch has always been a slow turner – as, indeed, it proved now. Before his batsmen walked out Wooller said, 'I want 320 by a quarter to six.' In fact they gave him 315 ten minutes short of his elected time.

Hampshire had an hour and a quarter to bat that night. Parkhouse made two brilliant catches – one off Wooller, one off Hever – to be rid of Rogers and Bridger, and Hampshire were 8 for 2 after half an hour. Then the off-spinners were called up; first Len Muncer, and then, to a round of nostalgic applause, John Clay, tall, thin, white-haired, plodding heavy-footed to the crease. Only McCorkell of the Hampshire batsmen could hold on. By seven o'clock they were 50 for 6. Yorkshire's match at Taunton was moving slowly and the Welshmen were tense with hope.

On Tuesday morning, with 4¾ hours to take fourteen Hampshire wickets, Clay and Muncer were thrown in at once. Still McCorkell played calmly and coolly until he allowed for Muncer's off-break: it went straight on and Haydn Davies howled with triumph for his second catch at the wicket. The longest partnership of the innings came from Leo Harrison and 'Lofty' Herman, but Hampshire were out for 84 and followed on 231 behind. Hever bowled Rogers, and then John Clay and Muncer took over from the new-ball bowlers. Almost at once Arnold, playing his characteristic and favourite hook, was brilliantly taken by Dyson at short leg. John Bridger set out to hit Clay off his length, but after one six he was bowled. McCorkell and Eagar stayed together for forty minutes as if to show how tame the wicket was. Willie Jones came on for Clay, and Eagar hit him for six. Muncer broke the partnership: he straightened one sharply to have McCorkell lbw; the hundred went up and then he clean bowled Eagar. Hampshire, 101 for 5 at lunch, were out forty minutes afterwards for 116. John Clay fittingly took the last wicket.

Bournemouth has never been truly a Hampshire people's – nor indeed a Dorset – town; it is too cosmopolitan for that. However, as the news came through of Somerset holding out, a remarkable number of the crowd at Dean Park revealed their Welshness in song. The BBC broadcast much of the last day's proceedings in their Welsh Service and for many years afterwards J.A. was hailed by Welshmen who had listened to his commentaries on that historic occasion. It made for much warmth, friendliness and a lifetime cricketing attachment to Glamorgan; not quite so close as to Hampshire, of course, but enduring.

Chapter 10

VOYAGE
TO SOUTH AFRICA

This was a period of four months of deep, new and mixed experiences for one still relatively ignorant of many matters. The trip was planned to give a short acclimatization period before the start of the Test matches and to end with them. So he went from a dull British mid-November to the quite unaccustomed luxury of a voyage on a Castle boat. He was treated handsomely on the trip, and such experiences as the ritual of 'Crossing the Line' were all pleasant fun. So, too, was the rail journey by Blue Train from Cape Town to Johannesburg, where he arrived in early December.

There was just time to have gone to see the MCC's match with North-Eastern Transvaal at Benoni, no distance away. To his regret he did not go and thus he missed Denis Compton's amazing performance of scoring 300 out of 399 in three hours. Compton had been for some time in magnificent form and this was in many ways near the crown of it.

For J.A. the trip brought yet another new experience altogether. On his first day in Johannesburg, instead of going to Benoni, he was walking along Commissioner Street when he saw a black man walking towards him in ordinary enough fashion on the outside of the pavement. Suddenly a white man walking in the opposite direction swung his leg and kicked the coloured man into the gutter. The victim got up and, apparently apologetically, walked away. J.A.'s stomach turned over; it was the first of a series of experiences which changed his entire outlook on a country with whose cricketing representatives he had spent such pleasant times in 1947 and where now people continued to bestow immense hospitality upon him.

There were many evidences of strange conditions. Consequently, one day finding – unusually – a coloured taxi driver, J.A. asked him to drive him to one of the coloured towns. The driver took much persuading, but eventually agreed. It was an amazing sight: the poverty, the filth. The houses were built of tar barrels hammered flat; single-room hovels for entire families. A narrow stream ran down through the settlement. The inhabitants used its head-waters for drinking and washing water, its end as a sewer. All this weighed much upon his mind and he persuaded a member of the touring side – S.C. 'Billy' Griffith – to come with him on a repeat visit to ensure that he had not been mistaken in the appalling degree of degradation. Billy suffered it and even long afterwards as Secretary of MCC said, unasked, 'I shall never forget what we saw in that compound in South Africa.'

During his stay, J.A. was constantly entertained in three- or even four-car homes where the coloured servants were housed in a hut in the garden – not allowed to sleep under the same roof as whites. Before the end of the tour there had been an election, Smuts was defeated and apartheid, already practised without acknowledgement by many of the population, soon became law. For J.A. this was new and left him immensely uneasy, with the result that the cricket of the tour never quite made the impact it should have done – or should it have done? If he had gone to Benoni to watch Compton and never seen the Bantu kicked into the gutter would his life have been different? Would he have been a less disturbed, if more ignorant visitor? That, though, is fruitless speculation. Happily for his peace of mind he was able very soon after his return to speak out in a very early edition of the BBC programme 'Any Questions?' on which he worked quite regularly, happily and freely for several years. He had been in the first programme of the series and felt absolutely at ease in it. There was quite honestly no advance knowledge of the questions. When the subject of the situation in South Africa was raised, he spoke his mind freely but, so far as some officials were concerned, over-strongly.

The whole matter was raised by the Director-General at his Monday conference. The point was made that J.A. had said nothing stronger than Lady Bonham-Carter had already done in another programme.

Commentating at Bristol on the match between Gloucestershire and the 1949 New Zealanders. Ian Peebles – former Test cricketer, fine writer and wine connoisseur – is also at the table *(Hulton-Deutsch)*

Veteran of a single season, the beginner-presenter introducing the Indian touring team waiting to send their messages home in May 1946 *(Hulton-Deutsch)*

Scarborough in the rain, during the Indian tourists' closing match in England, against Leveson Gower's XI: bliss compared with the hard discipline of police life endured for eleven years and left only eighteen months earlier *(F. Stanley Cheer)*

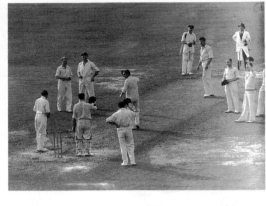

Bill Edrich and Denis Compton, who in 1947 kept high carnival during the first truly post-war summer *(Roger Mann Collection)*

No cricket side has quite matched the perform-ance of the 1948 Australians, outstanding in virtually every department. The England players saluted Australia's captain, Don Bradman, with three cheers on his arrival at the crease for his last Test innings; all those at the Oval on that evening were quite stunned when he was out two balls later *(Hulton-Deutsch)*

About to broadcast from South Africa during the 1948–49 tour, with *(left to right)* Len Hutton, Alec Bedser, Cliff Gladwin and Roly Jenkins

Talking to George Emmett and Jack Crapp (in blazer) during the tea interval of Gloucestershire's match with the New Zealanders, 1949 *(Hulton-Deutsch)*

Dylan Thomas *(left)* and Roy Campbell, two poets admired for their
work and relished for their company *(Hulton-Deutsch)*

In the studio for a 'Book of Verse' recording. Around the table: Hugh
Metcalfe, J.A., Preston Lockwood, George Robey, James McKecknie,
Dylan Thomas and Robin Holmes *(London News Agency Photos Ltd)*

George Rostrevor Hamilton, poet and epigrammist, and collaborator on the author's first published work, *Landmarks* (*Hulton-Deutsch*)

Michael Ayrton (*left*) – painter, poet, essayist, fine brain and a close friend from the early days in London – photographed with Madam Rambert and the Swiss artist, Rolf Durig (*Hulton-Deutsch*)

Neville Cardus, who effectively created modern writing about cricket, at Old Trafford in 1949 (*Roger Mann Collection*)

Bill Bowes: Yorkshireman, fast bowler, colleague and good friend
(Hulton-Deutsch)

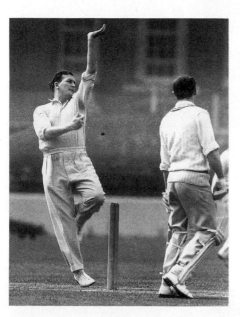

Jim Laker *(left)* and Fred Trueman, two of England's finest bowlers,
both of whom were to become colleagues in the commentary box
(Hulton-Deutsch)

Above left Basil
D'Oliveira, the young
Cape Coloured whom
J.A. had the privilege of
helping to his place high
in world cricket
(David Frith Collection)

Above right Sir Jack
Hobbs, Alf Gover, J.A.
and Leo Harrison at an
early meeting of The
Master's Club

Centre right
The Hampshire team
which finished third in
the County Champion-
ship, 1955: *back row, left
to right* N. B. Edwards
(Assistant Secretary),
James Gray, Alan
Rayment, Roy Marshall,
Malcolm Heath, Henry
Horton, N. Drake
(scorer); *centre row* Vic
Cannings, Neville
Rogers, Desmond Eagar,
Leo Harrison, Derek
Shackleton; *in front* Peter
Sainsbury, Mike
Barnard, Mervyn Burden
(Bournemouth Daily Echo)

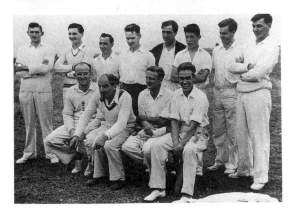

Above An Alderney side in 1956 featuring
(back row, left to right) Frank Tyson, Michael
St John Packe, Leo Harrison and the local
cricketer of all work, Joe Harrington
(Guernsey Press)

Liberal candidate for Epping in the 1955 General Election
(Hulton-Deutsch)

'After all,' said the Director-General, 'it is not as if he was still on the staff, is it?'

It was pointed out that he was; then said 'the old man', 'What's a member of staff doing on a programme where he can express editorial opinion?'

As a result it was ruled that J.A. should continue on the programme, and on any other where he was required, at an income not less than he had earned as a member of staff. In fact, merely by receiving the normal fees instead of the Corporation's 'SNF', he was better off than he had been: and free. This still seems to him to have been the best face of the BBC; better, perhaps, than its present character. He was on and off the 'Any Questions?' programme for some thirty years afterwards; last of all in Alderney after he settled there. Meanwhile, in South Africa he found it amazing that an entire section of the community could blot the majority out of its mind: that, though, is what racial dominance means.

To turn, however, to the original purpose of his visit to South Africa, the cricket was some comfort after the terrible mauling the English game had taken at the hands of Bradman's men. England contrived to go through the tour unbeaten and to take the Test series by two matches to nil. It must be observed, though, that those two wins were so narrow that they might until the very last moment have gone either way. It was apparent, too, that the general standard of cricket in South Africa was not high: very few of the provincial sides could offer the English team a serious game, though one or two could. As the following series against New Zealand in England was to show, this was something of a false dawn; for all its promise, English cricket was not really improved and its main strength lay in the batting of Hutton and Compton, the bowling of Bedser and, as a bonus of this tour, Jenkins.

Before the Tests started several factors limited the two sides' selection. On the English side, captained by George Mann, Edrich, Yardley and Hollies, for various reasons, did not make the tour. In fact the absence of Hollies enabled Roly Jenkins to make a considerable advance. As if he foresaw this contingency, Mann did not show Jenkins to the leading South African batsmen in the matches prior to the First Test. For the home side, Alan Melville, although he made 92 for Transvaal against the touring side immediately before the Tests, decided that he was not sufficiently recovered from a fractured wrist to play for his country. He was much missed, as person as well as player, but in his solitary Test appearance – the Third, at Newlands – he had little success and suffered much discomfort of the wrist.

The First Test was one of the most thrilling in the history of international cricket: when the last – eight-ball – over was bowled by Lindsay Tuckett all four results were possible and the suspense, as the rain drove in from the Umgeni Hills, was almost unbearable. Indeed, most of the England side in the pavilion found themselves unable to watch; the commentator had no choice.

When the Durban Test began, conditions were as humid as any could be in Britain and, as a result, both Bedser and Gladwin managed to swing the ball which they could rarely do in South Africa. In face of that attack, South Africa collapsed. After Jenkins had taken the wicket of Eric Rowan with his third ball in Test cricket, Bruce Mitchell batted patiently and Dudley Nourse demonstrated – one of the key factors of the series – the ease with which he – if only he – could play Jenkins. Then Nourse was out to Wright through one of the most brilliant catches anyone there had seen. Allan Watkins at short leg – who was in any event virtually picked for his fielding – took a far-diving catch from a push to leg in the instant before it hit the ground. Otherwise Denis Begbie and Ossie Dawson put together a few runs, but South Africa were all out for 161: four wickets to Bedser, three to Gladwin.

When England batted in a rain-interrupted innings they had to work for their runs as soon as they had dealt with the swing of Dawson, the pace of McCarthy and Tuckett. Then Athol Rowan and Tufty Mann bowled their spin in skilfully controlled fashion. Rowan bowled 44 of the eight-ball overs to take 4 for 108, Mann took 6 for 59 in his 37.4 overs. Characteristically on the tour, Hutton and Compton made the highest English scores, Washbrook a useful one. Otherwise the two spinners worked their way through. England came to within 15 of the South African score for the loss of two wickets, then the tail fell away and, apart from Hutton, Washbrook and Compton, Mann (19) and Bedser (11) were the only men to make double figures. Still a lead of 92 was useful: it soon became dire necessity when Nourse and Wade, the main South African batsmen throughout the series, scored respectively 32 and 63; and Denis Begbie weighed in with 48. Doug Wright, with 4 for 72, came out as the most successful English bowler and eventually England needed 128 to win. Their chances on a crumbling wicket did not look good. Two and a quarter hours were left for them and that was reduced to two hours by a couple of showers which also impaired the spinners' grip. So it was the pace bowlers, Cuan McCarthy (6 for 43) and Lindsay Tuckett, who fought it down to the end. Washbrook (25), Compton (28), Mann (13) and Jenkins (22) were the only men to reach double figures before the game moved into its final funnel. The stand between Compton and Jenkins was brave and crucial.

Lindsay Tuckett bowled the last over and with three balls left any result was possible. Then Bedser made a single, Gladwin missed the seventh ball and, as Tuckett came up to bowl the last, in a Scotch mist blowing down from the Umgeni Hills, the field closed in. In fact, and probably crucially, the rain on Tufty Mann's spectacles at short leg may have decided the match. Gladwin swung at the ball, missed and it ran off his thigh a few yards out on the leg side. The batsmen, though, had made up their minds to run whatever happened. They galloped through before anyone – least of all Mann at short leg – could do anything to procure a run-out. They went waving their bats and galloping on to the pavilion through milling crowds, with Gladwin, in his rich Derbyshire accent, whooping, 'Coometh the hour, coometh the man.' The tension was released over subsequent hours rather than minutes and the English team's hotel housed a series of semi-hysterical parties that night.

The SABC did not require broadcasts of the match between MCC and Natal Country Districts but it was splendid to be there because Maurice Tremlett scored the first century of his career. He had had a rough trip; on account of his reputation as a pace bowler he had been given the new ball, which he could not control. With Somerset, that was the province of Arthur Wellard and Bertie Buse, and Tremlett normally came on when the shine had gone and bowled his body-action off-breaks. Here he fired the new ball all over the place and became bitterly depressed. This innings did him a power of good. It required celebration and got it.

Hereabout there was a riot in Durban while Denis Compton was taking a few days off there. There was no reply from his hotel and Mike Green, the MCC team manager, asked J.A. to go down to make sure Denis was safe. He was located with no great difficulty, in fact with time for a rapid trip down to Les Payn's plantation. He had been the slow left-arm bowler played out of the action by Tufty Mann on the English tour. Philosophically, though, he accepted that, enjoyed the tour and became a good friend. Now, in a short space of time he provided some surprising information about plantation life. There were unexpected stories such as those of workers sitting eating their midday meal when they were 'cuddled' by constrictors but who wriggled out leaving their jackets behind.

Christmas was spent with Reggie Perks and his family at Brakpan. The Christmas dinner, eaten in a hotel in tropical heat, consisted of *hors d'œuvre*, soup, choice of chicken, turkey, duck, goose, pork or beef, Christmas pudding, fruit and cheese. Reggie was there as one of the English coaching team, which added to the company on the trip – also there were Emrys Davies, George Cox, Vic Jackson, Jack Walsh, Ray Smith and Sid Buller.

Then to the team's unofficial Christmas football match, in which Denis Compton was subjected to some terrific shoulder-charging by Jack Jardine, a former South African soccer captain. This, to the great anxiety of Mike Green, but Compton survived. J.A., unaccustomed to such exertion in the rarified atmosphere of the Rand, did not, and finished in a state of utter exhaustion.

The Second Test was played on Johannesburg's Ellis Park ground where the wicket was better than merely perfect. Hutton and Washbrook proceeded to enjoy themselves. They were confident from the start and they had both reached their centuries – Washbrook first – by tea at 236 for no wicket. They went on afterwards to beat the old record for a first-wicket stand in a Test Match – the 323 of Hobbs and Rhodes at Melbourne in 1912. Before Hutton (158) played a rather weary stroke at McCarthy, they had put on 359. Towards the end of the day, Washbrook was out for 195. There was time for Crapp and Compton to have destroyed themselves after such a performance, but they wisely played for the next day, when Compton came to a hundred and Crapp made 56, before the rest of the batting crumbled and England were out for 608. When Wynne and Eric Rowan were out with only 17 to show for their efforts, England suddenly perked up but Mitchell and Wade carried South Africa through to 315, though that was not enough to avoid the follow-on. On the morning of the third day the South African team for the Third Test had been announced and Eric Rowan was omitted. In their second innings – yes, you have guessed it – Eric Rowan made 156 not out and saw the game to a safe draw. When he reached his hundred he bowed to the pavilion and one could tell whom he intended the gesture to reach. After the match he held a celebration party – during which he fell asleep – and, of course, was reinstated in the side.

The team and their immediate followers flew down to Cape Town. It was something of a fresh venture for the BBC to send a commentator by air but with only one day to do it in they had little choice. There are few more lovely settings for cricket than Newlands. The Oaks enclosure, with Table Mountain seeming to rise out of it, is unforgettable. The match, alas, was drawn, when South Africa resisted the temptation to go for the ambitious target George Mann had set them, 229 in 125 minutes. Nothing in the game was more impressive than Denis Compton's bowling in the first South African innings when he sent down 25 overs of, not his usual Chinaman, but orthodox slow left-arm spin, to take 5 for 70.

It was more than a month to the Fourth Test and the time was spent partly in Rhodesia – a long train journey with the roar of lions to discourage excursions from the train when it stopped for rest.

The Fourth Test meant a return to Ellis Park, Johannesburg; and, once again, George Mann dangled the carrot of a declaration before South African noses but again they took no chances. For this match, Billy Griffith was brought in as wicketkeeper in place of Godfrey Evans. The combination of the stimulating rarified air of the high Rand and enforced idleness from cricket was too much for Evans. One evening he decided to go out some fifty miles from Johannesburg to a very highly recommended restaurant, and he insisted that his room-mate – J.A. – accompany him. Now, if ever cars were plentiful anywhere it is among the white community of South Africa, and Godfrey could be trusted to borrow a very fast one. The two made the journey swiftly indeed and a good evening was had by both. They left somewhat late, which Godfrey used as his excuse to see how fast the car would go. It would go extremely fast but, after a time, J.A. mildly suggested that they were going in the wrong direction – away from Johannesburg instead of towards it. The enthusiastic driver turned this over in his mind for some ten minutes – or twenty-five miles – before deciding, 'You might be right.' They turned about and, travelling even faster than before, they eventually reached the safety of Lutjes Langham Hotel as the sun came up.

The Fifth Test started stodgily and ended excitingly. When South Africa won the toss and batted, two difficult chances went down in the slips. The English fielding throughout was generally considered outstanding; the occasional fault in slip-catching was generally attributed to the glare, and it was virtually the only flaw in the performance George Mann pressed from his side. So South Africa went slowly to 219 for 3, largely through Mitchell, Wade and Nourse. On the second day, Mitchell went slowly – at about 15 runs an hour overall – to 99 before, almost incredibly, he edged Bedser to Billy Griffith, who confessed later that he was so surprised that he almost dropped it. Wade, however, continued to 125 and South Africa were all out for 379. England made 80 for 1 that night and were harnessed all the next day by some capable outcricket. Nevertheless, through firm-hearted resistance by George Mann (131 not out), Jenkins and Bedser, they reached 390 for 9 on the third evening.

The general opinion at the start of the fourth and last day seemed to be that a draw was inevitable. There was nothing in the early batting to suggest anything more. George Mann did not declare, as some expected him to do, but scored 5 more runs before McCarthy – the fastest bowler in the match – put out Jack Young.

Cuan McCarthy was tall, fair-haired and athletic, and by far the fastest bowler on either side during this series. After the South African tour of England in 1951, he played for Cambridge University and was top of their bowling figures in 1952. He subsequently played for Dorset but all through his career he was dogged by the fact that his action was suspect, which no doubt accounted for his eventual disappearance from the first-class game after his year at the University. He was also a very useful boxer, and good company.

The idea that Nourse was going to declare when South Africa went to tea at 187 for 3 was taken as a joke, only for – immediately after tea – the light roller to be put on. He left England 172 to score in 95 minutes: about 108 an hour. It soon became apparent that George Mann had told his batsmen to go for the runs, and he himself went in at number four as if to emphasize the urgency, though he was soon out to Tufty Mann for 2. In fact, the spinners, Athol Rowan and Mann, fought the battle down to the end. Hutton made 32, Washbrook 40, Compton 42, but then England were in trouble when wickets began to tumble: Mann 2, Bedser 1, Gladwin 15, Griffith 0, and England stood at 161 for 7. A leg-bye and they were 162, needing 10 to win in two overs with three wickets in hand. The ground was full of excited chatter as the thunder-clouds began to gather. Crapp and Watkins scored a single apiece – 164: 8 to win. Jack Crapp played two balls safely to the field. The light was going fast. It then occurred to Jack that Nourse would probably put on a fast bowler for the last over and both batsmen would have been vulnerable in that lack of light. He hit a long four to long-off, a two off the sixth ball and England needed 2 to win. On the seventh ball of the eight-ball over Crapp moved quickly down the pitch, Mann dropped it short, and the batsman's long arm-swing sent it humming through long-off; a single bounce and it split the boards in the back of the grandstand. England had won by three wickets and taken the rubber by two Tests to none. It was great credit to George Mann: his century had saved England's first innings and, in contrast to the South Africans in previous Tests, he pressed for a finish right down the order. Nourse, for his part, relied on the impressive spin attack of Athol Rowan and Tufty Mann but never was the contrast between the two sides plainer than in that fourth innings.

Staying with Charles Fortune in Grahamstown, J.A. drove Fortune's native cook back to her home through a thunderstorm. Suddenly they were in the native quarter: the thunderstorm itself was not more horribly chilling. Shame, hesitation, doubt, guilt, struggled in the mind. It asked a question South Africa has still to answer.

The return journey was an impressive one; surely the peak of luxury travel – by 'Speedbird' flying boat. To take off from the sea at the Cape was ordinary enough; so, in its way, was the landing on the Vaal Dam in Johannesburg with dinner and a bed at Lutjes Langham Hotel. On the next day – comfortably and not too early – they landed on the Zambezi near the Victoria Falls with a boat trip down to see them. Next morning they moved on to Lake Victoria and a war dance performed by locals before dinner. The third day was unforgettable. The flying boat came down on the Nile at Luxor and the passengers could ride on donkey-back to the unique and ancient City of the Kings. There was a tiny news-stall on the river's edge near the hotel. What odder place in the world to find a first edition of Cyril Connolly's *The Rock Pool*, published by the Obelisk Press in Paris in 1936? But there it was, marked 150 centimes and costing, in fact, a pound: a delightful and quite unexpected piece of loot.

The fifth was the longest flying day, encompassing tea at Alexandria – England's relations with Egypt were not at their best – and then across to Sicily, making what should possibly be called 'water-fall' at Augusta. There, in the hotel, he looked in the mirror. Now it should be said that whisky was still in short supply in Britain but not in South Africa, where it was also cheap. Unfortunately, there was rarely soda available to take with it, as a result of which he had tended to top up with bottled beer. The mirror showed that he had, in fact, spent his drinking time in South Africa the way he had spent his drinking time in South Africa. He rang reception. 'How long can I break my journey here on my ticket?'

'Not more than three months, Sir.'

'That will be enough, I think. In fact a week will be enough. Where can I stay?'

'You can stay here at the staff rates in the hotel.'

'But that would defeat the object of the exercise; where can I go that would be quiet and restful?'

'Shall I suggest Taormina, Sir, it will be full of flowers now.'

That was enough. He booked into the hotel at Taormina and found it a pleasing place next to the great theatre or small coliseum; there was a comfortable room and good cooking. The water, too, was good: he drank nothing else for his first three days. On the fourth, he put out his hand and took the carafe of wine which stood on the table as automatically as a water jug in an English boarding house. He has never drunk whisky or beer since.

It was a bland, characterless Muscat but he, in his ignorance, was completely charmed by it. The next morning he went down to the tiny seaside bar, bought himself a glass of white wine and settled to enjoy it while watching the water. Two Americans came up. Cheerfully extrovert, they explained they were on demobilization leave, but determined to see something of Europe before they went back home. The three settled to drink wine: 'Say, are you into this wine racket?'

'Not really but the owner of my hotel is.'

'We will move in there, then.'

Patiently but enthusiastically, that night the hotel owner explained to the novices about wine: his brother owned a vineyard up the mountain and he would take his guests there to be shown round. The offer could not be refused. By the end of the day the three thought themselves wine men. The landlord, though, counselled a visit to Augusta. The trip would not be easy (petrol was a scarce commodity in post-war Sicily) but a friend of his – an undertaker – was taking a corpse there the next day and undoubtedly he would be prepared to take three visitors as additional passengers for a few lire. They went, they tasted – still more Muscat – and returned with bottles for the homeward journey. Two days later he caught the flying boat back to England, Southampton in fact. His wife was at the landing-stage to meet him, to be amazed within a few minutes by the fact that he who had left her as a beer-drinker with a sneaking feeling for whisky, was now advocating sweet white wine – and passionately at that. It was an interest and a taste which was to alter, but also to develop and change his life in many respects in the days to come.

It was a matter of days indeed, for very soon afterwards he went to see Richard Aldington in Paris. This was one of the wisest mentors J.A. was ever to know. He himself frequently drank – and recommended – red wine, and J.A. followed him with the passionate belief of a disciple. Aldington also counselled 'with every glass of wine a glass of water', in which respect his pupil did not follow him.

Chapter 11

MAJOR CHANGE

He continued, it seemed, to make progress, but it was never steady and, at this point in particular, his career moved in a series of violent changes. South Africa had been a salutory political jolt: Sicily was a change of environment which although brief was far more than a holiday. Wine was a new experience and Richard Aldington proved the wisest of guides.

Richard was, of course, an outstanding novelist who had earlier been a promising poet but who made his first and major mark with *Death of a Hero* in 1929. He had fought in the First World War as an infantry officer, going through trench and open-country battles in France without ever firing his revolver. He had married the Imagist poet, Hilda Doolittle, but they divorced and he was living with Mrs Patmore of that literary family when he was invited to her son's wedding. He met the bride for the first time at the reception afterwards and a couple of hours later the pair eloped and went to America. In due course they married and the wife, Netta, proved a very sensitive artist. Richard, though, was in many ways too big a character for her. They came back to Europe, settled first in Paris and then in Le Lavandou, where J.A. became a regular and frequently amazed guest. There were other visitors from time to time, not only British and American but French, Italian and Spanish. It was, indeed, an international household, yielding a constant series of surprises – perhaps revelations is a better word. Netta, unfortunately, never grew out of her awe of her husband. It was no surprise when finally she fled to England, took temporary shelter in the Arlott household and then settled down with a man of literary bent but much less of a heavyweight in mind and character than Richard. It was not that affection had died but simply that understanding had become impossible. Her escape to the Arlott family meant the end, alas, of J.A.'s friendship with Richard Aldington, who did not easily forgive – at least not in the field of domestic affairs.

Until that split J.A. continued to go to Le Lavandou, where his respect for Richard grew immense but where, above all, he became conscious of his own English small-townness. He began to adopt a wider outlook and a greater tolerance of much that he had regarded as wrong-headed. From all this he came back home seeming, surely, to his family, a changed person as, indeed, he was. He had to take himself, as it were, by the scruff of the neck and push his face once more into cricket, but the zest for it returned instantly. Now, he was not simply an apprentice commentator following the touring side, but one constantly more involved with the counties. That summer saw quite strikingly his increasing acceptance among the county players, but that is not to say that he ignored the touring side. In fact, the New Zealanders were probably one of the most companionable teams ever to tour Britain. In some ways they were not particularly strong but they brought with them two left-hand batsmen, each in his way with a touch of genius, although they were quite different types of cricket characters. They were captained by Walter Hadlee, two of whose sons were to play for New Zealand, while one of them, Richard, became an outstanding all-rounder by world standards. Hadlee was thoughtful and shrewd, with a dry sense of humour. There was some discussion as to their allocation of Tests and it was probably Walter Hadlee who tilted the balance in favour of four three-day matches. He remarked one evening over a glass of wine, that if they had settled for three four-day games they would probably have lost the rubber but that, unless the weather intervened, they ought to have no difficulty in drawing four of three days each against the still limited England bowling.

Hadlee himself was only fifth in New Zealand's Test batting averages but he played one of the best innings of the season, against Surrey after the Oval pitch had been badly affected by frost! He went in at the fall of the first wicket and scored a match-winning 119 not out in a final declared score of 249 for 8: no one else on the side made more than 20 and extras were 33. It was, in many ways, as striking an innings as any played in post-war cricket. Of the two lefthanders, Martin Donnelly proved one of the most gifted batsmen of his period: yet, in a first-class career for Middlesex, Oxford University, Warwickshire and New Zealand, he took part in only 138 first-class matches. He had immense skill but, a rounded man, he always regarded cricket as a game simply to be enjoyed. Nevertheless, he could put his head down and battle for the sake of his side, as he did several times in that Test series. He richly relished the humour that a great player could extract from the play. For instance, against Gloucestershire at Bristol on a turning wicket he struck Tom Goddard – an off-spinner who had always and passionately fancied himself against lefthanders – for a crucial 89, mainly against the spin, which included all but one extra of the 45 runs put on for the last wicket. He liked to play strokes but he could defend most valuably at need. He played a few games for Warwickshire in 1950 but then went to Australia on business and did not appear in the first-class game again. He was, too, excellent company and, all in all, probably the greatest loss suffered by world cricket in the post-war period.

Bert Sutcliffe was essentially an athlete, fit, mobile, lean and strong, and he struck the ball with immense power. Hadlee, a most thoughtful captain, was at much pains to check Sutcliffe's impetuosity in trying to hook before he had picked up the pace of the pitch. He played some exciting innings and made more runs – 2627 – than anyone else on the tour. At the head of the Test batting averages, though, was little Brunty Smith, a bubbling, happy cricketer who, playing in only two Tests for three innings (including one not out), returned a figure of 86.50. Second in the Test averages and deservedly so, without the aid of not outs, was Martin Donnelly with 77.00. That figure was to a considerable extent attained by his 206 in the Lord's Test when he patiently played himself in – 3½ hours for the first hundred – but then opened out and used all his strokes.

They were a side full of character. Perhaps the unluckiest of them was Mervyn Wallace who very nearly made a thousand runs in May and then slipped away altogether; even so he made 1722 runs in all at 49.20 and enjoyed the tour up to the hilt. There was, too, Verdun Scott, a dogged opener, angular and determined. Geoff Rabone was a most patient batsman who always sold his wicket dearly. John Reid was an all-rounder, immensely physically strong, who would bat, bowl, field or keep wicket, and he was, of course, to come later to England as New Zealand's captain. Jack Cowie, though by no means the young player of his pre-war days, was top of their Test bowling with his game fast-medium bowling. He was closely followed by Tom Burtt who bowled slow left-arm, normally the stock break-away, but capable occasionally of slipping in one that turned the other way.

The rest of the bowling was not really impressive, or perhaps it might be fairer to say that it had not yet matured. Geoff Rabone did his best, and Harry Cave's fast-medium did not fully develop until the next tour. Fen Cresswell was a useful stock bowler who took 62 wickets on the tour, but he was already probably past his best and played only one Test match, bowling with his most unusual square-on action. It was characteristic of that side's humour that Cresswell was known as 'Ferret' because, in the words of the old cricketing chestnut, he went in after the rabbits. A kindly, friendly man, in 1966 he was found most tragically dead with a gun at his side. That would be altogether too sad a note on which to end a survey of such a companionable side, so it is fortunate that there remain several more. Cecil – 'the Burglar' – Burke tossed up his leg-breaks with cheerful good humour and without resenting the punishment he often received. He only ever played in one Test match – in Australia in 1945–46 – when he took 2 for 30. He was yet another character and, like so many of that team, happy with a joke however threadbare it might be. Frank Mooney was, on the field, a wicketkeeper and batsman who concentrated mightily. Once the day's play was over, however, he earned himself the nickname of 'Moonlight' and most certainly lived up to it. This was a side which never allowed cricket to become more important than life, but they did enjoy it.

In the First Test the bowling of Cowie and Burtt – five wickets apiece – was countered by the centuries of Hutton and Compton, while New Zealand were exhumed from 80 for 4 to 341 by

Donnelly, Smith and Mooney. For England, Washbrook and Edrich set a challenge which New Zealand could never reach and which never left the English bowlers room to bowl the tourists out. Trevor Bailey celebrated his first Test with 6 for 118 in the first innings. Lord's, too, saw a game too top-heavy with runs for any hope of a result: Compton (116), Bailey (93) and Robertson (121) could not tilt the scale against New Zealand's 484: Donnelly 206. At Old Trafford England, largely through Bailey's 6 for 84, put the tourists out for 293 and in return made 440 (Simpson 103) but Bert Sutcliffe's 101 and Donnelly's 80 wiped out all hope of a finish. Finally, to the Oval, the fourth and conclusive draw. Most of the New Zealanders made runs in a total of 345 in face of some useful bowling by Bailey and Bedser. England, though, with 206 by Hutton and 100 by Edrich, wiped out all possibility of a finish, especially when New Zealand went on to 308 for 9. As Walter Hadlee had forecast, there was never room on those four good pitches for a finish in three days between these two sides.

Meanwhile, away from cricket, life in the office went ahead absorbingly. Jim Pennethorne-Hughes proved the very negation of what the police force understood as a 'man in charge'. He became a friend in every way, not always understandable, for he had his eccentricities, but utterly likeable, frank and amusing. There is no doubt, too, that he saved his junior from a number of gaffes he might otherwise have made.

At home there was economic solvency thanks largely to J.A.'s writing – books and articles. Family life, too, was a joy – when he was at home – and the little boy gave both his parents immense happiness, so much so that they decided – wisely as it was to prove – that they ought to have another child. A move up the hill to Highgate Avenue was all part of the prosperity growth, and so were a series of motor cars. At the time they seemed like luxuries; now it is apparent that they were quite desperately cheap. Moreover, they carried him home at some speed from often highly inconvenient locations of cricket matches.

Book-collecting, too, began to assume a greater importance. The first editions of Richard Aldington had been something of a beginning but soon he began to develop a mixture of modern first editions and aquatints. The latter – mostly from the period 1775 to 1825 – were still relatively cheap. So, too, of course were the new – first – issues of the modern authors he collected: notably John Betjeman but also John Piper and Osbert Lancaster. These, in their turn, created a complete change in the look of the house – collecting books involved collecting bookcases as well. A few were huge and Victorian, most more modern, with sliding glass doors; indeed, they still occupy much space in his house.

Friendships, too, were growing up. Terry Delaney was the main personal bridge between the Southampton and the BBC days, especially when he made the leap from his public library into 'Radio Newsreel'. Julian Holland was another and as this is being written he is sitting in the garden taking the sun of an erratic summer. His eyesight is not now what it was but he had at one period an uncanny knack of dropping the needle of a BBC machine precisely in the groove he wanted to broadcast. It was a nerve-shaking experience but he rarely failed.

Writing books was now part of J.A.'s existence. His first prose work – *Indian Summer* – had been written by dint of spending an ordinary domestic evening, then starting on the book at ten at night and working through, sometimes until four or five in the morning. That could not be maintained. Indeed, it still raises the hairs on the back of his neck to contemplate it, but for those few autumn nights at least it was possible. Without doubt, he developed a writing habit which proved fairly painless. So, without real difficulty, by 1949 he had three books ready for publication. *Concerning Cricket* was a collection of essays gathered from the previous four or five years. *The Middle Ages of Cricket* was an editing of early classics of the game, and *Gone to the Test Match* was another in the series of season accounts published by Longmans. In the same year he was putting together a collected volume called *Cricket in the Counties*: a series of nine county match accounts with a general introduction. The accounts – essentially knowledgeable – were of matches of Yorkshire by Bill Bowes, Glamorgan by Wilfred Wooller, Sussex by Billy Griffith, Essex by Peter Smith, Lancashire by John Kay, Surrey by E. M. Wellings, Warwickshire by Crawford White and three by J.A. The book was launched with immense enthusiasm – by the editor-compiler at least. Yet, although it seemed such a good idea, it made little impact – certainly not enough to call for a repeat.

Gone with the Cricketers was an account of J.A.'s tour to South Africa and the New Zealand visit to England in the series of his season accounts for Longmans. Domestically there was much to be achieved and the only certain source of income was writing. It was not by any means a spectacular money-spinner, but it helped the house along and, crucially, it was done with appreciable pleasure.

Another book published at that time was *Wickets, Tries and Goals*. Football had long been an enthusiasm, compelling enough to cause J.A. in his schooldays constantly to cycle the sixteen-odd miles to Reading and back to watch League football there. That is how keen he was: and football certainly once weighed as heavily with him as cricket. Indeed for much of the year he lived football so intensely that a rough approximation to the Reading team of 1928 rests still in his mind. There was the excitable goalkeeper, Joe Duckworth; the cool, bald-headed captain and right-back, Bert Eggo; and his partner, Billy M'Connell, a tall, fair-haired Irish international, Corinthian in his type of play. He used to pick the ball off the toes of opponents at top speed and was the idol of the Reading crowd. Bill Inglis was right-half: sturdy, strong and with a bias towards defence. At centre-half was Alf Messer, later to join Tottenham Hotspur, tall, upright and not to be hurried: an imperious taker of penalty kicks. Dai Evans, a neat, fair-haired, quick-witted Welsh international, who went on to Huddersfield Town, and was succeeded as left-half by that wonderful shot on the volley, Meads. The forwards constantly changed but the best remembered of them were the wiry McDonald at outside-right; with Wally Baggett from Bolton, or Frank Eaton from Barnsley, inside to him. The centre-forward who constantly roused the crowd to irritation by missing open goals, but who always came out with a fair tally for the season, was Bill Johnston. Frank Richardson, who could play at centre-forward, was usually in those days inside-left, predatory, busy and a constant scorer. Finally, at outside-left, was Bill Robson, something of a heavyweight for a winger, but he used his bulk to force home some valuable goals. Reading winning promotion to the Second Division, and reaching the semi-final of the Cup, were proud memories for their young supporter from Basingstoke – and for many others.

With his transfer of work to Southampton, his loyalties were switched, though he still looks secondly for Reading's result in the newspapers. It remains a vivid memory from boyhood days that once, at a bank-holiday match at Elm Park – the Reading ground – a drunk ran onto the pitch at half-time and the crowd booed him off. That was not in those days the amusing action it seems to be today.

Football writing became increasingly attractive both for itself and for its financial return. A whole flood of schoolboy ambitions poured in upon him when he went to do a match at Reading and he made a point of meeting Maurice Edelston. That was to prove a key friendship in his life. Maurice was a mine of information on the game and a pleasure to watch in action. The pair often dined together – though Maurice was always concerned to keep his fitness – and, hence, his speed – at high condition. In fact, that friendship and another, with Wilfred Wooller of Glamorgan, led to J.A. proposing, and Sampson, Low & Marston accepting, a book on the three games called *Wickets, Tries and Goals* in which Wilfred Wooller wrote the rugby section, Maurice Edelston that on soccer and J.A. the cricket. It was not a success. A sports book needs to be either a major reference to many games or simply, and probably best of all, devoted to one. Neither Wilfred nor Maurice had ever appeared in book form before which was, in fact, a considerable advantage because they both had much that they wanted to say and which they now wrote in concentrated form.

Maurice Edelston worshipped Matt Busby, the Manchester United player and then manager, who had played with him at Reading when they were both posted to the Forces at Camberley, but he also had experience with Stanley Cullis, Stanley Matthews, Tommy Lawton and Peter Doherty. He had played with many of them in England wartime internationals. He settled with Reading because his father went there as manager. A schoolmaster by profession, he had until then been an amateur, but he now became a professional, and if ever a manager had a player who would not ask for a transfer it was Joe Edelston in Maurice. During the winter when the book was published – in 5000 copies on 8 December 1949 – the three had a party in London which, by the wartime economy standards which still persisted, was a luxury. The little restaurant in which it was held did not last for long but, for that time, it had amazing resources and, egging one another on, the three indulged in luxuries they had never eaten before, and certainly could not afford. They did, though, and it was worth it. So, too, was the talk over some four or five hours, with the head waiter from time to time joining in. Fortunately, they had had the forethought to book themselves hotel beds for the night. Those friendships lasted strongly and happily until Maurice's untimely death in 1956.

He had contemplated the cricket season of 1950 with a certain amount of doubt, which was to be replaced by deep impressions. First, though, came a little hint of history. Frank Owen was editor of the *Daily Mail* and, talking with him, J.A. quite casually – almost as a joke – put up the idea of seeing Harold Larwood off to Australia. They both agreed that probably so many journalists would deal with the occasion that it would prove worth only a few lines. Nevertheless, the evening was convivial, and it was agreed that J.A. should cover Larwood's departure next day for the *Mail*. He duly turned up at the *Orontes* in Tilbury Docks and, after a few enquiries, found Harold Larwood on the boat deck with his wife and five daughters, all sitting quietly without a single journalist in sight. It soon emerged that, journalists quite apart, J.A. was the only *person* at all there to see him off. The great bowler turned in his memory to the day, seventeen and a half years earlier, in September 1932, when he had sailed in the same ship with Douglas Jardine's side to Australia. Now the situation was very different. He had sold his little general store in Blackpool and was setting off to settle in Australia – perhaps the situation was best indicated by the fact that he was going to settle with the Australians. That he should be going there at all was ironic. It was doubly so in that he should be going at the suggestion and invitation of Jack Fingleton, on whom he had inflicted the second of a pair of spectacles in the

Third Test of 1932–33. 'Lol' had had no lunch and refused beer, which he had always said sustained his bowling. He consented, though, to come down to the tourist-class saloon where he took a cup of tea. It was inescapable that he was going with courage rather than enthusiasm. Wearing horn-rimmed spectacles, thin on top, pale and modest-looking, in what was obviously a ready-made sports coat, he looked far from the terrifying fast bowler of legend: rather a tragic, but brave, figure. For one who as a boy had watched him and been excited by his great speed, he seemed a different man; fragile in a way, yet admirable in his firmness as he set off with those six women into a new life. Encountered four years later in Sydney, he still looked frail but the old strength and power showed through; he had not surrendered.

Prior to the 1950 season, the picture of West Indian cricket to the English mind was a strange one. Since Tests between the two countries had begun in 1928 they had never lost a series at home and never won one in England, where, indeed, they had never so much as won a single Test. Indeed, to English cricket-watchers, they had appeared somewhat naïve; sometimes spectacular, but never commanding. George Headley and Learie Constantine had seemed to stand almost alone. Quite noticeably, if not pointedly so, they had once again been granted only four Tests.

In the first post-war series, against Gubby Allen's side in 1947–48, they had won the four-match series by two matches to nil and had created something of a legend with the 'three Ws': Weekes, Worrell and Walcott had become a cricket reporter's cliché. Surely enough, those three justified their considerable batting reputations; in addition, though, as few could have expected, Bob Christiani, Gerry Gomez, Roy Marshall, Allan Rae and Jeff Stollmeyer all scored a thousand runs and averaged more than 36; it was a ponderous batting performance. Yet that was only half the picture and not, by any means, the more surprising half. It had been expected that their main attacking strength would lie in the fast bowlers, Lance Pierre, Prior Jones and Hines Johnson. In the event they took only 91 wickets in first-class games, while the two unknown spinners, 'Sonny' Ramadhin and Alf Valentine – four matches between them prior to the tour – together took 258.

There was little at the absolute outset to suggest such a course of events. Worcester yielded a drab draw in which only eight wickets fell, and those cheaply; while Yorkshire were beaten by three wickets on a spinners' pitch. Then, suddenly, came the deluge. Against Surrey the tourists made 537 for 5 declared (Rae 96, Weekes 232, Walcott 128), but in cold weather they dropped enough catches to make only a draw of it. Cambridge was the first eye-opener. The University scored 594 for 4 declared and the tourists retaliated with 730 for 3 – Christiani (111), Worrell (160), Weekes (304 not out), and Stollmeyer a mere 83. Then, as if to prove something or other, MCC beat them at Lord's, by 118 runs, thanks to Jim Sims's eleven wickets in the match. The Cardiff match packed in another huge crowd to watch the batting of Worrell and Weekes and one of the few good performances by their fast bowler, Hines Johnson. Significantly, though, Ramadhin and Valentine took five wickets apiece.

They were an odd pair, who had to be coached on the boat trip in in signing their autographs. On arrival in London they spent hours on the underground completely unable to decide where they were and when they ought to get off. Ramadhin was christened Sonny when, in the autograph-signing practice, he was asked his christian name, looked baffled, and was asked what his mother called him. 'Sonny,' he said: and Sonny it has been ever since. A tiny man – no more than 5 feet 4 inches tall – he is a Trinidadian of Indian extraction, who had the rare gift of being able to bowl off-breaks and leg-breaks with virtually no change of action. He spun it, so far as could be ascertained, according to which way he wanted to turn it, off the inside of either his index or his second finger: he did so in a dark whirl which baffled batsmen. It was possible to identify his spin from the side (Jim Sims could do it) by the arc of flight, but not from the finger action. When he was said to have been 'rumbled' by May and Cowdrey in 1957, the explanation was that, on the advice of Bill Bowes, they played every ball as a leg-break. Ramadhin soon grew out of his innocence and became a highly professional spin bowler.

Alf Valentine, a Jamaican of extreme good nature, simply bowled the leftarmer's break-away. In fact, he bowled nothing else, and he applied such spin that throughout most of 1950 his index finger was bleeding as he bowled. During the Lord's Test of that series, J.A. asked him, 'Alf, do you ever *not* spin the ball, so that it goes with the arm, in to the righthander?'

'No,' said Alf, with his usual broad grin. The next day, though, he bowled one to Len Hutton, who was so accustomed to the mechanical turn that he left it alone and was clean bowled. That was not observed to happen again.

It was Valentine who made an amazing start to the First Test by taking the first eight wickets, quite unparalleled by any bowler on his first Test appearance. England were saved by a record sixth-wicket stand for matches between the two countries – 161 – by Evans and Bailey. Then Hollies and Bob Berry bowled out West Indies for 215, which gave England a first-innings lead of 97. The ball continued to turn. Valentine took three wickets, Ramadhin, Gomez and Worrell two apiece, but England's 288 was enough to give them a win by 202 runs – Hollies and Berry did the damage again.

The Lord's Test was historic, not only in event but in its completely novel atmosphere. John Goddard won the toss for West Indies; they batted. Allan Rae (in the first innings) and Clyde Walcott (in the second) scored centuries, and Weekes, Worrell and Gomez batted usefully. Washbrook made 114, and Parkhouse, too, batted well for England, but it was the two West Indian spinners who decided the issue. Valentine bowled 116 overs to take 7 for 137, and Ramadhin 115 to take 11 for 152. Lord's – indeed, English cricket – had never seen anything quite like it before. Suddenly it was a bi-partisan crowd – in itself remarkable – and the atmosphere was such as had never been known there before. Everyone within the ground and, it was said, many people listening in, were absorbed by the emotion. It was the West Indies' first Test match win in England and it was impossible not to be carried along by the emotions of their players and supporters. Among other manifestations, the match threw up, most fittingly, that unforgettable calypso, 'With those two little pals of mine, Ramadhin and Valentine'

The Third – Trent Bridge – Test was, by comparison, almost a sober-sided cricket occasion. Before a mainly English crowd, it brought West Indies another big win: England's brave attempt could not dig them out of a losing situation. Frank Worrell made 261, Everton Weekes 129, and despite some brave bowling by Bedser, Ramadhin and Valentine once again had the decisive word, with twelve wickets between them. In the second innings Valentine bowled 92 overs. A whole series of records for Tests between the two sides were created: the 558 scored by West Indies was the highest total by either side in England; Worrell's 261 was the highest Test score ever made at Trent Bridge; the fourth-wicket stand between Worrell and Weekes – 283 – was the highest for any wicket on either side in the series with England: it was also the highest stand for West Indies anywhere.

At the Oval, West Indies won the Fourth and last Test by an innings and 56 runs. Len Hutton carried his bat through the England first innings for 202 not out, but the West Indian 503 was too much – it included centuries by Allan Rae and Frank Worrell and conclusively, of course, fourteen wickets by Ramadhin and Valentine.

The bank-holiday match between the tourists and Glamorgan at Swansea was once more a national occasion. The crowd of 32,000 was a Welsh record, and so were the takings of £4660 for the first two days. Neither were the county shamed: West Indies batted first, but some useful bowling – Emrys Davies much relished his slow left-arm 4 for 18 – put the tourists out for 211. Then came some special entertainment for the crowd. In a stand of 132 with Gilbert Parkhouse, Willie Jones (105) hit a towering six on to the rugby stand, and Glamorgan's 322 saw them 111 in front. Finally, to leave the game an honourable and entertaining draw, Everton Weekes scored 147 in a couple of hours.

It was a vastly enjoyed tour: not least for West Indians living in England, with the crowds delighted by much spectacular batting and fascinated by the bowling of Ramadhin and Valentine, who appeared quite tireless: in the four Tests the pair bowled, between them, 800 overs. England, in face of such penetrative power, threw up little more than a series of game gestures – by Hutton, Washbrook, Bailey, Evans and Parkhouse as batsmen; Berry,

Hollies, Bedser and Jenkins as bowlers. Denis Compton played in only one Test and Tom Dollery, after such a fine season as a batsman and captain for Warwickshire, was dropped following two indifferent Test innings.

It was Len Hutton's benefit year and Yorkshire people served him well, by the standards of that time, with £9713. Leonard is a shy and likable man, one who overcame the injury to his left arm not only bravely but also with considerable skill and adaptation. From seeing him come exhausted into the pavilion after that innings of 364 against Australia at the Oval in 1938, through to the present day, he has never looked less than his own man. His honesty is not to be doubted and his humour is greater than some people think; not merely dry but often penetratingly witty. He served the game of cricket well, not least as a perceptive, and often subtle, captain.

By this time there was a steady flow of demands for help – usually an appreciative essay for a player's benefit booklet – or some subscription-raising venture for a club. J.A. made it a firm rule never to refuse such a request; the result is a file of such pieces large enough to make a book – though it is doubtful if many would want to read it.

Harry Craig remained a good friend, though not a regular scriptwriter for the 'Book of Verse' programme, if only because he had so many interests that it was never certain that he would be in London, nor even in England. He was perpetually footloose, even fancy-free – for he had many fancies, and he followed them up with charm, persistence and humour. He also contrived always to be down to his last few pounds, but never quite broke, and always generous. The time lay well ahead when he was first to make substantial sums of money from his films on the Crimean War. Occasionally he would create, if not havoc, at least much bafflement, especially among the young women in the BBC, by having his twin brother to stay. They were so nearly identical as to make it difficult to distinguish between them, and, to add to the confusion, they rarely appeared together. In general the difference was that Harry looked scruffy and his brother – who was in the Palestine Police – extremely spruce. The brother, though, had no civilian clothes and as he, obviously, refused to venture out in uniform, he used frequently to appear in Harry's only presentable suit. Since the twins were as close as two men could be, they would happily share young women who were often baffled by the resemblance – or something. The two were delightful company, though sufficient unto themselves. The sons of a Church of Ireland parson, their accents alone were sufficient to charm anyone. Add to that the fact that they had genuine humour and respect for their fellow men and you have the picture of two quite delightful human beings.

'Book of Verse' remained for some six years a source of interest, delight and learning. During the summer of 1950, however, there was a change. Jim Pennethorne-Hughes was offered well in advance – and accepted – the post of Head of BBC Staff Training. He suggested that J.A. should become his General Instructor, which he agreed to do late in the year. It was, in many ways, an agonizing choice. 'Book of Verse' had been a delight but Jim's friendship – his illuminatingly witty company, and general generosity – made him hard to part with. There was no real clash; perhaps there was a certain amount of self-seeking in his reluctance to lose a 'boss' so tolerant and so friendly; but the real basis of the decision to take the job lay in a friendship based on respect and admiration.

Jim suddenly, and to the surprise of his friends, parted company with his delightful girlfriend-secretary of many years and married an extremely wealthy young woman from Cairo. She eventually turned out, like so many young women, to be both charmed and baffled by him, but she made a good hostess and J.A. could rely on their flat for a glass of wine and conversation whenever he wanted it.

The new appointment as General Instructor was wide-ranging and quite profound in its effect. By taking the chair at expert lectures, J.A. learnt much about broadcasting that he had not known. In the course of his own lectures and demonstrations he discovered much about broadcasting that he had always previously found instinctive. That meant that he had to examine and define much that he had always done off the cuff.

In addition, he was free to undertake other work – in general, writing, though of course only out of office hours; fortunately, they proved extremely flexible. The most important of these odd jobs consisted of a column for *The Evening News* whose editor, John Marshall, became, though completely different in almost every way, as good and generous a friend as Jim Pennethorne-Hughes. He was easy to work for, receptive to ideas and happy to encourage his new columnist's enthusiasms.

He also proved something of a boon companion out of office hours and was, without great difficulty, persuaded to an interest in wine. There occurred another of the strange coincidences of J.A.'s career. John Marshall's wife, the charming 'Dave', eventually presented him with a child, to their joint and almost dizzy delight. At this juncture, the proud father turned up with a query. He wanted a wine for the reception that would appear to the guests to be champagne but cost much less; did J.A. know one such? By quite freakish coincidence, he had within the previous week met, drunk and talked with a wine merchant who had samples of, and was about to import, a sparkling Languedoc which was bottled like champagne and, though obviously not so good, fizzed, sparkled and was drinkable. It was also at the time in effect quite new to the London market and likely to be completely unknown to any of the guests at the christening celebration. The only question was whether an adequate quantity could be obtained, for John Marshall's idea of an adequate quantity of wine was by no means niggardly.

As it proved, just enough was available to go round the guests generously and at an unusually low price. It was drunk fairly ravenously and at the end when one of John Marshall's most influential directors was leaving, he said to his host, 'That was an interesting champagne, Marshall, you must give me the address of your wine merchant.' Fortunately for both the founders – or finders – of the feast, he never repeated the request. John Marshall, though, was utterly happy; so happy, indeed, that a few days later he turned to J.A. and said, 'Why don't you write about wine for the paper?' It was not, of course, a very extensive briefing, consisting mainly of a survey of wines suitable for Christmas drinking on a fairly economical basis. Of course the invitation was accepted.

As a result – another of these fantastic coincidences – he was noted down in some trade reference book as a newspaper wine correspondent. In that capacity he was invited to make a press tour – a month long – of the Bordeaux vineyards. He accepted, and dived home to beg that he might spend his holiday on the trip. The patient wife, also interested in wine, agreed, and arrangements were made.

In the meantime, J.A. was one day drinking with Laurence Gilliam – Head of BBC Features – and mentioned quite casually the Bordeaux project. Gilliam at once showed interest – what were the dates of the trip? Now, BBC Features was arranging its own Bordeaux visit, taking André Simon for expertise, Wynford Vaughan-Thomas as an on-the-spot broadcaster, and Laurence Gilliam himself to see that all went as he wished. This proved to begin exactly one month after the press visit. Would J.A. go as well? Alas, he could not get the time off. Of course he could, Gilliam pointed out, the BBC would give it to him for it was, after all, a BBC matter. So that was all arranged.

Chapter 12

BORDEAUX

In fact, this chapter is entitled to three headings – Bordeaux, claret and Daniel Querre. Yet another bout of amazingly coincidental good luck – in which Jim Pennethorne-Hughes played an influential part – made it possible to fill in the gap betwen the press tour of Bordeaux and the BBC trip, with a month spent at Château Monbousquet. It all fell out in this fashion: J.A. spent several days early in the press visit with Daniel Querre, the owner of Monbousquet. When he learnt that his visitor would be returning a month later, Daniel suggested, quite spontaneously, that J.A. should spend the intervening period as his guest. A telephone call to the Staff Training School and Jim Pennethorne-Hughes's instant reaction was 'Accept.' Some fairly elaborate financial and travel arrangements made it all practicable.

As a result, he embarked on a remarkable learning course. First, the press visit gave the relatively ignorant young man a grounding in the wines of Bordeaux. Then, a month with a highly knowledgeable mentor increased it. Finally, a third month with as outstanding a scholar of wine as André Simon multiplied the original smattering to a state which, the student at least, felt to be familiarity with the subject.

Daniel Querre was responsible for the post-war propaganda on behalf of Bordeaux wines – it was an urgent, if not desperate, situation, for the Germans had not been kindly disposed towards the French wine trade. Daniel was a stocky, ruddy-faced, quick-thinking, bustling enthusiast. Probably the best impressionist view of him comes in a story which J.A. had, eventually, the nerve to repeat to his face. It ran thus: Daniel went up to Paris to meet some influential American buyers; they entertained him in their hotel.

'Mister Querre, we understand you know all about Bordeaux wines.' Daniel, whose English was not very good, made a deprecating gesture.

'We want to see if you can identify these wines.' He nodded deferentially. A waiter appeared with a magnum, its label most painstakingly covered with a napkin, and ceremonially poured a glass of red wine from it. Daniel held it away at eye level; surveyed it; sniffed it: 'Ah, of my region.'

He tasted it, rolled it round his mouth; swallowed slowly and then, 'Latour – Château Latour 1926.' The Americans did not seem unduly impressed.

The waiter approached with another magnum, again its label carefully covered, and poured a second glass. Once more Daniel surveyed it – this time most thoughtfully – sniffed it and, 'Ah, not of my region.' He sniffed it again, 'Burgundy.' He sniffed again, tasted; tasted a second time and then, 'Chambertin . . . Chambertin Clos de Bèze, Chambertin Clos de Bèze 1929.'

There was a little applause from the inquisitors and the waiter approached with yet a third bottle. This time the process was very certain – he looked, sniffed, tasted and, 'Cheval-Blanc – Cheval-Blanc 1924.' Cursory applause. The fourth bottle was produced, and the Americans reacted with some interest. This time the identification process was lengthier but, finally, 'From the neighbouring district – Château Pétrus – Pétrus 1929.' This time the applause was unstinting; there was a celebratory dinner and Daniel departed with a most substantial order for clarets – and, for that matter, Sauternes as well.

'Was the story true?' J.A. asked. A modest nod. 'Then that was a remarkable performance.'

'Of course, I do not know all red wines; but I knew the only four that hotel kept in magnum.'

True? Certainly believed by wine men all through Bordeaux.

There could have been no finer, nor more enthusiastic, mentor for any man anxious to learn about wine. Daniel Querre was the eldest son of the châtelain of the Pomerol vineyard of Château Mazeyres. He grew up there and stayed on, even after his marriage, absorbing wine and knowledge of it through the pores until eventually he achieved his own ambition and was able to take over Château Monbousquet at St-Sulpice-de-Faleyrens. A series of absentee landlords had allowed it to run down and Daniel devoted his life to reviving it. In the meantime, while he was waiting for the vines to mature, he marketed his 'clairet' which was a commercial success in Paris, and kept him solvent. The business of producing and selling his own wine was a demanding task but not enough to satisfy his burning enthusiasm and use up his boundless energy. He became a key figure of the Bordeaux wine trade; the offices of the Conseil Interprofessionel de Vin de Bordeaux on the corner of the Allée de Tourny, facing the theatre across its imposing square, became almost like a second home to him and he was constantly busy about its affairs. Local parking regulations were waived for him. His next favourite rendezvous was the Plaisance with its tables, situated, oddly enough, on the roof of the ancient mono-lithic chapel in Saint Emilion. That was the hub of his social activities. Third came his merchandizing operation in the old port of Libourne. There his business – arrival, entry and departure – was most rapid of all. Nowadays his son Alain runs an office on the same premises.

Racing between these three ports of call – sometimes spon-taneously many others – in his very French motorcar which he drove as much on the horn as on the accelerator and the brakes, was an educational tour. If the subject of study was basically the Bordeaux wine trade it became also, force-put, one in the French language.

Most of all, Monbousquet itself was a lesson in French living – eating, drinking, the whole social pattern of a household which had no telephone, but where Daniel could drive up at the end of his day's work and tell his wife there would be four unanticipated guests for dinner without causing the least disturbance. The quite imperturbable, kindly Madame Querre ran the house with an easy but remarkable efficiency; training local girls, often as many as four at once, in the domestic skills of a French château. Of course it was not for J.A. a mattter of ordinary learning, it was a luxury education in French living – generous, wise, wide and utterly civilized. Often he found himself in a state of bewilderment. Life simply was so dif-ferent. That was never more apparent than during the vintage when his main duty was to remain out of sight and out of mind while, nevertheless, absorbing all he might. He was never allowed to feel in the way but he was conscious of weighty business being done: he kept his mouth shut – except for eating and drinking – his eyes and his ears open, and ended a wiser man.

It was all a completely different life: and the first impact was through food. Going out to the vintage he had expected something like British hop-pickers' food, only to find that most of the châteaux – even the smallest – prided themselves immensely on the way they fed those workmen. The *vendangeurs* had of necessity to be housed in quite simple accommodation but the food they were given was magnificent. The famous *soupe des vendangeurs* was regularly served and it was constantly followed with poultry, meat, cheese and generally the stock Bordeaux dessert of fresh fruit. There, too, he picked up *faire chabrot* – which consists of pouring wine into the last spoonful or so of soup and drinking it down. The French attitude to food indeed rendered it altogether different. Someone once said English people eat like children, French children like adults. After the soup of the *vendangeurs*, one of the strongest early impressions was that of oysters being casually regarded. Arcachon, which has oyster beds on the coast near Bordeaux is, of course, something of a freak so far as oysters are concerned. It is said that in the middle of the last century the captain of a merchant ship with a cargo of *Portugaises* (oysters) found his cargo somewhat high and dumped it overboard into the sea off Arcachon. As a result the beds there now yield both the original *gravettes* and *Portugaises*. Both are taken freely, and are certainly not regarded as luxuries in the restaurants nor even the bars of Bordeaux. That soon became an appetite indulged until it became a habit whenever he went there.

It is indeed a most handsome city, with the great theatre – so near to Daniel's CIVC office on the corner of the Cours du 30 Juillet – and a wealth of small and large historic buildings, wine museums, and restaurants, cafés and bars prolific and rich in their yield.

Madame Querre's kitchen was constantly redolent with rich and exciting smells, one of which was revealed as coming from the wood which she constantly used as fuel for grilling. It consisted of vine prunings, cuttings and even roots, with their own memorable odour. That method is called *aux sarments*. Experience taught the distinction between that and the method often encountered in wine merchants' establishments, where they used pieces of ancient wine-sodden casks for fuel – which is called *feu de bois*.

If Daniel Querre was a highly skilful teacher on wine matters, he was also a knowledgeable food enthusiast. One of his first lessons was on lampreys. These are eel-like creatures, not unlike the elvers of the Severn, which swim in the waters of the Gironde. They are not easy to come by and the close season for them is long. Happily, though, the prepared version, *lamproie à la Bordelaise*, can be bought canned. It is cooked basically in red wine, its own blood and leeks; it is delicate, not in the least fishy and somewhat compelling. There is a story, which may be fictitious, that Henry I died of a surfeit of lampreys, and another that Nero had his slaves bound and thrown into the river for the creatures to eat. However that may be, they are extremely tasty. Whichever sauce is used, *entrecôte à la Bordelaise* is an extremely handsome dish, so are the Agen geese stuffed with plums.

To travel the Bordeaux wine country with Daniel Querre was to be accepted; and the best bottles were produced for him, which extended the education. Others might perhaps have been able to obtain the same or similar facilities, provide the same or similar food and like information. There can, however, have been few such magnificent characters in Bordeaux or anywhere as Daniel Querre. It is rare indeed for a man of such enthusiasm and drive to be so uniformly good-tempered and so to retain a sense of humour – except when a level crossing or some heavy vehicle checked his headlong progress through the countryside.

The combination of the three Bordeaux trips – the relatively superficial press tour, the spell with Daniel Querre, and the tour similar to the first but far more profound with André Simon, made an ideal combination. André Simon was in many ways the effective missionary, not simply of champagne – which he sold for a living – but of all French wine and, indeed, all wine, to a whole generation of British people. He looked French and he sounded French but he spent the greater part of his life in Britain and understood it well. It might be argued that he did more for the drinking of wine in Britain than any other single person.

The trip of four such different people – André Simon, Wynford Vaughan-Thomas, Laurence Gilliam and J.A. – was convivial, enlightening and impressive. J.A., thanks to his stay at Monbousquet, was able to hold his own with his fellows from the BBC, while all three sat contentedly at the mental wine-feet of André Simon.

He arrived back in England to find his small son suddenly and impressively growing up; and most lovable. Excitingly, too, on 16 November, Timothy was born. It is true to say that at this point J.A. hardly knew whether he was on his head or his heels: there was so much freshness, stimulus, strangeness, his tiny successes, his loves and friendships.

Chapter 13

CRICKET OF MANY KINDS

Meanwhile cricket remained his main form of work – perhaps more accurate to say his main source of income – for it remained, too, extremely pleasurable. The South Africans were the touring side in 1951 and they came with high hopes but returned disappointed, having lost the rubber by three to one – though they might easily have done better. They had a young side, some of whom probably had a slight inferiority complex when facing seasoned professionals. The main interest of the tour was crammed into the Test matches. It all began dramatically enough at Trent Bridge when Dudley Nourse, who had been batting for over a fortnight with a fractured thumb, scored 208 in the first innings. It was a typical Nourse performance: he was in considerable pain throughout but ploughed determinedly on and, as a result, he was unable to bat in the second innings nor for more than a week afterwards. Centuries by Simpson and Compton helped England to a creditable reply, but the game was decided by two poor second innings and South Africa won by 71 runs. Bedser took nine wickets. McCarthy, Chubb, Athol Rowan and Mann all bowled well for South Africa. Tufty Mann, alas, died in the following year of a brain tumour. He was a most engaging man with a splendid capacity for amazement, humour, and general relish of life.

At Lord's England won by ten wickets on a pitch damaged by rain. Compton, and Willie Watson in only his second Test, both scored usefully (79 apiece), but the match was virtually won by Tattersall who took 7 for 52 and 5 for 49 with his off-breaks. Old Trafford brought another England win; this time by nine wickets. Again it was primarily a bowlers' match. Alec Bedser took 12 wickets for 112 runs in the match, exploiting his leg-cutter, which was for him then something of a new toy – and one which delighted him. For South Africa, Chubb took 6 for 51 in the first innings. Geoff Chubb, who played in spectacles, was, for all his forty-one years, a bustling enthusiast who bowled at fast-medium with unquenchable zest. He had a pretty sense of humour and it was a shame that this should be his only Test rubber. Headingley was a draw dwarfed by batsmen. Eric Rowan's 236 was the highest South African score against England: a rare competitor, he feared nothing and no man. Peter May achieved the rare feat of scoring a hundred in his first Test innings. Don Brennan, as wicketkeeper of course, Frank Lowson and, for South Africa, Percy Mansell also made their first Test appearances in a game in which 1130 runs were scored and only 20 wickets fell. It was back to the general pattern of bowling dominance at the Oval, where England recorded their first win at the ground since 1938. It will long be remembered for the first instance in a Test of a batsman being given out for obstructing the field. A ball from Athol Rowan bobbed up off Hutton's hand and, in pushing it away, it was decided that he had prevented the South African wicketkeeper, Russell Endean, from catching him. Athol Rowan took four wickets, Geoff Chubb five, but Jim Laker, in his first major Test performance, had match figures of 10 for 119.

Once more the Glamorgan match with the tourists raised immense excitement. In a low-scoring match which lasted only into the second day, Glamorgan won by 64 runs and Wilfred Wooller was chaired off the field by the crowd. Athol Rowan, batting at number nine, made top score for the South Africans – 49 not out in a total of 111. He also took eight wickets; Mansell had nine, but the game was decided by Muncer with eleven wickets and McConnon who, in the second innings, had 6 for 27.

For J.A., who had hitherto spent much of his season following the tourists, a fresh shape of cricket broadcast programming gave him more matches in the West Region. As a result he saw much of and developed a close relationship with Leo Harrison and Neville Rogers of the Hampshire side. Leo, who became his closest friend in the game, had been judged a virtual batting genius as a boy. He might well have justified all his promise but that his eyesight was neglected and deteriorated during his war service. From time to time all that ability came out and he would play a century of undoubted skill, and he became a good enough wicketkeeper to hold the place regularly for Hampshire and to be chosen for the Players against the Gentlemen at Lord's. Neville Rogers was unlucky never to play for England; he was an opening batsman of fine resistant qualities, with a notable ability to play fast bowling in a side with virtually no fast bowler of its own: every cricketer will know the significance of that judgement. The friendship between the three has never faded and not long ago it threw up a convivial evening as full of zest as any of their youth.

In this year, too, J.A. published a fairly slight but warmly felt biography of Maurice Tate, the Sussex and England fast-medium bowler. The making of that book was an immense pleasure. In his boyhood days staying with his grandmother at Eastbourne and watching Sussex matches, Tate had been a great hero. To watch him bowling on a 'green top' from behind the sightscreen, to see the ball angle off the pitch was a revelation. Now to meet the great man in his retirement to a Sussex country pub was to relish his recollections of the period which every cricket enthusiast holds greatest – that which occurred in the hero-worshipping phase of his boyhood. Maurice Tate lived life almost painfully openly; speaking his mind in any situation, unsubtle perhaps, but full of an almost boyish enjoyment. His family, too, wife and two sons, belonged most happily in the picture. To visit them and find oneself adopted into the circle was a rare privilege. To have played for Maurice's eleven against the local village and had him bowl at one in the nets remains a happy memory.

Charles Kortright was a different experience. The legendary 'fastest bowler of them all' was a pure Victorian figure. One conversation with him ran, 'What did you do, Charles?'

A pause, 'What do you mean, what did I do?'

'Apart from bowling fast, I mean.'

'Bowled leg-breaks when I couldn't bowl fast any more.'

'But what else did you do?'

Another long pause, then, 'Well, when I grew old I took to golf.' That had, in fact, been his life; a bachelor with enough money to play cricket and golf, drink in moderation and relish conversation and memories. He was, indeed, if not a profound, an uncomplicatedly happy man.

For every English cricket follower, 1952 was a year of immense excitement. The Tests were against India, and the fact that they had won the last match of the English tour there in only the previous February held out no great encouragement for the home side. Indeed, India had won that match by as wide a margin as an innings and 8 runs, scoring 457 which England, despite the efforts of Jack Robertson and Dick Spooner, could not match. So the home season that followed was one of excitement and surprise.

In the first place, England abandoned the tradition of an amateur captain and appointed Len Hutton of Yorkshire to take the side into the First Test, appropriately enough at Leeds. He was an ideal man for the post; a very complete professional, calm, thoughtful, much respected by his fellow players, both amateur and professional. It will seem amazing to younger readers that a number of spectators – not all of them of great age – were heard voicing regret and even anger at the appointment. If the point of the professional captain was to be made, there was no better time and no better man to make it.

As had happened after the First World War, England, after the Second, had experienced a famine of fast bowlers, while Australia had been so rich in that department as to rout one English side after another. England's great and trusty standby had been Alec Bedser, burly, tireless and strong – but not fast, not truly fast that is, only fast-medium. Now, upon his historic cue, and filling the rôle almost like a cartoonist's creation, came Fred Trueman, a fast bowler and conscious of it: a Yorkshireman and more than proud of it, he utterly routed an Indian side weaker than might have been expected.

Of the known Indian players of 1946, they lacked Merchant, Amarnath, Mushtaq Ali and, above all, Vinoo Mankad. Owing to some difference with officialdom, Mankad, unquestionably a world-class all-rounder, was not a member of the party. Instead, he was playing for Haslingden in Lancashire League cricket and merely appeared three times on the tour for his country. Those three matches, though, were Tests in which Mankad showed himself to be something much more than capable; the one player who looked really capable of turning a Test between the two countries. Reference to the Indian side would not be complete without mentioning their manager, the busy, bossy, often funny, Pankaj Gupta, who, when Hazare failed to match his playing ability with captaincy of comparable class, proved a considerable influence on the side.

Up to the First Test, at the beginning of June, India had played unexciting cricket and had drawn most of their matches, losing only to Surrey, and contriving to avoid defeat against a highly capable MCC side. England brought in Frederick Sewards Trueman for his first Test match and he took the wicket of 'Polly' Umrigar quite early, and India were 42 for 3. Then, though, came a most capable stand between Vijay Hazare and the twenty-year-old Vijay Manjrekar. They put on 222 before Hazare was caught by Godfrey Evans off Bedser. Then England broke through and Laker finished with 4 for 39. England made a poor start but Tom Graveney, Allan Watkins, Godfrey Evans and Roly Jenkins hoisted them from 92 for 4 to 334. All this was very interesting but gave no indication at all of what was going to happen. A lead of 41 was not very impressive and a large Saturday crowd settled itself, prepared to be entertained. In fact they were shocked into complete silence when the first four Indian wickets – three to Trueman and one to Bedser – went down without a run being scored. Pankaj Roy, D.K. Gaekwad, M.K. Mantri and the young Manjrekar were all back in the pavilion without scoring, before Hazare and D.G. Phadkar put on their face-saving 105 for the sixth wicket. There was, though, no real escape for them. Trueman this time took 4 for 27 – in only nine overs – and Roly Jenkins 4 for 50. So England needed 125 to win. May, like Hutton, was out early, but Reggie Simpson, Denis Compton and Tom Graveney tidily steered England home by seven wickets, and if ever a crowd was satisfied – much of it local satisfaction, too – it was that at Headingley in those early days of June 1952.

The whole summer was one of excitement and drama. Humbled

by their defeat in the First Test, the Indians went cap in hand to Haslingden and asked for permission to play Mankad in the Second Test. It was granted, and he produced the outstanding all-round performance of the match. He made 72 – their highest score of the first innings. In the tourists' best opening stand of the series, he and Pankaj Roy (35) put on 106, and quite early on he lofted Jenkins straight over the sightscreen for six. He was out to one of Allan Watkins's spectacular short-leg catches and, although Vijay Hazare hung on desperately for 69, the other eight batsmen could muster only 42 runs between them to take India to 235. At the end of the innings Godfrey Evans stumped Sadashiv Shinde, the leg-spinner, to become the first English wicketkeeper to dismiss a hundred batsmen, and to complete the wicketkeeper's double with his thousand runs; while in the England innings he scored 104 – 98 of them before lunch on the third day. Peter May (74) and Tom Graveney (73) also scored well, but Len Hutton played the innings of a master for 150, and England took a massive lead of 302.

Mankad then proceeded to make 184, then the highest Test score for India in England. He was simultaneously adventurous and certain; it was the innings of a class batsman. Meanwhile, his opening partner, Pankaj Roy, made nought – indeed he did just that in five of his seven Test innings of the series, which must easily be a record – perhaps the least enviable of all – for an opening batsman. Trueman took four wickets and, although they cost him 110 runs, he had now taken fifteen wickets in his first two Tests. Laker polished off India, and though Simpson was run out, Hutton and May virtually saw England clear to their win by eight wickets. Mankad ended his bowling in the match with 5 (half the English first innings) for 231 off 97 overs – altogether a most impressive return to Test cricket.

For a commentator, it was a series on which he could not go wrong. Event and variety dominated every Test. At Old Trafford in the Third, although rain interrupted the first day, Hutton made another century – 104 – and May and Evans batted brightly in a score of 347 for 9 declared, but that was only the more pedestrian part of the story. On the third day, Trueman ran amok, making the ball rear ominously off the damp wicket, to take 8 for 31. In the second innings, after an opening spell in which he completed the unfortunate Pankaj Roy's pair of spectacles, Hutton did not need to bring him back. Bedser took five wickets, Tony Lock, playing in his first Test, had 4 for 36. Thus India were put out twice in the day – as had never happened to a Test team before – for the meagre totals of 58 and 82. So England won by an innings and 207 runs, leaving the Old Trafford crowd somewhat breathless. Trueman, whose histrionics highly diverted the crowd, was now a national figure.

Almost immediately afterwards in that strangely varied season, India beat Surrey by six wickets. That was a remarkable feat since Surrey were eventually County Champions. The county batted first and were hustled out by the two brisker of the Indian bowlers – 'Buck' Divecha, who performed a hat-trick in the process, and Gulabrai Ramchand – before lunch for 71. In their second innings, Surrey reached 319 thanks largely to 143 from Peter May. Adhikari (98 not out) and Phadkar made the runs to see India home, but not before Tony Lock, only a few days after his first Test match, had been 'called' by Fred Price for throwing.

The Fourth and final Test might have been almost as remarkable but that after a spectacular opening, rain ruined it. This time Hutton (86) and David Sheppard (119) put on 143 for England's first wicket; Hutton declared at 326 for 6. Then, after Saturday was lost to rain, India were flung out for 98 (Pankaj Roy another nought). Alec Bedser took 5 for 41, Trueman 5 for 48 and heaven knows what might have happened to the bedraggled Indian side if the weather had not drawn a charitable veil over their struggles.

1952 was the first year of Surrey's great Championship-winning run of seven years. They won the title despite the fact that they constantly lacked Alec Bedser, Jim Laker, Tony Lock and Peter May – away playing for England. Probably the key to their success was the appointment of Stuart Surridge as captain. An immense enthusiast, a bold and capable close catcher and busy fast-medium right-arm bowler, he was, above all, a mighty competitor who inspired his players with something of his own fire. They were, of course, an immensely strong bowling combination, with Alec Bedser and the captain to open the bowling with the new ball – reinforced increasingly often by Peter Loader – and then the conclusive spin of Laker and Lock. The entire side was both competitive and hostile: the close fielding was of an extremely high standard. In the same year there were complaints about Lock's action, and both he and the South African Cuan McCarthy – playing for Cambridge University – were called for throwing.

When, in July, the touring side went to play at Northampton, the county's bowling was opened by an 'unknown' by the name of Tyson, F.H. His first ball whistled past a motionless opening batsman, Pankaj Roy. There was an instant intake of breath all round the ground, and instant conversation among the close fieldsmen: for Tyson was a stranger to them also. They at once dropped back some five yards but in that same over Roy held out his bat tentatively, the ball took its edge and the wicketkeeper took the catch. Over a drink after play – the first of many evenings with J.A. – he was not quite so surprised as his friend had been.

1952 was also the year when Surrey in their Championship dinner gave a quite echoing salute to Jack Hobbs and, on his seventieth birthday – 16 December – there was a special BBC programme in his honour.

Chapter 14

CORONATION YEAR

This was a year replete with event, especially for J.A. There was commentary on the Coronation procession, a broadcast which was simultaneously a challenge, memorable and, eventually, fun. Add to that an Australia series which may sound dull enough at one-nothing, but, in it, England won the Ashes after nineteen years – a record period – from a series of matches of constant switches of trend, excitement and even heroics. It saw the knighting of Sir Jack Hobbs and the foundation of the Master's Club. J.A. made a highly salutary visit to Germany and, even more important for the later years of his life, went for the first time to Alderney.

Lindsay Hassett brought to England an Australian team which seemed half naked without Don Bradman but the new captain won the toss in all five Tests, his side fielded brilliantly and provided event, not merely day by day but almost hour by hour. Surrey won the Championship for the second year in succession and, in the middle of May, actually beat Warwickshire in a single day: Alec Bedser took 8 for 18 in the first innings, 4 for 17 in the second, when Laker, who had not even got on in the first innings, had 5 for 29.

Even without Bradman, the Australians attracted vast crowds wherever they went. As a point of fact, the Fifth Test was the only match of the entire tour that they lost. To his great mirth, Bill Johnston achieved a freak figure of a tour batting average of 102. Bill, capable left-arm bowler as he was, had always seemed something of a comedy figure as a batsman, but this time he was only out once on the entire trip. Vic Cannings of Hampshire was the only man to dismiss him, which he passed as his favourite bowling joke of the season. Johnston unfortunately damaged his right knee in a practice match against East Molesey before the tour proper, which sadly reduced his bowling potential from its heights of 1948.

Keith Miller made an amazing start to the trip: in the first match, against Worcestershire, he scored 220 not out; in the second (Leicestershire), 42; then, against Yorkshire, 159 not out. After that, however, Hassett, through lack of Johnston's services, had to bowl Miller too much and, in the course of it, Keith tore muscles, so that the best of both his batting and his bowling was much missed in the Tests. In the tourists' match against Hampshire just before the First Test, Roy Marshall, the West Indian, not yet qualified, made his first appearance for the county, took four wickets – something he rarely did again – in the first Australian innings and, in Hampshire's second, scored a brilliant 71 out of 148 – with five sixes.

In the Test itself – at Trent Bridge – the first day, which was ended by bad light, was played out on a dead wicket on which Alec Bedser, labouring unstintingly, took the three Australian wickets that fell in a rain-punctuated day of 157 runs. The second day, characteristically of the series, provided complete contrasts. Hassett went on from his overnight 67 not out to 115 and Miller continued to 55. Then the rest of the batting fell apart and, in three-quarters of an hour after lunch, Australia lost six wickets for 6 runs (Bedser 4 for 2, Bailey 2 for 3). In that spell Bedser equalled Sydney Barnes's record for the most wickets taken by an English bowler in Test cricket, which then stood at 189. His complete figures for the innings were 7 for 55 which, on so sluggish a pitch, represented mighty effort. So Australia were out for 249 and England, with Don Kenyon of Worcestershire opening with Hutton, and Reggie Simpson coming in at number three, were soon in trouble against Lindwall. They ended the day 92 for 6, which seemed disastrous enough in all conscience. They 'recovered' to 144, whereupon Bedser, 7 for 44, and Tattersall, 3 for 22, bowled them back into the game. There was no play on Monday – never any chance of play – because of the rain. Indeed, Nottingham had its heaviest day's rainfall for a year. On the Tuesday, after the captains had disagreed and the umpires had thought for a long time, there was play at half past four. Kenyon was out fairly early, but Hutton and Simpson held out for the inevitable draw at 120 for 1. If a result never appeared probable, it could be remembered as Bedser's match – he took fourteen wickets for 99 runs.

So to Lord's, with England holding something of a moral advantage from Trent Bridge. They brought in Freddie Brown and Willie Watson for Simpson and May. That gave them some extra bowling strength but Brown bowled more seamers than spinners – apparently he did not enjoy bowling his leg-breaks to lefthanders – and he was, therefore, inhibited against Morris, Harvey and Davidson. Hassett with his neat – almost finicky – footwork played beautifully, though he had the luck to survive a chance to Compton at fine short-leg off Bedser. In the course of the day five catches went down – four of them at backward short-leg. It was Bedser who, as usual, did the major part of the early work and he put out Morris and Harvey, though not without cost. Hassett came to his hundred and then hobbled off with cramp and a pulled muscle. Miller struck Wardle for a mighty six on to the top tier of the Grand Stand, played back to the next ball and was bowled. Benaud was at once lbw to Wardle, who also had Hole caught. Hassett did not return: Davidson played himself in with Ring, and Australia were a fairly healthy 263 for 5 at the end of the day. It had, surely, been a good toss to win; the pitch had never been green as it so often can be at Lord's, and Australia had runs in the bank. On the second day, Davidson struck out lustily but Bedser accounted for him, Langley and a returning Hassett (104) in total figures of 5 for 105, and Australia were a useful 346 all out. Talking to Hutton afterwards, he said, 'I have played in over sixty Tests and dropped more catches today than in all those other games put together.' Those chances – at backward short-leg – brought him some ungracious treatment from the Lord's crowd. By the end of the day, though, he had played himself back into respect and changed the shape of the game. Kenyon was once more out cheaply to Lindwall, but then Hutton (83 not out) and Tom Graveney (78 not out) lifted the score to 177 for 1 by the close; only for the game to be completely upset again on the Saturday. Hutton played on calmly to 145 but Graveney was out early, and otherwise only Denis Compton (57) made any substantial contribution to the total of 372. By the end of play Morris and Miller had taken Australia to 96 for 1.

On Monday, Miller went an entertaining way to 109, Hole to 47 and Lindwall to a hectic 50, in a total of 368. Freddie Brown took 4 for 82, and the ever reliable Bedser 3 for 77. The last hour of the day saw another dramatic reversal of trend. Lindwall bowled and the ground dropped into silence: he removed Hutton and Kenyon quickly and Graveney was quite brilliantly caught at the wicket by Gil Langley off Johnston. The score stood at 12 for 3. The chill deepened when Watson was dropped at short leg off Ring, as he and Compton defended desperately down to 20 for 3 by half past six. Surely that was a losing position but, as was apparent throughout this series, no game ever went as it promised. It was not simple, though, for Englishmen to appreciate that at the time, and the huge crowd went slowly and unusually quietly away that night.

After the throngs of the earlier days, the Tuesday attendance reflected the general English pessimism. In the press box there was talk of a finish by – or even before – three in the afternoon. Compton and Watson went, heads down, with painful care for an hour and a half. Then a ball from Bill Johnston squatted and Compton was lbw to let in Trevor Bailey. Denis Compton had by now, in two innings, played his way back into something like Test match form. By this stage, though, Bailey and Watson were the last two worthwhile defensive batsmen left. Brown, Evans and Wardle could lay a lusty bat to milder bowling, but no one fancied them much against Lindwall or Miller: and there were almost five hours of the playing day left. As Bailey came in, someone pointed out that in his nine innings against Australia he averaged less than eight – with a highest score of 15.

Willie Watson – bare-headed, fair-haired and handsome – batted uprightly, Trevor Bailey with his characteristic pendulum of forward defensive. They carried on soundly after lunch and some English hopes began to rise; but they were not logical. Midway through the afternoon Hassett took the new ball and called up Lindwall and Miller, who both bowled flat out with every ounce of pace and artifice they possessed. That included the bouncer, and three times Bailey was hit on the hand on the defensive stroke. He did no more than rub the hand. For three-quarters of an hour that peak attack continued. England scored only 12 runs. They had, of course, no chance of winning; all at once, however, hope began to dawn that they might save the game.

As the mood gradually changed even maiden overs were applauded. Then, suddenly, just as the tension seemed to be falling, Hole caught Watson off Ring. Watson had batted for nearly six hours and made 109, but all at once the door was open for Australia again. Within a few minutes Bailey, too, was gone – caught by Benaud off Ring for 71, after 4¾ hours. He seemed positively angry with himself for having weakened but now there was little over half an hour left to play; Ring and Benaud were turning the ball and anything might happen. The tension mounted once more. It went down to the last over when Brown was caught by Hole off Benaud. Such was the feeling in the crowd that the possibility of Benaud taking the three outstanding wickets in the remaining four balls was talked about with a certain amount of awe. Wardle, though, saw it out to as epic a draw as might possibly be imagined.

So, with the most open of minds, it was on to Old Trafford and the Third Test. There the constantly surprising pattern of the series was continued. It was, so Southerners alleged, not surprising that, at Manchester, out of the possible 30 hours, rain reduced the actual playing time to just under 14 hours. One was constantly amazed by the patience of the crowd waiting for hour after wasted hour for play to start.

Hutton, who was given Bill Edrich to open with him in succession to Kenyon, lost the toss again. Hassett, poker-faced as ever, decided that Australia would bat. Statham was injured, Trueman was called up, and then left out. Within a few minutes England regretted that fact. Almost at once Laker, slipping on the muddy ground, pulled a muscle in his left leg. Under England's policy of the time, they had gone into the game with only three main bowlers and an all-rounder (Bailey), so now they were reduced to Bedser, who bowled Morris and Miller, while Hassett was out to a splendid break-back by Bailey. At 48 for 3, England could feel happy. Then Harvey edged Bailey to Evans: it was so easy a chance that the wicketkeeper was throwing it up when he dropped it, and England were promptly in trouble. Harvey, the good-looking little lefthander whom the English public had decided to like, and Hole put on 103 that day before the rain finished play. On Friday, Harvey and Hole spent an in-and-out day before rain ended it all again. On Saturday there was sunshine after floods but play started at midday. At 221 for 3, the faithful Bedser had Hole caught by Evans, who also made some amends by catching Harvey, but that after he had made 122. Following his dismissal the innings fell to pieces and they were all out for 318. The crowd were at last rewarded when, after Edrich and Graveney had gone at 32, Hutton and Compton batted at their handsome best. However, there was only a quarter of an hour to go, and the pair had put on 94 when Compton nicked Archer to Langley and, instantly, Hutton was lbw to a splendid ball of high pace from Lindwall.

Even a Manchester crowd did not expect play on Monday and, in fact, Hutton and Hassett called it off before eleven. Again, on the Tuesday, there was no play until after lunch, when England safely avoided any possibility of following on through some neat work by Simpson and Bailey, and a few hearty thumps by Evans. The innings was ended by one of those happy moments that befell so frequently in that series, when Arthur Morris bowled his constant tormentor, Alec Bedser. There was no possibility of a finish but Bedser (2 for 14), Wardle (4 for 7) and the hobbling Laker (2 for 11) reduced Australia to 35 for 8 by the end, leaving the spectators once again to say 'If only'. So still there had been no result in the series when the two sides went to the Fourth Test, at Headingley.

There again Hutton lost the toss: he threw the coin away: Hassett unwinkingly invited England to bat. In another of the great vignettes, Ray Lindwall allowed himself one sighter and then, with his second ball, yorked Hutton, middle stump. This was Leeds; and Hutton; and the silence was almost painful. The effect on the England team, too, could almost be felt. The batting fell entirely on the defensive, and the rest of that first day yielded no more than 142 runs and saw the loss of seven wickets. England were all out for 167 the following morning. Graveney was top scorer with 55; Watson made 24 and Evans 25 in a stolid rearguard action. Lindwall, though, once again, was master with 5 for 54, and Miller weighed in with the wickets of Edrich and Graveney. This time Bailey was not fully fit and bowled off a short run, so England leant again most heavily on Alec Bedser, who once more played an heroic part with 6 for 95. Bailey helped out with 3 for 71, but Australia led by 99 with three days left, which seemed to give them the advantage although they had to bat fourth. England, however, batted gamely while rain reduced cricket on Saturday to less than two hours, and another sad but patient crowd drifted away wondering what might have been. Compton had to give up with a hand injury but Bailey did it again, batting for 4 hours 22 minutes in which he received 215 balls and made just 17 scoring strokes from them. This followed Lord's as the classic Bailey defensive innings. Edrich had made 64 early on; Compton (61) and Laker, with a most impressive 48, also contributed to a total of 275 made as dourly as its timing – nearly ten hours – would suggest. So Australia wanted 177 to win and had five minutes less than two hours in which to make them.

Hutton began his bowling with Bedser and Lock, preferring to rest Bailey who, of course, had been on the field, batting, all day. Lock was heavily punished. Laker took a wicket, Bedser bowled tight. Crucially, however, as Australia neared their total, Hutton consulted with Bailey, who proceeded to bowl outside the leg stump to a stripped-down off-side field. Indeed, once the batsmen ran a leg-bye from a ball that landed in the middle of the pitch. Hole hit one ball from Bailey high to square leg, where Graveney held it spectacularly – and importantly – over his head. Only 12 overs were bowled in the last 45 minutes, the steadiness of Bedser and Bailey was decisive and the two sides went to the Oval for the Fifth Test – which it was decided to play to a finish – without either having achieved a win.

A Saturday start to a six-day Test to decide an Ashes series conjured up visions of crowds that frightened many people away from the Oval that day. In the event, the ground was only comfortably full when Hutton lost the toss for the fifth time in the series: there was no doubt that Hassett would take first innings for Australia.

For the first time in the series England played five bowlers in Bedser, Trueman, the two Surrey spinners, Lock and Laker, plus the invaluable Bailey. Bedser and Trueman began the bowling to Hassett and Morris, and England's catching weakness of the series persisted when Morris was dropped – at short leg, of course – in Trueman's first over.

For the fifth time in the series Morris was out in the first innings to Alec Bedser – this time lbw turning his back on a sharp inswinger. Miller was soon lbw to Bailey but Hassett and Harvey settled in convincingly. They put on 66 and seemed to have taken the initiative when, first Hassett was picked up at the wicket off Bedser, and then, in the next over, Harvey was brilliantly caught by Hutton running with his back to the wicket. There was an interruption for rain and then de Courcy was taken at the wicket. That meant 118 for 5, but Hole and Archer proceeded determinedly to play Australia part-way out of trouble. Hole went for his strokes until he gave Evans his third catch and, at once, Bedser caught and bowled Archer. That wicket was Bedser's 39th in the series and beat Maurice Tate's 38 of 1924–25 which had previously been the highest figure for a bowler in an England-Australia series. These Tests never ran uniformly and now Lindwall batted most handsomely and aggressively – to make, in fact, the highest score (62) of the innings. Davidson gave him good support and so did Langley, but at length he was last man out – Evans catching him off Trueman – to the high delight of the crowd. The Australian innings of 275 left everything open – with no apparent advantage to either side. There was time for Lindwall and Miller to bowl an over apiece before bad light ended the day. In that time Lindwall's second bouncer took the edge of Hutton's bat but fell short of the slip field because it hit – and removed – his cap on the way.

The manageable crowd of Saturday gave way to an absolute mob on Monday, when the gates were closed more than an hour before the start. Edrich batted usefully with Hutton, but was out at 37, giving way to Peter May whom the Australians had done much, all summer, to blast out of the Test running. The pair put on exactly 100 before May was caught off Bill Johnston, who bowled with considerable skill all through. Compton was manifestly uneasy, and that seemed to unsettle Hutton who scored very slowly for some time before Bill Johnston bowled him for 82 – England's top score. It was slow going when Compton and Graveney were together against Johnston and, rather more surprisingly, Hole.

They held the game almost static until Miller and Lindwall were fresh enough for Hassett to bring them back. Lindwall removed both Compton and Graveney, but Bailey once more dug in and Evans gave him good support, with a brief attack on Lindwall for good measure. When he was run out and Laker caught at the wicket off Miller, Lock leant upon defence while Bailey rolled out some attacking strokes, and by the end of the day there was, once again, very little in it with England at 235 for 7.

On Tuesday, Bailey did it again. Lock was quickly caught at short leg off Lindwall, but, first Trueman, and then Alec Bedser stood by until Bailey was bowled by Archer for 64 (made in just under four hours) at 306. England's lead of 31 was small enough but it could prove valuable, their friends felt, since they had to bat fourth.

There had been showers of rain since the game started and the pitch was slow. This was, though, the Oval, the home ground of Laker and Lock where they had already achieved much and were, of course, to achieve more. Alec Bedser had little opportunity to add to his record, for Hutton brought on those two spinners and they served him characteristically and utterly effectively. The Australians, after all, had pinned their faith largely on speed – the strike power of Lindwall and Miller who remained a classic shock-attack pair. England, with their constant round of fast-medium, followed by spin, had seemed at times rather flat. Now it was all changed. The successful spin attack was started by Laker who had Hassett lbw and, in the conclusive spell of a quarter of an hour, four wickets went down for 2 runs, and half the Australian side was out at 61. Briefly Archer succeeded by aggressive methods and he was well supported by Davidson and, to a degree, Lindwall. Eventually, though, the spinners broke through and, to the delight of England and their followers, Australia were out for 162. That, surely, meant victory – but in this series almost anything might happen. Certainly Hutton was run out going for a second run but May, until he was caught off Miller, and then Compton, bore Edrich company until the end, a few minutes before three o'clock. It was England's first Ashes win since 1932–33 – the Bodyline series – and their first at home since Chapman's side won on the same ground in 1926.

The crowd swept over the ground like a wave and stood jammed in front of the pavilion calling for the players. The formal speeches by the captains emphasised the good feeling between the two sides. Then the crowd contentedly left the Oval to hectic and often prolonged celebrations elsewhere.

It had been a grand summer for J.A., but so many activities and, indeed, financial considerations beckoned that he, for the first time, forsook his father's dictum and gave up his pensionable employment – leaving the BBC with sentimental regrets and economic fears, though, on the surface, the promise of an appreciable income.

Forces lectures took him into Germany by the night train – with its blinds drawn – through the Russian zone to Berlin. It was illuminating in many ways, but mainly depressing. Russian look-out posts were everywhere through the city, including the British sector. One old friend, now a member of the British Military Police which, by agreement, had the right to travel inside the Russian zone, took him on a long journey into it. It was there that one of the East German People's Police – *Vo-Pos*, as Berliners called them – stepped out into the road and stopped their patrolling car. The English Military Policeman looked at J.A. ironically and said, 'You – Police, Special Branch, Liberal and BBC – I don't think he will fancy you.' When they stopped, the East German policeman walked over and the English officer said to him, 'Where would you sooner be, then, here or in Nottingham?' 'In Nottingham, my oath I would,' was the answer from one who had been a prisoner of war in that county. War was over but one could feel it still, especially in the young People's Policemen of East Germany. There were a few memorable meals, for the British sector of Berlin still retained a somewhat French influence in its restaurants. To visit the city many years later was to find it much changed but still, somehow, not a happy place.

A more attractive visit, and one which was to have an immense effect on his future, was a holiday trip to the Channel Island of Alderney. It all fell out very oddly. At a party in London, Bill Tayleur asked, 'Have you ever been to Alderney?'

'No,' said J.A., 'but I don't in general like the idea of the Channel Islands.'

'Channel Islands be damned,' said Bill, 'I am not talking about the Channel Islands, I am talking about Alderney and there is nowhere else in the world quite like that.' So the family went there for a holiday and found it enchanting, so much so that J.A. made up his mind one day to settle there. In fact, he bought a house – a three-storey elderly one – in the Huret for £32, only to sell it again by post a year later for £350. It would run to many thousands now. Alderney was rest, but companionable, frequently vinous, rest. The beaches were safe for small children, which attracted a family man who also found mixed, interesting and convivial adult company there. It is now home.

For several years up to 1953, J.A. had often had lunch with Jack Hobbs, 'the Master' batsman, in the Wellington Restaurant next door to the great man's shop in Fleet Street. The Wellington was kept by a Belgian, Emil Haon, who used occasionally to supply Jack with a bottle or half bottle of champagne – which the Master would never think of buying unless he was going to share it. In 1953, on the spur of the moment, 'The Master's Club' was founded by Kenneth Adam, John Marshall, Alf Gover and J.A. With the passage of years it acquired other members who were also admirers of the Master – Frank Lee, Tom Pearce, John Bridges, Doug Insole, Greville Stevens, Harold Redding, Bev Lyon, Alec Durie, Hugh Metcalfe, Colin Cowdrey, Morley Richards (who had reported the historic 127th century at Taunton), Arthur Gilligan and Tom Wisdom. Its fixed occasion was 16 December – the Master's birthday – but, in his lifetime, it had many other lunches to coincide with visiting Test teams, or the presence in London of one of the Master's friends. The menu varied from time to time but basically – and always on his birthday – it consisted of his favourite meal: soup, roast beef and baked potatoes, apple pie and cream, cheese and celery; with a white wine as an apéritif, Burgundy with the beef and port with the cheese.

When Emil died and the Wellington was closed, the club moved around until eventually – at the invitation of Raman Subba Row, who became a member – it settled at the Oval, which offered a promise of continuity. Its guests were an impressive list of men, most of whom had played with and against the Master – Herbert Sutcliffe, George Brown, Maurice Tate, 'Plum' Warner, 'Tich' Freeman, Jack Crawford, Patsy Hendren, George Geary, Ian Peebles, Bert Strudwick, Arthur Wellard, Bob Wyatt, Bill Hitch, Frank Woolley, George Duckworth, Leslie Ames, Walter Robins, Sir Learie Constantine, Sir Norman Birkett, Arthur Mailey, Don Bradman, Frank Tyson, Jack Mercer, Tom Webster, Ted Dexter, 'Father' Marriott, Sir Jack's two sons, Jack and Len, and, of course, his old partner, Andrew Sandham, who, after Sir Jack's death, proposed the single toast – 'The Master' – every year. There were no speeches except when once Sir Jack stood up and, to everyone's amazement, went round the room naming everyone and attaching to each a memory. It was, and remained, a simple but moving and friendly, warm and easy occasion.

After the generously spread interests of Coronation year, 1954 seemed oddly lop-sided. A short holiday at the wrong – early – end of the year confirmed enthusiasm for Alderney. It was, though, a lamentably wet summer, and cold as well, certainly not cricketing weather for the touring Pakistanis though in this, their first Test tour of England, they won the last of the four-Test series to draw the rubber with England. J.A.'s mind, though, was very firmly fixed on the coming tour of Australia.

The Pakistanis made many friends, and two at least of their players – Hanif Mohammad and Fazal Mahmood – were of world class. In the First Test, which could not begin until late on the fourth day, they were fired out by Statham and Wardle for 87; and England did little better with 117 against the bowling of Fazal and Khan Mohammad, the latter borrowed from the Lancashire League. Hanif, Waqar Hassan and Maqsood Ahmed made them safe from defeat. At Trent Bridge, though, they came in for a most terrifying mauling. In the first innings of the match they were bowled out for 157, largely by Bob Appleyard, who took a wicket with his second ball in Test cricket and 5 for 51 in the innings. Then they ran into some immense England batting. Reggie Simpson made 101 and

Graveney an utterly brilliant 84, but the decisive innings of the match was 278 made in less than five hours by Denis Compton, in a total of 558 for 6 declared. An abiding memory of that game is that of the forlorn figure of the sixteen-year-old Khalid Hassan, the youngest player ever to take part in a Test match. He had been battered for 116 runs off 21 overs – though he did take two wickets – and after Compton's onslaught he wandered looking almost stunned in the outfield. Bedser, Statham, Appleyard and Wardle shared the wickets in the second Pakistan innings of 272, which left England the winners by an innings and 129. It threatened to be a short match at Old Trafford, too, but rain allowed play on only two days in which England made 359 and Bedser, Wardle and McConnon (3 for 19 in his first Test) bowled them out for 90; they were 25 for 4 in their second innings when the match ended.

So on to the Oval, where England brought in Peter Loader and Frank Tyson for their first Test matches. That was largely as a trial for the forthcoming tour of Australia and they and Statham put out Pakistan for 133. Then, though, Fazal Mahmood, a police inspector at home, and a man of mighty stamina who bowled a shouldery fast-medium, took 6 for 53 and 6 for 46. Despite the efforts of Compton and May, each of whom made 53, the touring side won by 24 runs. Historically they became the first country to win a Test match in their first rubber in England. The tiny Hanif, still not quite twenty, and of a family of cricketers, opened the innings and batted imperturbably in match after match.

In the county matches Surrey, with an immense late effort by Laker and Lock, won a third Championship. Four of their bowlers – Bedser, Laker, Loader and Lock – each took a hundred wickets.

Before J.A. went to Australia he made an absorbingly interesting tour of English cheese regions. There was a growing recognition of the merits of English cheeses and he found it not merely illuminating but most attractive to write about. He undertook the work for the English Country Cheese Council, who were generous in their travel and hotel allowances. They also provided for a secretary and he took with him Valerie France, who had worked for him in the Staff Training Department and moved with him into his funny little office off Charing Cross Road.

For some two years before this, he had become increasingly involved in politics – Liberal politics – and had entered into an agreement with the Epping Liberal Association. His mother approved heartily. For his own part, he enjoyed political meetings and found the people he met in that association extremely pleasing and of a like mind to his own. It was agreed with the committee and, probably, most importantly, with that good man Norman Hoddell, the local party agent, that J.A. would stand as their candidate at the coming election. Of course, no one at this time had any idea when the election would be and he set off to join the MCC party in Australia with politics by no means his overriding consideration.

Chapter 15

TO AUSTRALIA

It was an exciting and, of course, for him, a completely novel, trip to Australia. Giving Services lectures in Singapore and Hong Kong on the way meant quite fresh views and experiences. Singapore was deadly hot but yielded one old school friend – 'Bunny' Lunn – who apparently counted double time (he was in the Services) for his willingness to work in the heat. His guidance provided a geography lesson not to be forgotten; it is most spectacular.

Hong Kong was more comfortable. Bev Lyon had made arrangements through his firm – Rediffusion – for J.A. to be shown round the city. Although, of course, it was only a minor aspect, one evening which remained long in the memory was that of a Chinese meal of many courses and as many subtleties. On the other hand, almost every step on every day revealed something fresh and unexpected in that strangely cosmopolitan city.

Eventually he reached Australia, with the sharp, bright impact – briefly – of Sydney and then up to Queensland and cricket. Len Hutton, as captain, knew that there was still some criticism of, and opposition to, his appointment in England and, in any case, he always played his cards close to his chest. Nevertheless, he was infallibly courteous and, when he felt like it, informative. George Duckworth, the baggageman, and one of the wisest, as well as the most humorous of cricketers, was also a great help.

The tour was already fairly well advanced and the side was still unbeaten when J.A. caught up in the latter half of November for the match with Queensland at Brisbane – in fact, Woolloongabba – locally, 'the Gabba'. Hutton did not play in the state match when the tourists met Lindwall for the first time on the trip. Cowdrey, Bailey and May were out quickly, then Simpson and Compton weighed in with hundreds, but only two others even made double figures. The batting was constantly to prove as erratic as that and they were all out for 304. Queensland made 288. Some good second-innings batting by Bailey, May and Compton made comfortably sure of a draw as a preview to the First Test on the same ground.

Not everyone took the heat well and before the match Evans went sick with sunstroke. Many of the first-morning pitches of the tour had been greenish and helpful to the seam and it is virtually certain that Len Hutton had made up his mind in advance to put Australia in if he won the toss. No England captain had ever done such a thing before in that country and the consequences were dire. On the first morning Denis Compton, running round the outfield, collided with the wooden fencing and broke a bone in his left hand. In the tiring weather four England bowlers conceded over a hundred runs each. In their defence, though, it must be said that some dozen catches were dropped. Australia, captained by Ian Johnson for the first time, made a towering 601 for 8 (Morris 153, Harvey 162). When England went in, a start of 25 for 4 with Compton missing – he would bat only 'in emergency' – was more than any England side could withstand. Cowdrey and Bailey made gestures in the first innings and, after England followed on, Edrich and May in the second, but Australia won – as indeed they had been doing since the first morning – and the margin was an innings and 154 runs. Alec Bedser suffered to the extent of one wicket for 131 runs and a fair proportion of those dropped catches. He had sustained the England bowling ever since the war and at last his labours took their toll and he only played in one more Test match (that, incidentally, against South Africa at Old Trafford in 1955). Coming upon Len Hutton standing alone in the bar with a half pint of beer in his hand after the match, J.A. could only put a sympathetic arm round his shoulders and utter words of commiseration. Hutton gave the wryest of smiles, but refused a second half.

At various points during the First Test, Frank Tyson had reduced his normally extremely long run in the effort to achieve accuracy in face of the punishment all the Englishmen were suffering. Before the next Test he and Hutton were constantly in consultation. As a result of their deliberations, Tyson appeared against Victoria nine days later bowling off a short run, and was immensely effective with 6 for 68 in the first innings of a drawn match ruined by rain.

So it was Sydney and the Second Test when, quite amazingly after Hutton's desperate experience at Brisbane, Arthur Morris, acting as captain in place of Johnson, won the toss and put England in to bat.

On the selection side, with Johnson and Keith Miller unfit, Australia brought in Alan Davidson and that dour batsman and humorous character, Jim Burke. In addition to Miller, another major character was missing from the match in Denis Compton, who still had not recovered from his hand injury, while Simpson was dropped and Wardle, Appleyard and Graveney came in. Virtually historically, England left out Alec Bedser, though Evans came back. England made a hard-grinding start, especially against Lindwall bowling with the famous Hill green behind his right shoulder. Surely enough, he yorked Bailey for 0, May was caught off Archer for 5, and England were grimly 19 for 2. Hutton, Graveney and Cowdrey all grafted, but were never really 'in', and 58 for 2 became 111 for 9 before Wardle, hacking and carving rustically, and Statham hoisted England to 154 – meagre enough in all conscience and deadly slow. Lindwall's 2 for 47 was better than it looks on paper; he bowled highly skilfully on a not particularly helpful pitch. There was time that night for England to enjoy one piece of cheer when, from the last ball of the day, Hutton at leg slip caught Morris off Bailey – 18 for 1.

Through the morning of the second day England bowled indifferently and Burke, Favell and, finally, Harvey batted happily enough to 88 for 2. Bailey was accurate and thoughtful but not fast enough; Tyson was fast but not accurate enough. After lunch, though, all was changed. It was not spectacular, but it was workmanlike and Tyson was truly fast. He and Bailey came by four wickets apiece and suddenly England were their own men again.

It did not seem like that next day when, in yet another of England's tragic starts, Johnston and Archer reduced them to 55 for 3 with Hutton, Bailey and Graveney gone. English spirits, though, were revived by the two young men of the side – Peter May (104) and Colin Cowdrey (54) – with a stand of 116. Bill Edrich made 29, but May had to wait overnight on 98 and things went slowly. Lindwall began the morning with the new ball fresh and full of fire. May reached his hundred before a break-back beat him, but Tyson batted well, defensively, until he turned his back on a bouncer from Lindwall, was hit on the head and taken off the field. When he returned, Lindwall bowled him. England were extremely grateful for 46 for the last wicket from Appleyard and Statham and, by the end, had climbed to the comparative respectability of 296 – setting Australia a possible, if not certain, 223 to win.

That evening, Tyson and Statham took a wicket apiece in Australia's 72 for 2. There was rain in the night but the covered wicket played easily next morning when Tyson yorked Burke and then Hole. Soon it became a question of Tyson against Harvey. The game could have gone either way. Tyson grabbed himself a piece of Test match history with 3 wickets for 41 runs in 7 overs – altogether 6 for 85. No one could stay with Harvey, who was left with a determined – indeed mighty – 92 not out in their second-innings total of 184. England won by 38 runs in the middle of the fifth afternoon. It was by no means completely satisfactory: the margin was narrow; the game, like so many England had played of late, fluctuated: there had been flaws in their batting and bowling as well, but at last their confidence was renewed and the team's Christmas was a riotous celebration.

Off the field – and there were many days of minor matches when J.A. was not wanted – other interests grew up. A series of letters of introduction, and the company and shared enthusiasm of Bill Bowes, led to some highly informative vineyard visits. Australian wine-making had far to go in those days – many of their products were sugary imitations of the French or of sherry and, as such, were all but undrinkable. But there was good stuff to be found and it was duly discovered, enjoyed and remembered.

One morning, J.A. was prowling round the shops when he went into a secondhand bookshop and was delighted to find Frank Tyson there. Before the end of the tour they had together visited every secondhand bookshop they could find in Australia and came back with their luggage much the heavier.

Sydney is a city that never seems to take rest. For miles along the coast and inland it is devoted to small housing, and dotted – as one appreciates when arriving by air – with a welter of white concrete wicket-strips – a breeding-ground for cricketers. It is, too, a place of great speed, with aircraft coming in and out like a bus service. 'Our bridge' and 'our harbour' really are as impressive as Australians constantly tell the rest of the world they are. Sydney is the most cosmopolitan city in Australia. Perhaps, especially, that character-istic was apparent in King's Cross which, in those days, was rather more 'respectable' than it now is, and where J.A. and Bill Bowes found a useful flat in which they cooked rather badly. It was, too, a city where the taxi drivers knew absolutely everything and insisted on communicating it to their defenceless passengers. It was brightly and crisply sunny when the party left it and went on to Melbourne where the heat stoked up heavily and stickily.

Melbourne Cricket Ground was already the largest in the world before work started for the 1956 Olympics, with the aim of a capac-ity of 120,000 people. On the playing side, Compton and Miller came back to contribute their particular charisma, while Johnson was fit to take over the Australian captaincy again: and, although Bedser was included in the England party, he was once again left out, which seemed nostalgically sad. This time Hutton – who was suffering from a cold and general malaise and only decided at the last moment to play – won the toss and batted. He went in first with Edrich who was soon out in yet another of England's disastrous starts – this time 41 for 4 with Hutton, Edrich, May and Compton gone. This was largely due to a superb spell by Keith Miller who, although in pain from an injured knee, in an hour and a half before lunch look three wickets for 5 runs. Colin Cowdrey (102), who seemed to bat better match by match, and the dogged Bailey did their best to patch things up. Those two, and Godfrey Evans, made 152 of England's 191 – not impressive but much better than it might have been.

Oddly enough, on the second day large cracks could be seen on the pitch yet, despite the great heat, they had closed up by Monday! The Melbourne Club held an official enquiry which denied that the pitch had been watered! The first day's play ended with the England innings. Next morning, their bowlers – primarily Tyson and Statham – set about trying to play England back into the game. Although constantly in this series Tyson achieved spectacular figures, everyone on both sides and those who watched with any perception realized that Statham's sustained pace and accuracy were an essential factor of the attack. Moreover, the pair, both Lancashire born, enjoyed each other's company and bowling together. They, with intelligent support from Appleyard and Bailey, had Australia 188 for 8 by the end of play. The figures indicate the slowness of the batting.

On the third day Maddocks, Johnson and Johnston put on another 43 useful runs and faced the England batting yet again with a burden. This time Hutton (42) – patiently despite his ailments – and May (91) contrived for them at last a fair start to 128 for 3, but it needed small, useful innings by Compton, Bailey, Evans and Wardle to lift them to 279. That left Australia 240 to win, which hardly looked to be an advantage when Benaud and Harvey carried the score to 75 for 2 by the end of the fourth day and Australia – according to Australians at least – were all but home. Then, though, in another spectacular burst of pace, Tyson took 6 for 16, Statham 2 for 19 and England, to everyone's amazement, including their own, were home by 128 runs.

Adelaide – 'city of churches' but with plenty of pubs and some very interesting and well-wined clubs – housed the Fourth Test where England placed so much hope. It has been described as the hottest white city in the world and – no obvious connection – it has a very large number of post-war German immigrants. England played the same side as at Melbourne. Australia left out Hole who frankly could not cope with the pace of Tyson who had clean bowled him three times in five innings, when he was sheerly unable to get his bat down in time. They had, though, no choice about missing Lindwall who had injured a leg in a state match. The heat was immense and neither side particularly wanted to bowl. Johnson was lucky in that respect: he won the toss and Australia took

first innings. Hutton nursed Tyson and Statham, and it was a
toughly contested first two days. England suffered in the heat.
Statham had had a toenail removed a day or so before the game;
the fieldsmen flagged and Evans was unusually remiss with several chances. Only two Australian batsmen – Davidson and
Johnston at numbers nine and eleven – failed to reach double figures but Maddocks's 69 was their highest score. Tyson, Bailey and
Appleyard took three wickets apiece by sheer hard labour, and
Australia totalled 323. England, by way of a change, started well
and, although Hutton, Edrich and May batted desperately slowly,
they were undoubtedly more comfortable in Lindwall's absence.
Benaud took 4 for 120 with his leg-spinners but, with Hutton
making 80, Cowdrey 79 and several others helping out, England
mustered 341 – a lead of only 18, but, as somebody remarked at the
time, better than nothing.

Early in the Australian second innings Hutton whipped off
Statham early and brought on Appleyard, who promptly, pitching
in the bowlers' footmarks, took 3 for 13 out of Australia's 69 for 3
by the end of the day. All the talk that night was of Hutton's use of
Appleyard, who, all the pundits predicted, would prove unplayable next morning. In the event, he never bowled at all that day.
Statham, his boot doctored to accommodate his battered toe, and
Tyson polished off the Australian innings in 14 overs: Statham 3
for 12, Tyson 3 for 17. It was never easy for England but May,
Compton and Bailey substantially made their 97 runs to win by
five wickets and take the rubber for the first time in Australia since
the Bodyline series. The celebrations that night were strenuous
indeed.

Those were quite special celebrations, completely different
from the pattern of 1953 when England had won at home. A member of a touring party abroad is in a very special position; one of a
small, isolated group which becomes the stronger for its smallness
and concentration. So it was with Hutton's party; the Australians
are nothing if not partisan and Australian humour can be very
heavy indeed. Every triumph is shared by all the members of a side
over there. Writing many years afterwards, one suspects that that
old sentimental, communal feeling may now be appreciably less

strong than it was, but in 1955 it was powerful indeed. The party was a substantial one, the players were eighteen strong, when Vic Wilson of Yorkshire was added as insurance against a recurrence of Compton's knee trouble. Geoffrey Howard, the manager, from Lancashire, George Duckworth and Harold Dalton, the masseur, were also deeply involved members, and the pressmen on the tour were more closely incorporated in terms of feeling than they seem to be nowadays.

Len Hutton was a thoughtful captain; quiet, indeed, but courteous, and a major influence on the side's success. He and his players lived down that terrible defeat of the First Test to come out as the better and more successful side. Hutton was not the prolific scorer he had been, but he constantly made runs far more valuable than they may look on the scoresheet, at the vulnerable start of the innings.

The Fifth Test was played at Sydney with never any real chance of a finish. The first three days were wiped out by the freak rainstorms which caused flooding, especially serious in the Hunter River Valley where it was more grave – even dramatic – than anyone could remember. In the event, play did not start until two o'clock on the fourth day, when Johnson, winning the toss, sent England in to bat, no doubt in the wild hope of achieving an innings win in the thirteen hours that were available.

Hutton was out early but Tom Graveney, whom he had taken in with him, proceeded to play probably the most handsome innings of the series. He made 111 with utter elegance, power and perfection of timing. England batted into the second actual playing day; May scored 79, Compton an eventually breezy 84, and Bailey amassed 72 before Hutton declared at 371 for 7. Due mainly to a dogged innings by Colin McDonald, Australia were 82 for 2 overnight but on the last day Wardle had a party. Bowling the Chinaman and its complementary googly as distinct from his normal orthodox slow left-arm, he puzzled – indeed frequently baffled – all the Australian batsmen. He took 5 for 79 in their first innings of 221 and when, for the first time since the war, an England captain enforced the follow-on, he took another 3 for 51. When time ran out, Australia were 118 for 6. Thanks to Wardle's bowling, it was an unusually entertaining draw and, for England, the end of a happily triumphant series.

It would be difficult to argue that these were two great teams, but there were some fine players among them, though, at that time, some were past their best and others were still developing. Such names, though, as Harvey, Archer, Miller, Burge, Benaud, Davidson, Lindwall and Johnston on the Australian side, and Compton, Hutton, Statham, Tyson, Bailey, Bedser, Cowdrey, May and Graveney on the English, have an epic ring about them. It was important, too, that of the England players, Graveney, May, Cowdrey, Appleyard and Tyson were at the outset of their careers. It was most happily a tour on which the players and what Brian Sellers used to call their 'circus' mixed freely to their mutual comfort. It was, too, an historic tour in that England won a rubber in Australia for the first time for twenty-two years.

For J.A. it was fresh, and virtually inspiring, to be one of a party which succeeded so strikingly as to compel reluctant respect even from Sydney taxi drivers. It contained, too, for him a quite unusual amount of completely spare time. Part of it he filled in by writing a book on the tour, but far more was enjoyed in prowling round Australia. Up-country he made some initially interesting trips, but most relishable were the major cities. He was to return to yet another fresh experience.

First, though, came the journey back which he contrived to make by way of Fiji, Hawaii, San Francisco, Chicago and New York. Rugby in Fiji – played bare-footed by the Fijians, the mud squeezing up between their toes; sunbathing and over-eating among the skyscrapers of Hawaii; gawping at the sights and meeting some old friends in San Francisco; being warned not to turn right outside the hotel in Chicago for fear of his life. The journey effectively ended with a most illuminating week in New York, with John Marshall as host and guide, to relieve the previous vast jumble of impressions: and then home. Wherever he went he had paid his way by writing. It was superb to be back.

Chapter 16

THE HUSTINGS

Back to England and the family and the almost childlike delight of a father in the development of his children: the two little boys had flourished and developed most happily. Now there was talk of a General Election, which meant for him an unusually indecisive phase. After much doubt and much pondering, eventually he took the decision that, whenever it came, he would fight the election for the Liberals at Epping – though he added a mental rider that he prayed it would not coincide with a Test match. When eventually a date was decided upon – 26 May 1955 – he realized that he would miss county matches, and that he would miss them indeed, but the decision had been taken, and he would not regret it.

Epping is a large and rambling constituency, including the town, a number of villages, some semi-suburbia, forest, and much farmland. One of the great chuckles of the campaign resulted from coming upon Alan Gibson, fellow commentator and friend, in a loudspeaker-van, practising a speech on three cows looking over a hedge: to his credit, though, the beasts looked interested.

The campaign involved canvassing, which he hated. In point of fact, he canvassed only two houses, at the first of which he was told, not very politely, that the family voted Labour; at the second he was met with, 'What election?' It must be confessed that he never canvassed another house. Canvassing is a depressing, worrying and uncertain business at which some people excel, but J.A. certainly did not. He did his best to make up for his deficiency in that direction by working hard in others, leaving supporters, who seemed to enjoy it, to canvass for him. He cheerfully made speeches – often three or four a night – travelled constantly about the constituency in a loudspeaker-van and was always available for questioning or consultation.

The Liberals had not contested the constituency at all in 1951 or 1954; prior to that the Liberal candidate had forfeited his deposit and that, J.A. was determined, should not happen to him. The speeches must have helped because attendances at them grew – if only from the negligible to the mildly respectable and, it must be said, rather encouraging. Lots of friends helped out and other Liberal candidates who could not really afford the time turned up to speak or take part in the 'Any Questions' sessions which proved extremely popular. On one occasion, Gilbert Harding insisted on joining in – not, he said, because he was a Liberal, but because he would always oppose Conservatives anywhere. The other two candidates were Graeme Finlay, the sitting Conservative, and Mrs – later Dame – Leah Manning. Finlay was a 38-year-old barrister, and had had a majority of over 4000 at the 1951 election. Leah Manning, who had been President of the National Union of Teachers, was the Labour candidate, with her feet most firmly on the ground. She talked cheerful sense, and when J.A. met her they got along well together. He barely saw Finlay. Leah Manning, a former school-teacher, had in fact been MP for the constituency from 1945 to 1950 and she had some loyal supporters.

It was a friendly enough election and J.A. was inordinately proud to see his mother sitting in the audience at meetings. Norman Hoddell was an absolutely tireless agent; cheerful, encouraging and happy to work all the hours of the day. Indeed he was, in many ways, more thorough than the candidate. The meetings varied from a few people on uncomfortable schoolroom forms to extremely comforting meetings in Epping itself. J.A. did not spare himself, for, increasingly, the idea of failing – which, of course, he understood not as losing the election but as forfeiting his deposit – drove him on to virtually everything or anything except canvassing.

However hard or long the day might seem, he always returned to the committee rooms or a supporter's house bearing a goodnight bottle of wine. Then the humours of the day would come out from everyone present – once indeed as many as sixteen people – in an atmosphere which produced warming and worthwhile friendships, which even today are recalled by letters and greetings cards from those who stood with him both in that campaign and the one of 1959. Had it been bitter he might well have pulled out of politics there and then, but it was – by the standards of today – almost friendly. There was no jeering, no catcalling, and while at meetings some opponents might come out with testing questions, they never made the atmosphere impossible for the speaker. Dawn, his wife, and Valerie, his secretary, and though he did not know it at the time, later to be his wife, were both helpful and comforting when he became depressed, doubtful or simply tired. The few weeks of the campaign proved quite surprisingly tiring but were made more than bearable – something approaching enjoyable – by the fellowship, wise counsel and good humour of his helpers.

When polling came on 26 May he felt like a pricked balloon. Never through all of it was it harder to show a cheerful smile. When eventually he stood up by the Returning Officer he realized that he was trembling and sweating – where was his confidence now? In fact, though, he saved his deposit relatively easily. Graeme Finlay was top of the poll with 26,065 votes, Leah Manning second with 22,542, while J.A. brought up the rear with 7528. There were tears on some unexpected faces; congratulations from some pressmen who had seemed extremely dour during the campaign. Leah Manning, obviously downcast and disappointed, turned to J.A. and said, 'And I thought you would take votes from him but, in fact, you have taken them from me.'

Then it was on to a party of unquestionable fellowship and happiness. The Liberals unanimously, so it seemed, regarded the saving of the deposit as something of a minor triumph. It had been a rare experience; there is a strange exhilaration about holding an audience, working up to a climax and then to a strong or, sometimes, extremely gentle, close. There is no doubt that a candidate in an election feels unjustifiably puffed up – few, surely, can resist that strange stimulus which comes from having and holding – even changing the feelings of – an audience of people who are, at least, interested; on the same wavelength and, for the moment at least, politically motivated.

Chapter 17

MIXED CRICKET

After Australia and the hustings, the prospect of English home cricket was restfully attractive. The early days of the 1955 season, which were lost to the General Election, were compensatorily cold and wet, so they seemed little cricketing loss. South Africa were the touring team, while, for J.A., the advance of Hampshire was a major pleasure of the summer. As well as a book of the tour of Australia, he wrote a King Penguin called *The Picture of Cricket* which showed – far beyond the ability of any author – the charm of that series, which he found himself collecting out of the sheer pleasure, as well as the pertinence, of its illustrations.

It had become the pattern of BBC county cricket broadcasting to divide it off into regions, so that he found himself invariably – unless Test matches intervened – attending the games between Sussex, Hampshire, Somerset and Gloucestershire, with occasional 'home' fixtures for Hampshire against other sides such as the tourists. However, he was fortunate in his mission to catch up with a sight of the South Africans in watching Paul Winslow mount the first of his hectic assaults on bowling at Old Trafford. The tall, personable young man struck Jack Ikin for 30 (4-4-6-6-4-6) in a single over, which he followed in the next – bowled by Goodwin – with a four and a six – 40 off eight consecutive balls received.

The First Test match was, as usual, at Trent Bridge; but, before it started, the face of the English game was historically changed when, first Len Hutton, the chosen captain, stood down suffering from lumbago; then Alec Bedser, as in Australia, was left out. They had been two major figures in post-war English cricket. In fact, although he had been nominated as captain for the series, Hutton did not play in a single Test of the season and, at its end, he announced his retirement: while Bedser, as previously mentioned, played only once more for England before his Test career, too, ended. Peter May was made captain while Colin Cowdrey was not considered since he had not yet played that season. On a sodden pitch it was an important question as to whether Tony Lock or Frank Tyson would have the last place. Perhaps surprisingly in view of the state of the wicket but, as it was to prove, happily for England, the selectors gave it to Tyson.

May made a good start to his Test captaincy by winning the toss, and sent in a most unfamiliar pair in Don Kenyon and Tom Graveney. It was a slow beginning as the two played themselves in. Then, while Kenyon, May and Bailey all made useful runs, the rest of the batting was disposed of by the five South African bowlers of whom Adcock was by far the fastest, Goddard and Fuller, steady, and Tayfield, as ever, diligent and dangerous though his figures do not look impressive. England, though, could be satisfied with their total of 334.

Hugh Tayfield was a major figure of South African cricket; an off-spinner with the somewhat extravagant characteristic of kissing his cap before handing it to the umpire at the start of each over. He had, too, the mannerism of stubbing his toes into the ground before he began his run; hence his nickname of 'Toey'. He was a bowler of monumental accuracy, patience and persistence. He took 170 wickets in his 37 Test matches.

Jackie McGlew, as usual on that tour, made a solid start to the innings but otherwise only the captain, Jack Cheetham, put up any substantial resistance to an attack in which the slow bowlers, Bob Appleyard and Johnny Wardle, cleaned up. McGlew and Cheetham between them made 122 of South Africa's 181 before May asked them to follow on. Again the dogged McGlew held on, this time for 51 in a total of 148. No one else faced Tyson with any competence or confidence and he finished with an analysis of 6 for 28. It was not a particularly exciting match except for the spectacularly fast bowling of Tyson. The crowd was small and unhappy – a poor advertisement for the Second Test.

During the Trent Bridge Test, though, J.A., at least, spent much time finding out the scores in the match in which Hampshire beat

Yorkshire by an innings and 43 runs, the first time they had won against them since 1932. Marshall made a hectic 52, while the young Peter Sainsbury took 5 for 19 and 4 for 43. That performance, in his first full season, no doubt did much to gain him his place the following winter in the MCC 'A' side to Pakistan.

The Lord's Test was an altogether more absorbing match than that at Trent Bridge. Again May had the luck to win the toss but the England batting fell back into its old habits and the first wicket went down at 7; Ken Barrington was top scorer with 34 and they were all out for 133. This was the first major sight the English public had had of Peter Heine who, from well over six feet, made the ball lift menacingly. England, without Tyson, failed to reply in kind. South Africa lost their first two wickets for 7, but then a rumbustious 142 by Roy McLean, 48 by Russell Endean, and 57 by the perpetually useful Headley Keith, took them to 304 and a lead of 171. Again an English wicket went early – Kenyon was out for 2 – but then Graveney (60), May (112), and Compton (69) revived them to 277 for 4. Once again the start was not maintained, the pertinacious Tayfield took 5 for 80; but England's second innings of 353 set South Africa a by no means impossible 183 to win. Before the end of the third day Statham had put out McGlew and Goddard while a short ball from Trueman had chipped Cheetham's elbow so that he was unable to take any further part in the game. Statham (7 for 39) carried on on the fourth day: South Africa were out for 111 and England were two up with three to play.

For the Third Test, at Old Trafford, England at length recalled Alec Bedser to replace the injured Statham; this was to prove his last Test. Tyson and Cowdrey returned, but Cheetham had not recovered from his damaged elbow, so McGlew took over as captain, and Winslow came in. The match was played throughout in glorious sunshine but on a diabolically fast first-day wicket. The ball rose snarlingly from it, and there was a high proportion of hand injuries, including one in which Godfrey Evans sustained two fractures of his right little finger. Graveney, his deputy as wicketkeeper, damaged a thumb in taking Tyson while there were at least nine other casualties of varying degrees of gravity.

May won the toss but taking first innings did not prove an

advantage to England: the pace of Heine and Adcock, the nip of Goddard and, as ever, the accuracy of Tayfield, were all difficult to handle. Kenyon and Graveney were both out by the time the score reached 22 – in fact those two batsmen scored only 7 runs between them in their two innings apiece of this match. May and Compton repaired the damage, Compton moving up from uncertainty to something like command. They put on 48 before May was out: Cowdrey soon followed him but the painstaking Bailey, as so often in this series, showed a dogged and correct defence. Once again, though, England's batting was – actually as well as metaphorically – in and out. Four men scored 255 out of a total of 284.

The pitch had eased a little by the time the South African innings began, though McGlew and Goddard were both missed before McGlew retired with a damaged right hand. Mansell, Endean and McLean were all out cheaply but, just when it seemed that England might gain some slight advantage on the first innings, John Waite (113) and Paul Winslow (108) came together in a record South African stand for the sixth wicket. In each case it was a maiden Test century, and Winslow's was most spectacular. Tall and lithe and with natural timing, he struck the ball with immense power: one mighty blow cleared the sightscreen. Then, as if the suffering of the England bowlers had not already been enough, McGlew resumed his innings and became the third man to score a hundred – in fact 104 not out – in a total of 521 for 8 declared. Another 18 runs would have given South Africa their record Test score, but, as matters turned out, that would have been damaging to their prospects.

So, England batted again, 337 behind. In another disastrous opening, they were 2 for 2 but once again May (117) and Compton (71) conducted a rescue operation and, at the end, Evans, despite his injury, thumped and hammered 36 in a last-wicket stand of 48 with Bailey. South Africa thus required 145 to win in 135 minutes. Tyson took a useful 3 for 55 but Bedser could not quite hold back the opposition in his old fashion, and McGlew (48) and McLean (50) enabled Waite to make the winning hit – a four off Tyson – in what must have been the last over but one. Thus the timing of that first-innings declaration of McGlew's eventually proved a decisive stroke.

A mere nine days later, the Fourth Test began at Headingley. Cowdrey, Evans, Tyson and Appleyard were all absent injured; so was Watson, who had been chosen to go in first: he was replaced by another Yorkshireman, Lowson. In little more than half an hour of the start of the England innings, Neil Adcock had to retire with a fractured left foot. He batted, but could not bowl again in the match: that was indeed a heavy handicap to impose on any team in a five-day match. Cheetham had not recovered from his elbow injury, thus McGlew captained the side. Short, fair-haired and perky-looking, he was a consistently quick-footed, but largely defensive, opening batsman: immensely fit and fast over the ground he was a keen and highly capable fieldsman. Few men played their cricket harder nor more bravely, and he stood up to short-pitched bowling quite fearlessly. Characteristically he did not allow the setback of Adcock's injury to sap his spirit; indeed he seemed to play the harder for it. He needed all his determination when South Africa lost their first six wickets for 63. McLean, the hitherto unlucky Endean, Tayfield and even Heine helped in a minor repair operation by the standards of Test cricket, but the accuracy of Statham and Loader's subtleties put them out for 171.

England made their now habitual dismal start, for the trial pair of Bailey (who could not really be spared from lower down) and Lowson were put out for 23 and, after them, only May (47) and Compton (61) so much as reached 25. Heine was always hostile, Goddard, as ever, steadily defensive and Tayfield – the inevitable Tayfield – took 4 for 70. So England, with 191, achieved a lead of only 20 on the first innings. South Africa, at the second attempt, made an altogether better fist of their job. McGlew scored 133 and shared an opening stand of 176 with Goddard. Keith batted valuably once more, but then there was something of a slump. It was, dramatically speaking, the cue for Russell Endean, who had not yet on the tour shown his best form. Waite, Tayfield, Heine and even the injured Adcock – batting without a runner – stayed with him while he made 116 not out and saw South Africa to an imposing 500, which set England 481 to win. This time Graveney opened with Lowson but it was the old tale – England 3 for 1. May's 97 was the main resistance with some help from Graveney, Compton,

Insole and Wardle, but it was not enough. Goddard and Tayfield took five wickets apiece, Goddard in 62 overs for 69, Tayfield in 47 for 94. Tirelessly and accurately they worked their way through the English batting to give South Africa a win by 224 runs so that the sides went level to the Oval for a decision.

This fifth and final Test was a striking example of the fact that a cricket match can be slow moving, low scoring yet sustainedly exciting. England were without Evans, Cowdrey and Tyson – all unfit – but brought back Bailey, who ought never to have been dropped, and Graveney. The selectors, in their obvious respect for the left-arm medium-pace leg theory of Goddard, played four left-hand batsmen in Ikin, Close, Watson and the wicketkeeper Spooner. South Africa brought in Fuller for the injured Adcock and also – which seemed extremely rough luck after his great innings at Old Trafford – left out Winslow to accommodate the returning Cheetham. It was a most unfriendly day on which to start any cricket match, with lowering clouds and the promise of rain. The conditions were bound to help swing but May, when he won the toss, had no hesitation about batting. Ikin was hit by a number of bouncers from Heine, one of which struck him in the stomach so that he had to retire temporarily. May took his place, but almost at once was taken at slip and a few moments before lunch Close went in the same way for a useful defensive innings of 32. After lunch Ikin took up his innings again but soon was well caught by Waite down the leg side. Then the rain came, with England 70 for 3.

Several times over the weekend it seemed doubtful whether play could be resumed on the Monday, but the weather cleared and Compton and Watson took up the innings on an altogether lighter and sunnier day. England made slow going of it; in an hour and a quarter they scored only 35, but those runs were precious; then Compton was taken by the wicketkeeper off his characteristic leg-side sweep. That was 105 for 4 and more trouble was to come. Tayfield put out Watson, Bailey and Spooner for one run and England were 122 for 7 at lunch. Goddard justified the selectors' fears by mopping up the innings and finishing with 5 for 31.

Briefly at the start, South Africa in the persons of McGlew and Goddard held on, but when Bailey had Goddard lbw at 22 they fell deeply into trouble. May was now using the two Surrey spinners, Laker who was monumentally steady and Lock who turned his left-arm spin sharply and took the wickets of Keith, Endean and – to an utterly suicidal stroke – McLean; that made the score 33 for 4. South Africa were grateful for a brave little stand of 44 between Waite and McGlew, but Laker broke it when Lock caught Waite acrobatically off him at short leg. Immediately, McGlew was caught at the wicket, in a brief spell by Statham, for 30, which was to prove the highest score of the innings. Cheetham made 12 in an hour but Laker, Statham and Lock took wickets at the other end and they were all out for 112 which gave England a lead of 39: negligible in most circumstances but surely crucial here. The innings ended, conveniently for writers, with the end of the second day's play.

England took their slight advantage into the second innings, but they were at once in trouble when Goddard caught Ikin off Heine for nought. Close was eventually bowled by Goddard – whom the lefthanders were brought in to muzzle – and Graveney came in in place of the hobbling Compton. He and May effectively made the match-winning stand, lifting England to 95 before Graveney was bowled by Tayfield in the course of an amazing spell. He bowled from 12.30 until the close of play without relief and it would be hard to remember him sending down a loose ball. He finished with figures of 5 for 60 in 53 overs. Once again, Compton joined May in an important stand. Someone remarked that Denis's running between wickets was bad enough when he was fit, but that now – for he refused a runner – he was a hostage to run-outs. When eventually Fuller had him caught at the wicket, England were 157 for 4. After that it was a question of May and no one else, though Laker did contribute 12 as Tayfield tidied up the England innings for 204 (May 89 not out).

So South Africa needed 244 to win. Compton was unable to field: his bowling might, in fact, have been useful, for the ball turned but, once again, the two Surrey spinners, Lock and Laker, were enough. McGlew and Goddard hung together for an hour before Lock made the initial penetration by having Goddard caught at slip – 28 for 1. After that it was 28 for 2, 29 for 3, 33 for 4.

McGlew, though, was still there and Waite played an outstanding innings. Lock found McGlew lbw for 19 and no one else could stay with Waite, whose cool and correct batting took him to 60: no other batsman scored more than 20 in the innings. Lock took 8 for 101 in the two innings, Laker 7 for 84: those figures tell the story. The same two had been together at the Oval when Australia were beaten and now they were bowling in harness when England won by 92 runs and took the rubber by three-two. As a matter of interest it was the first time that all five Tests had reached a positive result in an English Test series. May with 582 runs at an average of 72.75 and Compton, 492 at 54.66, were the decisive influences on the series. Although McGlew made 476 at 52.88, no other South African averaged 30.

It was a match to hold the attention from beginning to end, though on its last day J.A. could not resist giving some attention – on other men's telephones – to the match between Hampshire and Somerset when Shackleton had the bewildering figures of 8 for 4 in the first innings and 6 for 25 in the second. Somerset were put out for 37 and 98 while Hampshire made 154 and 245 for 7 declared; the latter set of figures merely indicate that the Weston-super-Mare wicket was not responsible for such an amazing achievement.

The South Africans made a close thing of it in the rubber, showed a healthy profit – crucial in modern cricket – and they were a popular side. The fifth of the prestigious 'County' cricket cups went to them as 'a special award for the year's outstanding performance'. Although McGlew as a batsman, Goddard as an all-rounder and, because of his immense accuracy, Tayfield as a master off-spinner, might be regarded as defensive players because they kept the game in such tight control, the South Africans were not a dull side. The reaction of the small boys to the entry of Roy McLean or Paul Winslow indicated the excitement of their batting; and Heine, too, struck some mighty blows. Their fielding was at times quite spectacular, and the presence of the leg-spinners, Smith and Mansell, also tended to keep the game moving rather faster than was merely interesting.

To revert to Hampshire, they finished third in the County

Championship where their previous highest position had been sixth. They, too, proved an attractive fielding side. Ever since his appointment as secretary-captain immediately after the war, Desmond Eagar had done his best to compensate for weaknesses in other directions by tightening that department. If not the key to their success, the cue to it was probably the full availability, for the first time, of Roy Marshall, the West Indian Test batsman, who not only finished at the top of their batting averages with 1890 runs at 36.34 but invariably attacked the bowling. He had all the strokes and a perpetual urge to use them, but he was by no means as relaxed as he sometimes appeared. Such, indeed, was the degree of his tension that he constantly wore the rubber handle-grips of his bats baggy by the working of his hands on them. Henry Horton, the unique 'H' of the peculiar stance and unrelenting defence, was also a batting success of the season for the county.

The major achievement, though, was Derek Shackleton's with his uncanny accuracy and constant variations on the theme of fast-medium – which was often much faster than it looked. His faithful henchman was Vic Cannings, also of fast-medium pace. In the familiar language of their opponents and colleagues, they were 'Shack and Vic', and they were sufficiently different in method to work effectively together. The tall young Malcolm Heath also proved a valuable acquisition, a bowler of sufficient pace, as Neville Rogers once remarked, 'who gives us the chance, for the first time, to see batsmen on the other side duck from a fast short ball from one of our bowlers'. Jimmy Gray scored a thousand runs for the season, and so did Neville Rogers, that valuable opening batsman who was unlucky never to play for England and who at the end of the season, though still only thirty-seven, announced his retirement from cricket to go into business. For J.A. that meant the loss of one of his best friends from the cricket scene, though Leo Harrison – steadily improving as a wicketkeeper and by no means negligible as a batsman at the pinch – remained to share their well-worn jokes.

The young Peter Sainsbury in his first full season had already made his mark as an all-rounder – 488 runs and 102 wickets. Mervyn Burden of the ready laugh and useful off-breaks; Alan

Rayment, brilliant cover point and stroke-playing batsman; and Mike Barnard, who in addition to his batting and certain slip fielding, also played football for Portsmouth, virtually completed the fourteen players who were all that Hampshire used that season. The last, who only played one innings – of 34 – was Colin Ingleby-Mackenzie who was in due course to become the county captain. They were a happy bunch, surprised by their success in a way, but they did beat both Yorkshire and Surrey, the two sides who finished above them in the table. Local pride, too, was stimulated by the fact that seven of those players were born in Hampshire.

For the fourth successive season Surrey won the County Championship. Stuart Surridge captained them with his usual immense spirit: he was only interested in twelve points for a win, and was prepared to risk losing in order to get them. Tony Lock had the astronomic return of 183 wickets at 12.22: Alec Bedser and Jim Laker both took over 100 and Loader 88. It was easy enough to say that Surrey were just a bowling side, but that is not true. Four men scored over 1000 runs and four more over 700. They retained the advantage of magnificent spin but, given conditions for pace, there were Alec Bedser and Loader, while Surridge himself could turn a lively, useful arm. One was tempted sometimes when watching them to say that they won because they expected to win, and Surrey under Surridge's influence certainly did.

This year, 1955, J.A. left *The Evening News* and crossed the road to *The News Chronicle*. That had always been the family's newspaper; both his grandfathers and his parents took it; he had grown up in its Liberal tradition and did his utmost to maintain it. That was a good newspaper and working for it, he covered cricket, soccer, wine and such other subjects as caught his attention. He had long written about football; and had broadcast commentaries on it, though with no particular success – it simply did not lend itself to such broadcasting aptitudes as he had – but his match summaries for the idiosyncratic Angus MacKay were well received. His first entry into football reporting for *The Observer* was an amazing one for, in the match at White Hart Lane he watched and reported, Tottenham Hotspur beat Everton 10-4. He continued indeed to write about the game occasionally for *The Times* (for that paper and several others he used the *nom de plume* 'Silchester') and also, later and regularly, for *The Guardian*. For that paper he covered international matches and was even known to scrounge a match in Scotland to watch Hearts, Glasgow Celtic or Rangers. For long he enjoyed it and was proud to write about it, but the pleasure did not last. He had grown up in an age in which, if a spectator ran on to the football field, he would be booed off by the other members of the crowd. So, when it became a game in which a minute proportion of those who attended could spoil the flavour of it for the others, he gave up. He continued, though, and still does, to follow in the press the doings of Reading and Southampton.

It was in *The News Chronicle* that he settled as a wine correspondent with ample opportunities of travelling the vineyards and sampling their wares with no small enthusiasm. As a member of the Wine Writers Club he still receives, and reads with interest, the utterances of the better makers of wine. On the *Chronicle*, too, he sat in on editorial conferences and began to learn how a newspaper is made, for although it 'folded' in 1960, it had high standards; perhaps, indeed, that was one of the reasons that it did fold. While it lasted, though, it was a friendly paper with no backstabbing or spite and many of its staff maintained – even maintain – friendship, although they no longer work together. In 1955, however, it was for him a new experience, not merely to contribute to a newspaper, as he had often done before, but to be closely inside it, so that he understood its workings and looked at his copy each morning with a completely fresh understanding.

Meanwhile it was a matter of picking up the strings of cricket for 1956. It was a phenomenally wet summer, in which Jim Laker achieved unparalleled bowling performances. It is usual for cricketers to call any cricket season short of a heatwave a horribly wet one. This, though, certainly was wet: day after day, week after week, it seemed the downpour went on and, statistically, it was a year of remarkable rainfall. That was reflected in the whole year's cricket. For instance, in 1955, Surrey achieved a positive result in every one of their Championship matches. In 1956, although

Surridge continued his urgent drive to win even at the cost of losing, six matches had to be left drawn. Crucially, the weather
cleared for decisive Test matches but left behind pitches on which
the English spinners – Lock and Laker in particular – butchered
Australia. Indeed, in the seven matches (two of them for Surrey) in
which he played against the touring side, Laker took 63 wickets out
of only 132 for the entire season. Thanks largely to that pair of
spinners – but not forgetting Alec and Eric Bedser – Surrey
achieved the fifth of their now unique run of Championship wins.

Leonard Hutton was knighted in the Birthday Honours. He had
followed Jack Hobbs as the outstanding English professional
batsman and now he became the only other professional cricketer
to be thus honoured. The distinction was, of course, later to be
extended, notably to the West Indians, Frank Worrell and Garfield
Sobers. Sir Len and Sir Jack had it in common, not only that they
were pre-eminent in their profession, but that they were quiet,
modest men. Hutton, though, was a much more anxious, worried
person than Hobbs: perhaps that was a product of his period rather
than a characteristic, though that may be doubted. He kept his
head and his temper through some very trying situations and was a
most distinguished captain of England, an honour never bestowed
upon Sir Jack.

The Australians were captained by Ian Johnson, an off-spinner
who tended – as is a characteristic of off-spinners – to bowl slow
outswingers, but, in his case, rarely genuinely biting off-breaks. He
lacked the personality of his predecessors, Bradman and Hassett,
and his side had notable weaknesses: in particular, its best players
had aged. The whole party, in any event, was out of its element in a
wet English summer which produced conditions a number of
them had never experienced before. The only other finger-
spinner, apart from Johnson – the left-arm Jackie Wilson – was
completely out of his depth, so they went basically handicapped
into all their matches, for a natural, finger-spin bowler is a first
necessity for any team in English cricket.

That fact was emphasized in mid-May when, not only did Surrey
win their match with Australia by ten wickets, but they also
became the first county to beat an Australian touring side for forty-

four years. In a quite spectacular hint of what was to come, Jim Laker took all ten wickets in the tourists' first innings. He himself always rated that a finer technical performance, higher than his all-ten in the Old Trafford Test. Undoubtedly, he based that opinion on the fact that the wicket was not particularly affected by the weather. As evidence of that, Jim Burke (28) and Colin McDonald (89) made 62 for the opening partnership when Australia won the toss and batted first. Indeed, Laker insisted that five of the ten wickets were taken with straight balls and certainly he did not achieve any remarkable degree of turn. It was, of course, the more formidable achievement for the fact that Tony Lock was attacking furiously from the other end (he returned figures of 0 for 100). In the second innings, though, Lock took 7 for 49; and he was to achieve an all-ten for Surrey against Kent at Tunbridge Wells in June; on that occasion Laker was not playing.

It is not difficult to believe that the memory of that match, bringing a consciousness of their weakness against finger-spin, remained with the Australians throughout the series. The rain pursued them – indeed the whole of English cricket – down to the First Test match, played at Trent Bridge, when more than twelve hours were lost to rain. England went into that match with three spinners – Laker, Lock and the Yorkshire off-breaker who bowled mainly cutters, Bob Appleyard. An outstanding performance in that match was the batting of Peter Richardson, the quick-minded and lively-moving Worcestershire left-hand opening bat who, in his first Test, scored 81 and 73. Colin Cowdrey had 25 and 81 and May, in his only innings, 73; otherwise only Trevor Bailey (14) scored double figures. England were without the injured Tyson, and Trueman. In fact, it emerged as a rather flat season for Frank Tyson, who would have been essential in a dry summer but who, in this series, played only once and then bowled only fourteen overs.

On the wet pitch, Miller did well to take 4 for 69 and Archer, bowling largely cutters, had 2 for 51. England, though, declared at 217 for 8 hoping, no doubt, to force a win on a drying pitch. In those conditions, the pace bowlers, Moss and Bailey, sent down only seven overs before Laker, Lock and Appleyard were brought on to take four, three and two wickets respectively, and Australia were all out for 148. As England looked for the opportunity to declare and force a win, Richardson and Cowdrey largely built the score to 188 before a second declaration. Then, however, Burke and Burge made Australia safe. Jim Burke, a dry-looking opening batsman, with a good sense of humour and a tough defence, was always useful, even when the ball turned, and finished at the top of their Test batting averages. In this second innings, he was at his best. If May hoped the wicket might turn sticky, he had no fortune, and the time lost made it a certain draw.

Australia won the Second Test at Lord's and, for the remainder of the summer, they and their followers were content to say that, on the only honest pitch of the series, they had had a sound and certain win.

The Australians came to that Test match without having beaten a county side, but they won most handsomely when, at last, they escaped from that English 'summer'. Lock, to his bitter disappointment – for he had never played a Test at Lord's – and Tyson, injured, were not in the England side; Trueman and Wardle came in. For Australia, the injured Lindwall and Davidson were replaced by Mackay and Crawford, both playing in their first Tests. This was one of the few reliefs from rain and, on a firm pitch with a degree of 'green' on it, the pace bowlers had their way. In fact, the two England spinners, Laker and Wardle, took only four wickets between them in the two innings.

Australia took the toss and after England had missed two half-chances, McDonald and Burke gave them a strong opening with 137, before Bailey nipped in with two quick wickets – of McDonald and Harvey. Australia soldiered on: McDonald's 78 and Burke's 65 remained the two highest scores, but Burge, Miller, Mackay and Archer all made their contributions to a total of 285, in which all five English bowlers took a wicket or two. It seemed a meagre enough total but England never really got a start. Australian supporters had been disappointed with their total, but all such matters are relative and now, in the absence of Lindwall, Miller rose to his best, moving the ball through the air and off the seam and, above all, bowling with the nip off the pitch that was his immense gift. May was, in fact, dropped off Miller in the course of making England's top score of 63, and Bailey put together a patient 32. Only two other England batsmen so much as achieved double figures. They were all out for 171 – Miller 5 for 72. That left Australia with a probably decisive lead of 114.

Then, however, Trueman proceeded to have one of his high-fire afternoons and to put England definitely, albeit only briefly, back in the game. He knocked down four good wickets for 38 runs and left Australia at 115 for 6 – only 229 ahead on Friday evening. The game twisted again on Monday when Benaud, who had never scored more than 34 against England in a Test, played substantially the highest and, as it was to prove, conclusive innings of the match. With typical Benaud panache, though, when he was on 97, he tried to go to lunch with a hundred, top-edged his attempted big hit and was caught by Evans. Bailey (4 for 64) tidied up; but Trueman's 5 for 90 included good wickets. England were thus set 372 to win in just under nine hours and they never really got their teeth into the task. May's 53 was their only innings of more than 27 and Miller again, bowling with skill and life to take 5 for 80, was the bowling match-winner, though Archer's 4 for 71 was useful. The green character of the pitch was indicated by the fact that twenty-one batsmen were out to catches behind the wicket. In fact, Langley set a new Test record for a wicketkeeper by dismissing nine men – eight caught and one stumped. Australia's was a decisive win, by 185 runs. That was, incidentally, Willie Watson's last Test match; it was ironic that it should be on the ground where he had saved England against Australia so recently. He was a better batsman than his general Test figures indicate; kind, gentle, a superbly stylish and handsome-looking batsman; perhaps he tried too hard.

It is a matter of custom, nowadays, to blame selectors for teams failing, wherefore those responsible for the England side in this series – 'Gubby' Allen, Les Ames, Wilfred Wooller, Cyril Washbrook and, automatically as captain, Peter May – deserve credit for their highly successful series of recalls to this England side. For Headingley, they brought back one of their own – Cyril Washbrook – who had not played a Test for over five years. For more than one critic, this seemed nepotism, which increased the burden of responsibility on Washbrook himself.

May was rarely luckier to win the toss than on this occasion, though it did not seem so at the start. Miller was not fit to bowl, and his place as opening bowler with Lindwall was taken by Ron Archer who, in a remarkable opening, knocked down the first three England wickets to reduce them to 17 for 3 by half past twelve. At that point, Washbrook came in to join Peter May and their partnership was virtually to decide the match. They batted together until almost the close of play, when May shovelled Johnson to Lindwall at long leg: by then, though, he had made 101, and the scoreboard showed 204 for 4 at the close of play. Next morning Washbrook, who had had two lives, laboured diligently for his hundred, but when he had come to 98, he missed a long hop from Benaud and was lbw. He was, nevertheless, a happy man that night; contented and justified; all hint of nepotism banished. Lock, the nightwatchman, firmly, Bailey patiently, and Evans briskly, carried England to 325 before Lindwall, at high speed, finished off the innings by the middle of Friday afternoon.

When the Australian innings began, Trueman, swinging the ball to a full length, soon had McDonald caught but Burke and Harvey batted usefully for almost an hour. Burke, that man of honour, always had a basis of style about his batting even when he was at his most dogged, while Harvey, essentially a strokemaking batsman, was much more than merely happier on true and fast than on turning wickets. Lock had him caught on the leg side, while Burge and Mackay were both accounted for by Laker. The ball was turning and the left-handed Mackay, who had been exaggeratedly defensive – yet effectively so – at Lord's, was manifestly uncomfortable. Laker had him taken at short slip. After making 41 of the 59 for the first four wickets, Burke was lbw to Lock, and Archer played on to Laker before Miller and Benaud came together in a stand of good sense in which they took every opportunity to score. They were still there – and grateful to be so – when bad light stopped play a quarter of an hour before time with the score 81 for 6. Weekend rain meant that there was no play on Saturday and more than an hour was lost at the start of Monday.

At that juncture, Australia needed 95 to save the follow-on, on what was, for the moment at least, a damp, easy wicket. Miller, by judicious hitting, and Benaud put on a further 61 but, as soon as the sun came out, the pitch began to dry and the ball to turn. At once Benaud gave a chance off Laker and in the next over he was caught and bowled. The Miller-Benaud stand had been worth 73 and only 34 were now wanted to avoid the follow-on. In the event, the last three wickets added only 1 run. Maddocks was caught, Miller bowled round his legs – after batting over 2 hours 10 minutes for a highly disciplined 41 – and Johnson was caught in the deep field. So Australia, 182 behind, followed on. Trueman soon put paid to McDonald, but Burke batted characteristically doggedly, while Harvey, with mounting and efficient mastery, played probably the best bad-wicket innings of his career. So long as he and Burke were together Australia threatened to save the game. After over an hour, though, Burke picked the wrong ball from Laker to hit and was bowled for 16. That brought in Miller to play another highly responsible innings, so that Australia lived to the end of the day at 93 for 2. On Tuesday, Laker bowled without relief from the pavilion end and, after more than two hours altogether, Miller was brilliantly caught off his gloves by Trueman at short leg. The ball was now turning reliably for the spinners and Laker put away Burge, Mackay and Johnson. Crucially, though, Lock took the wicket of Harvey, hurling himself acrobatically down the pitch for a remarkable caught and bowled. The little lefthander had made 69; otherwise Burke's 16 and Miller's 26 were the only double figures in Australia's second attempt. Lock and Laker polished off the rest fairly easily for 140, giving England a win by an innings and 42 runs.

Pleasing as it may have been for Englishmen, it was, to the unbiased, an unsatisfactory match, not only because so many of the Australian batsmen were out of their element on a wet English pitch, but also because so few of them had the ability to bowl effectively on it. In that latter respect Johnson was a bitter disappointment. Although May and Washbrook gave England a major early batting dominance, the effective match-winners – who are, of course, always bowlers – were Laker with eleven wickets and Lock with seven. England had, in fact, had luck with the weather – not, as some of the Australians argued, in the incidence of rain, though they had been lucky with the toss, but they played in conditions which the Australian bowlers simply could not use. So, ominously for those of the tourists who were now nerve-racked at the thought of rain and wet wickets, the sides went to Manchester for the Fourth Test.

This was one of the most remarkable games of cricket ever played at any level – leave alone in a Test between England and Australia. If the scorecard is looked at cursorily it may seem one-sided but, particularly towards the end, there was much suspense. It will always be remembered for the bowling performance of Jim Laker; indeed it has been called 'Laker's match' and many people seem to think only of that when they recall him. In fact, it was a peak performance in helpful conditions by a very great bowler; probably the greatest off-spinner who ever lived. Tell him a thing like that and his tongue would go into his cheek, his expression grow even more wry, and he would wriggle out of the conversation. Now, pace bowlers may achieve considerable performances with occasional lethal deliveries. A major ingredient of Jim Laker's success in the summer of 1956, and especially in matches when he played against the Australians, was that he barely bowled a bad ball; he flighted, varied and spun his off-breaks, and his accuracy again and again completed an armoury more effective than a side of Test batsmen – the old enemy – could withstand.

Even before the match started, there was a surprise for the general public when David Sheppard, of Sussex, was included in the twelve from which the team would be picked. He had gone into the Church and had not played a Test since he captained England against Pakistan two years before: moreover, he had played only four first-class innings thus far in the season, though one of those was of 97 for Sussex against the Australians. He replaced the injured Graveney; Statham came in for Trueman. For Australia, all seventeen were fit for selection except Langley, who had damaged a hand by sleeping on it – surely a unique Test cricket injury! Maddocks took his place and Burge was left out for the young Craig. The other essential preliminary to the play was the toss, which May won and he took first innings for England: that was to prove conclusive.

Richardson (104) and Cowdrey (80) gave them a fine start with an opening of 174: and once again the selectors were vindicated when David Sheppard at number three scored a most felicitous 113. England finished the day at 307 for 3 with dust rising ominously from the pitch of the ball. That continued on the second day, though May (43) and Evans (47) served to lift England's final total, made in good time – little more than eight hours – to 459. Australia began their innings soon after lunch on the Friday. McDonald and Burke started solidly enough with 48 for the first wicket but, as soon as May called up his two main spinners, Laker and Lock, they were struggling. There had been some to prophesy a long Australian total but certainly Jim Laker, studying the wicket the day before, was confident that the soil was loose and it would be a turner: so it proved. May constantly switched Laker and Lock from end to end, and one must wonder whether it was merely by coincidence that Laker took all his nineteen Australian wickets from the Stretford end. It was the more amazing that he took so many when Lock – who in fact bowled one more over in the match (69 to Laker's 68) and who made the ball leap, bounce and turn in the most astonishing manner – took only one. Sometimes, indeed, Evans had to make a remarkable amount of ground to the off-side and often was taking the ball in front of his face. Lock's solitary victim was Burke – the third wicket to fall in the first innings. That Australian innings was simply a rout, as if their nerve had been broken by that simply unplayable ball from Laker which pitched on Harvey's leg stump and hit the top of the off. In any case, after McDonald's 32 and Burke's 22, no one else achieved double figures. Laker, indeed, finished off their first innings by taking 7 for 8 in less than four overs, and they were all out for 84 – Laker 9 for 37, Lock 1 for 37. Then, following on 375 behind, they reached 51 for 1 at the close on Friday. The wicket to fall was that of Harvey, who had come out to replace McDonald when the latter had to leave the field with a knee injury.

Next day – Saturday – rain washed out all but three-quarters of an hour of playing time. Even that wind-harried few minutes sufficed for Laker to have Burke caught in the leg trap – by Lock. There was rain again on Sunday and a bare hour's play was possible on

Monday, in which time Craig and the returning McDonald took the score on to 84 for 2. By some remarkable skill, the groundstaff contrived to have a slow, easy wicket fit for play only ten minutes late on Tuesday, when Craig and McDonald held on until lunch at 112 for 2. Then the sun came out and once more the ball began to turn spitefully and Laker put out Craig, Mackay, Miller and Archer for 3 runs inside nine overs. Benaud stayed with McDonald for over an hour, and the conclusive breakthrough came when McDonald, after batting resourcefully and skilfully for over five hours, was caught by Oakman in Laker's leg trap. Laker inflicted a 'pair' on both Craig and Mackay before Johnson and Lindwall staged a quarter of an hour's resistance. By then Laker's spinning finger was beginning to tire and time was running out for England's deserved win and Laker's all-ten wickets. Johnson, in particular, used every conceivable form of gamesmanship in playing for time: he even complained to the umpires that the sawdust which had been sprinkled on the pitch was unsettling him when it was blown about in the breeze. Those two old hands, Frank Lee and Emrys Davies, though, were not to be deceived. Laker bowled one ball to Lindwall which went the 'wrong' way, took the edge of the bat and was caught – by Lock. A maiden from Lock to Johnson and then a ball from Laker hit Maddocks on the pad: an appeal and he was given out lbw. England had won by an innings and 170 runs; Laker had taken all ten in the second innings; nineteen in the match. A comparison of the figures of the two spinners – Laker 68 overs, 19 for 90; Lock 69 overs, 1 for 106 – is almost ridiculous. One might suspect connivance, but that could not be the case: Lock tried his heart out.

It was, indeed, a match of records, with the first actual result in a Test between England and Australia at Old Trafford since 1905. Laker's ten wickets in a Test innings and nineteen in a match were both unique – and, surely, will remain so. He had now, too, taken all ten Australian wickets twice – once in Surrey's match with them. If the first Australian innings at Old Trafford had been quickly dealt with, the second was gamely played out, especially by McDonald, but also by Burke, Craig and Benaud to within just about an hour of the allocated match time. Laker was so heavily engaged with press, radio and television interviews that he did not leave Old Trafford until after eight, when he drove home. He stopped on his journey for a beer and a sandwich in a Lichfield bar, where a crowd of drinkers discussed his performance without recognizing him. It was past two o'clock when he reached home, and he was due at the Oval the next morning to play for Surrey – against the Australians! He was always drily shy about his performance: indeed, too modest; but there is no doubt that he was quietly proud of it – almost as proud as his wife.

After all that, the Fifth Test, at the Oval, was something of an anti-climax; though it need not have been if the weather had not filched twelve hours of it. Australia, of course, needed to win it to draw the series, though England were already sure of retaining the Ashes. When the match was eventually closed by rain Australia – 27 for 5 in their second innings – were in a losing position against, once more, Laker (3 for 8) and Lock (1 for 17). Yet again, the selectors turned up a trump card; this time in Denis Compton, who was recalled after the operation that had removed his kneecap in November 1955. He, like David Sheppard at Old Trafford, made top score – in this instance 94. May made 83 not out but, from 222 for 3, England subsided to 247 all out. Heavy rain on the first night left Australia once more to face a turning pitch. Brave batting by Miller, Benaud and Lindwall saved them from the follow-on, which was threatened when their score stood at 47 for 5. Laker had 4 for 80, Lock 2 for 49 and Statham, with a pitch on which the fast bowlers could at least be used, came out with 3 for 33. Laker set yet another record with his 46 wickets in the series; he took them, too, at the remarkable average for modern times of 9.60. It was the most extraordinary Test series J.A. had ever seen.

Chapter 18

THE 1957
CRICKET SEASON

1957 was a cock-a-hoop year for English cricket. It stood then at a peak it has rarely achieved since. England had not lost a series since they were beaten by West Indies in 1950. Len Hutton had led them up to a high peak, and Peter May had contrived to keep them – and Surrey, County Champions for the sixth consecutive year in 1957 – at the top. Perhaps in terms of history it was not the greatest of all teams but, for the moment, it was without doubt the best in the world.

This was never more clearly exemplified than in their defeat of West Indies by three Tests to none in that season. Some of the batting looked quite prodigious on paper: for instance, Tom Graveney averaged 118.00 with only one not out; Peter May 97.80; Fred Trueman – not out in three of his four innings – 89.00; Colin Cowdrey, a genuine 72.50; Peter Richardson 58.71; David Sheppard 54.00 (in only two innings) and Godfrey Evans 50.25: that is to say seven men with figures over 50. Yet it could be argued that the main strength lay in the bowling – a mixed bag of Loader, Trueman, Statham, Bailey, Lock and Laker, all took ten wickets or more, and five of them did so at better than 25 apiece. Add to that the fact that the catching – except in the Third Test – was superb and the ground-fielding keen, and the picture is complete of a competent, all-round, successful side.

The West Indian side was interesting in its successes, its failures and its promise. Top of the batting was the merry little 'Collie' Smith. A bright stroke-playing batsman, bowler of wily off-breaks and a good field, he was tragically killed in a car accident in 1959 while playing for Burnley in Lancashire League cricket. Worrell followed him in the figures and also made an impressive mark when, in the absence of John Goddard, the captain, and Clyde Walcott, the vice-captain (the latter often injured), he took over the captaincy. Undoubtedly his manner and performance in that office took him on to the captaincy of his country – the first non-white cricketer to lead them on tour – and an eventual knighthood. He also proved a valuable bowler – fast-medium or slow left-arm. Gilchrist was the first of their modern breed of West Indian fast bowlers but Ramadhin, though he was at last 'read' and mastered by the English batsmen, proved their most successful Test bowler. Their ultimate lack of success derived from the poor form, after some initial successes, of Alf Valentine whose accurate slow-left-arm had been such an immense asset to them in 1950 – he commanded much sympathy in his loss of absolutely all he had possessed in bowling terms. Extremely promising were two young players, the all-rounder Garfield Sobers and Rohan Kanhai, a batsman, both of whom, of course, were to play importantly in English cricket in later years. There are many who believe that Sobers was the finest all-rounder who ever played: he batted most handsomely, though he could defend at need. Even on this tour, while still only twenty, he made its highest score – 219 not out – against Nottinghamshire. He bowled left-arm, fast-medium or spinners; he was also a brilliant and prehensile fieldsman. Cricket to him was indeed a game and, if necessary, a gamble, for he insisted on enjoying it: and he was most cordial company. Rohan Kanhai, of Indian extraction, was a neat, small, dextrous batsman who made runs against all types of bowling on every kind of wicket, and who was to enjoy a long cricketing career, although he fell out drastically with some of his political masters.

For the First Test, England went back to Birmingham – Edgbaston – after twenty-eight years – and they played a most remarkable match. May's luck held: he won the toss yet again, and took first innings for England. It proved of little advantage, for Ramadhin proved as mysterious as ever to the English batsmen. In front of a Saturday crowd of 32,000, the biggest that had ever watched at Edgbaston, his 7 for 49 proved murderous even on that good plumb wicket, and England were all out for 186. That night, in the hotel where the team were staying, Bill Bowes talked deeply to several of its members – including Richardson, Close, Bailey and, as was to prove most significant, May and Cowdrey. Meanwhile, however, West Indies were to take their innings, and in his first Test in England Collie Smith scored 161: he had already made a century in his first appearance against Australia. Walcott made 90, Worrell 81 and Sobers 53 in a total of 474 which seemed to have given them an overwhelming advantage. When the wickets of Richardson, Close and Insole went down for 113, that opinion seemed confirmed. Then, however, came an amazing stand of 411 by May (285 not out) and Cowdrey (154). In other words, Bill Bowes' advice, basically to treat Ramadhin as an off-spinner who often simply went straight through – though there were variations and elaborations on that theory – had borne remarkable fruit. May had made his highest first-class score and Cowdrey his first Test century; there were then only two higher stands in the history of Test cricket than their 411. Meanwhile, Ramadhin sent down 774 balls, the greatest number ever bowled by anyone in a Test match. That left West Indies 296 to make in 140 minutes, and Trueman, Laker and Lock made life more than a little uncomfortable for them, reducing them to 72 for 7 by the close of play: tight passive defence by Goddard and Atkinson saw them safely through to a draw.

On to Lord's, and there England, now freed from their awe of Ramadhin, won by an innings and 36 on the third day. Both Lock and Laker were unfit. It was England's good fortune that it proved a characteristic Lord's wicket, fast and lively, absolutely right for the pace bowlers. Bailey, in his fiftieth Test match, took seven wickets in the first innings and four in the second, and was the chief destroyer; but Statham and Trueman were also effective in his support. So, West Indies, ousted for 127 and – despite a brilliant 90 by an injured Everton Weekes and 66 by Sobers – 261, were thoroughly beaten by an England side which, thanks largely to Cowdrey's 152 and a lively 82 by Evans – who was dropped five times – totalled 424 (Ramadhin 1 for 83) in their only innings.

The Third Test was drawn but, nevertheless, remarkable for several performances. Three of England's first four batsmen – Peter Richardson, Tom Graveney and Peter May – made respectively

126, 258 and 104. In the midst of those scores (the board showed 360 for 2 at the end of the first day), poor Don Smith, the Sussex lefthander at number two, looked forlorn with his 1. Incidentally, that did not cost him his Test place, though nought in the next Test did. Cowdrey was run out for 55, and May was able to declare at 619 for 6. When West Indies batted, Worrell carried his bat for 191, an innings of both skill and dignity; Collie Smith yet again played magnificently in their second innings when he made 168. Trueman took five wickets and Laker three in the first innings, Statham five and Trueman four in the second, when Goddard played a defensive innings of 61 of quite sterling quality. England, though, had really only themselves to blame for they dropped more catches than at any other time in the series. They still needed 57 when time ran out on them; May was simply determined not to risk losing.

Any man needed to be a fervent English partisan – and not proposing to see anything after the first half of the match – to enjoy the Fourth Test at Headingley. It finished in the middle of Saturday afternoon with a win for England by an innings and 5 runs; and it must have given immense personal pleasure to Peter Loader and Godfrey Evans for their performances. There was very little satisfaction indeed for West Indies: only Walcott contrived to make double figures in both innings, or fifty altogether. Advance bookings to the impressive tune of £20,600 included a disappointed number for the Monday and Tuesday. The match began as a perfect setting for seam bowling, with a heavy atmosphere and a cross wind and Peter Loader, coming in for the first time in the series, made the most of it. Trueman took the seventh wicket, that of Pairaudeau, with the last ball of an over. Then, with the first three balls of the next, Loader bowled Goddard, had Ramadhin taken at short leg and hit the stumps of Gilchrist, to perform the first English hat-trick in a Test in England since 1899. Before that, there had been some resistance from Worrell, Kanhai, and Walcott, but otherwise only Collie Smith (15) made double figures, and they were all out for 142. Umpire Dai Davies cautioned Trueman for intimidatory bowling when he sent down four bouncers in a single over to Kanhai.

England batted usefully: May, Cowdrey and Sheppard – the three Blues – batting at numbers four, five and six, all reached the sixties. Worrell bowled his fast-medium seamers persistently, steadily and sharply to the tune of 38 overs to take 7 for 70. Gilchrist, though, possibly not completely fit, disappointed: but Sobers bowled a long, steady stint of slow left-arm, the real merit of which does not show in the figures. In their second innings, West Indies fared somewhat worse – they were all out 132. Only Sobers – who was freakishly run out – and Clyde Walcott, made any real impression on the English bowling, in which Loader took 3 for 50 and Trueman, Smith, Laker and Lock all weighed in. When he caught Collie Smith off Don Smith, Godfrey Evans became far and away the first wicketkeeper to make 200 dismissals in Tests. He celebrated the fact that night quite riotously, not because it was particularly important to him but simply because he loved to cele- brate. Godfrey made his mistakes – some of them so elementary that they seemed to be sheer carelessness. Throughout his career, though, he had communicated enthusiasm to the bowler at the other end: he was perpetually convinced that cricket was fun, and, perhaps largely for that reason, could prove a great psychological fillip to an entire fielding side. If this seemed a rather hollow win, historically its importance lay in the fact that it gave England their first rubber in this series since 1939.

So the series was settled before West Indies went on to prove even more vulnerable at the Oval. May won the toss and England batted; Richardson made a briskly taken 107, Graveney a hand- some 164 and England scored 412. West Indies then proceeded to record their two lowest totals against England. In the first innings only Asgarali and Sobers scored double figures: in the second, only Sobers and Walcott. They were out for 89 and 86. Once more they had little luck. Goddard fell ill at the end of the first day and did not bat in either innings (Walcott took over as captain); they were without the injured Atkinson and they obviously and pain- fully did not believe in themselves. On a pitch responsive to spin, Laker took 5 for 77 in the match; but Lock – in addition to two bril- liant catches – had 11 for 48, which set a new record for either side in these Tests. West Indies' few satisfactions included the wicketkeeping of 'Gerry' Alexander, who had come in for the first time at Headingley and who communicated his enthusiasm to the fielding in general. Even more impressive, probably, was the responsibility of the young Sobers as both batsman and bowler. There was little else to arouse enthusiasm, though Ramadhin bowled 53 overs to take 4 for 107. This represented the nadir of West Indian cricket for, as history shows, within a few years, fired by their perpetuating battery of fast bowlers, they had begun their great sweep to supremacy in world Test cricket.

Chapter 19

VALERIE

The move from production to the Staff Training School had retained Jim Pennethorne-Hughes as J.A.'s immediate superior, but changed all else about his BBC situation. It meant, which seemed relatively unimportant at the time, that the Corporation issued him with a new secretary. She was short, with gentle, direct eyes, a humorous, easy-smiling mouth, and a good sense of fun, as well as sound commonsense, and she was utterly reliable and efficient at her job. Her name was Valerie France; she came from Bromley in Kent, where her father was a GP; her sister was also a doctor and her younger brother was to become one. When J.A. left the Corporation, he took a tiny office in the suite – if that is not too grand a word for it, and it probably is – of his accountant, in Cecil Court, off Charing Cross Road. It seemed only reasonable – and certainly convenient – to offer Valerie the job as his secretary there. She agreed to go with him and thus they continued what had become a sound and friendly working relationship.

In 1957 she asked permission to take about a month off during July-August, to join the crew, recruited from the Island Cruising Club of Salcombe, of *Provident*, a Brixham trawler, in what was, in fact, the first 'Tall Ships Race' from Salcombe to Lisbon. That was no trouble because for most of the period he was engaged on cricket commentaries. It remains vividly in the memory that, driving down for the Glamorgan-West Indies match at Swansea on the Friday before the game, it occurred to him that she had said she would be back about August bank holiday. Quite suddenly it dawned that he was in love with her. He sent her a telegram at the Island Cruising Clubhouse, asking her to come at once to Swansea. Surely enough, she arrived at the pavilion there on the Saturday afternoon. He went down to her, asked her in and, on the way up the stairs, told her he loved her and asked her to marry him. 'I thought you would never ask me,' she said, 'I have been in love with you for years.'

He had come a long way from the provincial policeman who had married Dawn, to the experienced cricket commentator and journalist he now was. It had meant, too, that he had been much away from home and, much as people can grow together, the pair of them had grown apart. The two boys, Jimmy and Timothy, had remained a strong link, but on the holiday in Alderney in 1957 when they, Dawn and Valerie made up the party with him, it became plain that he had to tidy up the matter. As soon as they returned home he told Dawn; a fact that she probably knew or felt already. She was understandably bitter, and it became clear that the only thing for him to do was to live the peculiar night-monastic life of a resident member of the National Liberal Club.

The whole process of divorce is horrid and should only be undertaken by anyone when it becomes completely necessary. Even for one who wants a divorce, it is highly distasteful; and however one may tell oneself that there is light at the end of the tunnel, it is often difficult to descry. For the partner who does not want it, it must be unutterably cruel. When that was over – in 1959 – he duly married Valerie and they went to live in George Street, off Baker Street, in a flat on two floors. Then began the seventeen years of marriage to her which was beyond all argument the happiest period of his life. At the end of 1960 she gave birth to a baby girl – hastily christened Lynne – who died within a few days of her birth. It was only then that the gynaecologist told him – amazingly in one who was a doctor's child – that she had hypertension to such a degree as to amount virtually to a death sentence. She chose never to discuss it; to move to different ground if he introduced the subject. Nevertheless, they went ahead with the idea of another child – Robert – who was born on 4 February 1963. They both doted upon him, the more so when the delightful Jimmy was killed in a road accident on New Year's Eve, 1965. He was, indeed, an extremely nice person and the coroner at his inquest was at pains to state that there was no question of his being under the influence of alcohol when he ran into the back of an unlighted vehicle.

In 1973 Valerie came to him and said of Robert, 'I am sure that boy is going to be all right.' On 14 March 1976 she died, as she knew she would do, of hypertension. She was just forty-two and she had put a remarkably brave face on it all. For all that Pat was later able to do to repair his life, he never quite recovered from the loss of Valerie; perhaps, indeed, he was too old to do so. This is an inadequate memorial to a woman of honour and humanity, who had a superb capacity to love; it can only say that her loss was a genuine loss; the world was the poorer for her going.

Chapter 20

YEAR OF EVENT

The year of 1958 was, in many ways, the most eventful, and probably the most informative, of his life. It saw the break-up of his marriage to Dawn and, if neither gave many signs of its emotional effect, it was traumatic and its echoes hung around the remainder of his life. After the divorce, both continued a close relationship with Jimmy until his death, and still with Timothy.

J.A. had, for some time, been writing the Friday soccer lead in *The Guardian* and now became number two to Donny Davies, that paper's soccer correspondent. Donny had won an amateur cap and wrote under the *nom de plume* 'Old International'. His standing among soccer journalists was high and he was also a capable broadcaster of match reports, to which he gave something of a literary bias, invariably including a quotation from Dickens. No one relished that Friday soccer stint: after a couple of years most people were completely fed-up with scrabbling for subjects left over from the previous weekend which others had milked dry. In January, with soccer news hard to come by, J.A. asked the Sports Editor, Larry Montague, if he might go to one of the club matches in Europe to increase and enhance the material for the Friday piece. Surely enough, about the end of January, Larry rang up to say, 'You can watch Manchester United's match in Belgrade next week. It will probably give you a fair information lever if you go to United's game with Arsenal on Saturday.'

That seemed a pleasant and useful arrangement. He duly wrote the Arsenal-Manchester United match piece and rang on the Sunday to check his copy as usual. Thereat, Larry said, quite casually, 'Donny now finds it possible to go to Belgrade to take over that match.' To J.A.'s protest he countered with, 'Donny is the soccer correspondent: you are his number two: if he wants the match, he must have it.'

J.A. swallowed his indignation in spluttering, but through the match day on the Wednesday, the matter still rankled. It lasted until the next day – Thursday 6 February – when, unable to settle to work, he said to Valerie, 'I'm going out to buy a book – and probably shall not hurry back.' He made his way down through his favourite London secondhand bookshops. When he reached Vigo Street he went in, as usual, to Bertram Rota's shop. He was looking along the shelves there when Miss Jones came out of the office to say, 'There is a phone call for you, Mr Arlott.'

'There can't be, nobody knows I am here.'

'It is for you, though; you will take it, I presume?'

It was Valerie, who had traced him, north to south, by way of his usual book-buying resorts. 'John – you are to go down to *The Guardian* Fleet Street office: the Manchester United plane has crashed and they want you to write the obits as the names of the dead come through, players and journalists as well.' In a very subdued voice, she added, 'Donny was among them.'

He could not say more than, 'All right – I will go down there.'

The sickness lay in his belly all that afternoon and evening, through paragraph after paragraph about the dead: his friends, his footballing idols, and men who only the previous Saturday he had watched playing a fine game of football. *The Guardian*, being *The Guardian*, accepted all of it and constantly asked for more. Alcohol was no answer: he plugged on until far into the evening but the piece about Donny was not easy to believe. Some time later Davies's widow mooted to the Sports Editor the idea of a collection of Donny's football writings. Larry agreed and thought that J.A. might well collaborate. Mrs Davies, however, said simply and categorically, 'John Arlott must not have anything to do with it.' What, J.A. has constantly wondered since, was the explanation Donny gave to his wife for going on that trip to Belgrade? For several days to come, J.A. had almost to pinch himself to believe in that reprieve.

The cricket season was therapeutic. The New Zealanders were the tourists: cheerful and companionable but not particularly strong. They lost four and drew the other of their five Tests, and lost another two of their first-class matches. Bert Sutcliffe was hampered by an injury but batted well when he was available. The captain was that immensely strong man, John Reid, who could last out the longest possible day. 'Mac', the tireless Tony MacGibbon, who took twenty wickets in Tests, was another fairly inexhaustible and capable player, good company and always ready for a joke and a drink, even when the game was running against him. So, too, was Alex Moir, the humorously disposed leg-spinner, while Harry Cave, tall and lean, already gave promise of the valuable medium-pace bowler he was to become. There was little wonder that they were defeated by an England batting side which included, in that season, by remarkable coincidence, three double internationals: Arthur Milton and Willie Watson, cricket and soccer, and Mike Smith, cricket and rugby. Peter May, Colin Cowdrey, Peter Richardson, Willie Watson and Tom Graveney were the senior batsmen; while the bowling had those formidable spinners, Tony Lock and Jim Laker, Trevor Bailey and Peter Loader at fast-medium, and Fred Trueman and Brian Statham to bowl at pace. Of them, Lock took 34 wickets at 7.47 in the Tests; the other five bowlers took upwards of six apiece for averages below 20. There was a pleasantly relaxed atmosphere about their matches.

For J.A. the most important aspect of the season seemed the success of Hampshire, who, winning thirteen matches and losing only six, became runners-up in the Championship, the highest position of the county's entire history until then. In Roy Marshall, the West Indian opening batsman, they had recruited an attractive and fast-scoring strokemaker. He was backed by that most enthusiastic captain, Colin Ingleby-Mackenzie, who cared much more about the game than his casual witticisms sometimes suggested. They had the solidity of Henry Horton, the all-round ability of Peter Sainsbury and Jim Gray; the pace bowling of Malcolm Heath was a genuine acquisition, and Shackleton emphasized his right to be regarded as the steadiest bowler in the country – and, in addition, a mighty penetrative one. In fact, from June until the middle of August, Hampshire made most of the running but, in the end, Surrey came through to win the title for a record seventh consecutive year. Nevertheless, there were some happy days – and, indeed, some even happier evenings – for Hampshire, delighted by their success, even if they did at the end fall short of their hopes.

The job of soccer correspondent for *The Guardian* was not available in double harness with writing cricket leads. Just when he was revolving this in his mind, there came an invitation from Chris Brasher – Sports Editor of *The Observer* – to report the main Saturday-for-Sunday soccer match of the week. That at least partly relieved J.A. of the shivery feeling he had not cast off since the day of the Manchester United crash. He agreed, took the job – and on 11 October 1958 he reported his first soccer lead for that paper. He had his pick of the fixtures and most fortunately settled on Tottenham Hotspur's home match with Everton, went to it and was duly, shatteringly and gloriously happy with a match which Spurs won 10-4. Little Tommy Harmer – that ingenious waif of the midfield – constantly produced the impossible. It was the period not only of Harmer but also of the wing-halves Blanchflower and Iley, Medwin at outside-right, Bobby Smith at centre-forward and George Robb at outside-left. After the game Tommy Harmer said to his manager, Billy Nicholson, 'We shan't score ten every week, boss.' In fact, and incredible as it may seem, that immensely talented side finished only eighteenth in the league and were knocked out in the fifth round of the Cup. Amazingly enough, too, only three members of that extremely gifted side survived as regular members in their remarkable 'double' season two years afterwards.

One event of that year which seemed quite minor at the time was to prove the most important in – if not of – his life. He received a letter from South Africa quite handsomely written in green ink. It was an immensely courteous request for help in obtaining a coaching post in England – 'To enable me to pass on the knowledge to my fellow Cape Coloureds' – from a man named Basil D'Oliveira. It appeared to be a mild request but he soon found out that it was not by any means easy to satisfy. J.A.'s efforts were given some impetus by the appearance, in a somewhat obscure magazine called *World Sport*, of the same young man's cricketing performances.

The visit to South Africa a few years before had left J.A. with a deeply engraved consciousness of the fashion in which Cape Coloureds – indeed, all non-white residents of that country – were treated. Their cricketers generally had to play their matches on matting or merely rough earth pitches. It transpired that the young letter-writer, though still only in his early twenties, had scored fifty-odd centuries, once an amazing 225 in 70 minutes, and also 46 from one eight-ball over. On the other side of the coin, as an off-break bowler, he once took 9 for 2. J.A. did his level best for him but with little luck, and the fact that he had played on goodish pitches against the Kenya Asians and for the Coloureds against the Malays, the Indians and the Bantu in South Africa seemed to carry no weight at all. Lord's simply did not wish to know him nor anything about him. There was similarly little luck around the counties. Cite his batting achievements and a county secretary would retort, 'Of course, on plumb wickets.' Point to his bowling figures and they would say, 'On rough pitches, of course.' The letters from South Africa came regularly but not frequently enough to seem nagging.

Eventually it became clear that the only hope was to find him a post as a league professional. There, too, luck was scarce. John Kay, a fellow journalist, and his brother were closely connected with the Middleton Club which played in the Central Lancashire League. They had dismissed their professional, the West Indian Roy Gilchrist, and had sought to replace him with Wesley Hall. Hall, trying anxiously to keep on the right side of the West Indian authorities, had constantly put off the decision and when he informed them that he could not come, it was late in the day to sign a new professional for that coming season. At this point John Kay wrote to J.A. that 'We can give your man a job at £450 for the season.' It was not much but it was the only vestige of encouragement that had so far emerged from his efforts. After some doubts and thoughts he wrote to South Africa telling the young man, 'It is not an earth-shaking job but I don't think you will find a better one and I do recommend you to accept it.'

Basil D'Oliveira did accept it: J.A. was blissfully ignorant of all the efforts being made on Signal Hill, Cape Town, to raise the money to pay his fare to England. He duly arrived, was met at

Heathrow by John Kay and brought to J.A.'s London flat. He was pleasant-looking, with a neat moustache, and he moved well with, obviously, plenty of muscle. It emerged that he was uneasy at being asked into a white man's house and he needed reassurance. Middleton, when he arrived there, must have seemed even more puzzling to him, but the season was about to start and now a man who had never played on English pitches was thrown in at the deep end of the league. Every Saturday night J.A. rang Middleton – but not Basil directly – to find out how the young man had performed. Five matches, though, in the hostile Lancashire climate were enough to discourage anyone: they yielded just 25 runs and it transpired subsequently that, at that juncture, D'Oliveira all but made up his mind to return to South Africa. Then Eric Price, the slow left-arm bowler, formerly of Lancashire and Essex, and a former Middleton professional himself, with quite striking generosity, gave the young man all the help and advice he could. From that day the sun shone on what had been an unfriendly season: Basil D'Oliviera made runs. At the end of the season he was top of the Central Lancashire League averages – ahead even of Garfield Sobers.

In a way, that is the end of the story, but he went on and on; during the second of the Commonwealth tours Tom Graveney, who played with him, suggested that he sign for Worcestershire. Once more the young man's modesty made him to a degree suspicious but he agreed, and spent the 1964 season qualifying for Worcestershire by playing, highly successfully, with Kidderminster. More importantly, though, playing for the county in non-Championship matches he averaged 61.66 which included a score of 119 at Hastings for Arthur Gilligan's XI against the Australian tourists captained by Bobby Simpson. In 1965, duly qualified, he was one of only two batsmen – Tom Graveney was the other – to score more than 1500 runs in the English season.

He became a British citizen and in that same first season played for England and, as he pointed out, in his blissful delight, he had shaken hands with the Queen. He went on, as is common knowledge, to play in, altogether, 44 Tests for England and to become the chief coach to Worcestershire. As he showed when his selection for England to South Africa was announced and aroused so much controversy, he remains the modest man he has always been, reasonable, pleasing and easy company. His son, Damian, now plays for Worcestershire. Essentially and significantly, though, the career of Basil D'Oliveira offers hope to those coloured people of South Africa who are excluded from normal human rights. John Arlott is proud to have rendered that service to Basil D'Oliveira and to all his kind.

Chapter 21

ALDERNEY

From 1953, Alderney became a regular annual part of life. After cricket tours and even wine trips – both comfortably on expenses – the island was utterly refreshing. For a chronic bronchitic, its splendidly clean, fresh air was, in itself, a tonic. There was, though, much more than that. It had, and has, the habit of gossip and of scandal. In an English village of the same population there are always escape routes to neighbouring, near, or even relatively distant, places. On the other hand, an island is an island is an island: short of leaving it altogether, there is no escape. For those who have a romantic attachment to the whole concept of islands, as J.A. has, it is ideal. For some years, though, domestic upheaval prevented him going there. The Isles of Scilly provided a pleasantly gentle substitute; moreover they prompted a genuine enthusiasm, reflected in the book called *Island Camera*. This was virtually entirely an appreciation of the photographic work of four generations of the Gibson family who had been the principal photographers since the early 1860s when John Gibson began to take portraits in a studio in Penzance.

Delightful as those islands were, they lacked the colour, genuine character and, at times, it must be admitted, quite lurid characteristics of some of the Alderney people. The island is utterly distinctive. It is the nearest of the Channel Islands both to France and to England, with France the nearer and, for an enthusiastic Francophile, it has always been attractive on that ground alone. It is ringed by fourteen forts, all but two first built in the 1850s as protection against the forces of Napoleon III, and subsequently, during the Second World War, reinforced by the Germans – the Victorian work is in the local granite, the German in reinforced concrete: they present a bewildering variety. There are, too, eleven pubs, some of them hotels – of varying degrees of social aspiration and catering. There is a relatively old section of the main town – St Anne – and a rash of buildings on the north side in the modern style. The church – St Anne's, by Gilbert Scott – is as fine as any in the Channel Islands. Behind it there is a small network of ancient houses, many of which date from the fifteenth century; several of them were the central houses of the farms which once radiated out from the hub. The island has a population of over two thousand, a number of them retired from England; though there is still a substantial residue of earlier islanders, some of families which had been there for many years, others sprung from the soldiery who manned the forts in the mid-nineteenth century. The island was vacated by its own population and occupied by German forces during the Second World War and, for that reason, feels itself to be, and in fact is, quite different from Jersey and Guernsey – or, for that matter, from Sark and Herm. After the war when some of the earlier inhabitants – though by no means all of them – returned, Mr Chuter Ede, the then Home Secretary, disappointed at the Aurignacs' failure to make collective farming work on the island (though if he had known their character he would have realized that that was never going to be successful on Alderney) tied it to the apron strings of Guernsey.

In an island of only about two thousand people everyone is much closer to everyone else than would be the case in a British village of the same size. There is small opportunity for the average person to get away from it, with the result that everyone knows everyone else's business. For instance, in those early post-Second World War days, only a teetotaller was likely not to run into the President, Captain Sydney P. Herivel, CBE, DSC, RNR, generally known as 'Toby', on his daily round of the island. He used to come out of his handsomely impressive house, Mouriaux, and stride off. He kept an interested eye on all the affairs of the island and initiated several of its most important activities. Elected the first President in 1949, he was told then by Chuter Ede that no President of the island was likely to hold that office for more than a year at the most. Mr Ede little knew his man. Toby was re-elected, generally unopposed, in 1951, 1954, 1957, 1960, 1963, 1966, 1969, and resigned a fortnight before his death – which befell precisely eleven days after that of his wife, Edith. It was like the old epitaph: 'He for a little to live without her tried, liked it not and died.'

Toby's first port of call on his daily tour was always the Campania, kept by Jack Hammond, a descendant from one of the British soldiers who had manned the forts – unnecessarily – against Napoleon III, had married an island woman and stayed on after his service. Jack became a local hero in the early 1920s when he virtually won the Muratti Vase – the inter-island soccer competition – for Alderney: that was the only time they have ever won it. Jack was that rare character, a teetotal landlord, which, to be accurate, meant only that he never drank on his own premises. He was a reliable fount of island knowledge with a shrewd ability to separate truth from rumour.

After the Campania, Toby strode off on his long, thin legs, drainpipe trousers barely flapping, and showing his bony ankles, back along High Street and down Victoria Street, where his next port of call was the Albert. Incidentally, at each of the pubs he visited he partook of a pink gin. After the Albert he called at the Victoria, not strictly licensed as a pub but always keeping a bottle for him. Then the Bellevue and up to the Butes to the Grand, where that famous air pilot and convivial character, Tommy Rose, ran his bar; those two were intimates. Then, turning about, Toby made his way down the steep slope of Braye Hill to the Divers and then the Seaview, where Percy Collenette was, after Jack Hammond, the President's best informant. Then back up Braye Hill, a short diversion to the Harbour Lights and then back again, long legs eating up the hill, along Victoria Street and, turning right down the High Street, to the Coronation, the Rose & Crown, to the Marais Hall and back home without a quaver or a wobble.

In his later years – and we are talking of a man born in 1890 – he made the circuit in his ancient Daimler. That car became almost a symbol of the island. After Toby's death his son sold it to a newcomer to the island for a negligible sum. That newcomer – Geoffrey Rennard – had been driving it for several days when he was approached by a senior islander: 'To see that car going round the island is like seeing a ghost.' As a result he exchanged it for another slightly younger but less impressive vehicle. In return, he was invited to the breakwater the next day, where he saw the car, started up, accelerator and steering locked, chug slowly off into the sea.

Once, as Toby made his way back home, J.A. asked him in for a drink and gave him a fair-sized glass of sherry; he drank that at a gulp, accepted another, larger glass and swallowed it just as rapidly. Thereafter there was always a pink gin for the President's acceptance wherever the Arlott family stayed in Alderney.

Once, drinking a sherry which Toby provided for him in the sitting-room of Mouriaux, J.A. said, 'Now, Toby I know you were in the Navy in the First and Second World Wars but you did not serve in it in peacetime, did you?'

'No,' said the great man.

'What did you do, then?'

'I ran guns into Mexico and liquor into the United States,' was the answer.

Incredulous, his guest looked across to the great lady, Edith, who was the very picture of an English *grande dame*. With half a smile, she said, 'Yes, Mr Arlott, that is true.' Toby simply grinned and introduced a fresh subject to the conversation.

He was a wise man; certainly shrewder than some took him for at first encounter; humorous, a good friend, but utterly ruthless if anyone tried to outwit him. He did much for the good of the island and, so far as could be ascertained, did it no harm. His death was mourned by many people.

Another Alderney resident in those days was Michael St John Packe. He had captained the Leicestershire county cricket team in 1939 and, as a reservist, went away to join his unit on the outbreak of war. Although he played cricket once or twice for the University, he did not get a Blue for it as he did in hockey. He was a history scholar of Magdalene College, Cambridge, who wrote several books which reflect considerable scholarship and an immaculate style. His first was *First Airborne*, describing the history of that regiment from its foundation in early 1942 through to its great stand at Arnhem in 1944. The second was his major work, *The Life of John*

Stuart Mill, a penetrating and understanding study which remains the authoritative work on Mill, his period, and thought. The next was *The Bombs of Orsini*, a well researched biography of that tragic figure and his amazing escapades. When Michael Packe died, he was working on a life of Edward III, of which he had finished the first two books, and most of the third, while he had made extensive notes for the fourth and last. Those notes were expanded by L.C.B. Seaman, who edited the whole of that first attempt at a full-scale biography of Edward III since Victorian times. It is a work of scholarship and feeling.

Michael settled in Alderney as soon as was possible after the war and lived a well planned life. In the morning he worked on his market garden, which he planned, planted and reaped with immense skill and impressive results. Then, at midday, he showered, had two pints of beer with his lunch and settled down to write for the afternoon. At seven o'clock he finished that work, poured sherry for himself and his wife and took a relaxed dinner, often with friends.

Michael's father was almost a caricature of the military gentleman and a cricket fanatic. Though he himself never played first-class cricket, to his pride and delight his three sons all did so. They were Charles, the eldest, Robert, the middle one, and Michael, who all turned out for Leicestershire. Michael captained the Alderney team against visiting sides with humour, ability and acumen. It was a pleasure to play under him, especially when he went on to bowl. He had virtually never bowled in his rather brief first-class career, and in club cricket for the island he did not use himself very much. He would, however, go on when an appreciable stand was mounted against his side, and frequently succeeded in virtually thinking batsmen out. His was a happy and occasionally highly effective team. He was also one of the island's *Jurats*, or magistrates, a duty he discharged sagely. He died in 1978, at the age of sixty-two, and it was one of J.A.'s major sorrows that, by the time he could settle on the island, Michael Packe had died, for he was a good man though never in the least priggish; indeed he was invariably cheerful, and an extremely good companion.

One of the best of friends to many people on the island was

Tommy Rose, who once won the Cape to Cairo Air Race and, in Alderney, became a hotelier. His bar was always full of good cheer. Though he himself did not always prosper financially, he was always ready with a friendly word or a joke for a friend.

One of his constant bar customers was T.H. – 'Tim' – White, the author of *The Once and Future King*. Stories about him abounded. For instance, when he first landed on the island – having come by boat to accommodate his huge Irish setter, Killy, and also because he hated flying – his prolific and carefully curled beard prompted someone on the quay to say to the captain, 'My word, you must have gone deep, you have come up with Old Father Neptune.' Another story about him which may be accepted as authentic recounts that a couple of tidily dressed young men one day knocked at his door in Connaught Square and announced that they were Jehovah's Witnesses. 'Right,' said Tim, 'I am Jehovah, what is your evidence?' He was undoubtedly a most eminent writer of prose, probably at his best when on various themes from the Arthurian Legend but he also wrote a number of amusing and witty novels and some extremely fine short stories. He produced some good light verse as well, and illustrated the fine calligraphy of his amusing letters with capable, simple drawings. He was a fine conversationalist. Unhappily, he used to become extremely drunk: in fact, one story runs that he lurched home from Tommy Rose's bar one Saturday night, collapsed inside the door and was found still there when his cleaning woman came in on Monday morning. He would have been quite capable of staging that, of sleeping in his bed all day and night on Sunday and then going downstairs and posing collapse. He often, too, used to assume drunkenness and collapse for dramatic effect. He craved affection, from both men and women, and that hunger drove him to many stupidities: he estranged many by his demanding expectations. He was, for all that, the best of company so long as he remained even remotely sober.

All those characters now are dead but they remain in the island's historic sense. Before Alderney was evacuated, in 1940 – just two farmers remaining – under the threat of German occupation, the population of the island was slightly over a thousand. By the end of

1946 fewer than five hundred – about a third of the earlier population – had returned. It has subsequently filled with retired folk from the mainland and others, younger, who have taken businesses such as shops, hotels, and, at one time, a meat-canning factory which did not flourish. That influx of non-islanders explains why Alderney alone among the three larger Channel Islands speaks no *patois*. The Alderney Society, however, has confirmed that it once existed by producing a cassette recording of one of the last men who spoke it.

The newcomer to the island will be at once struck by the forts which encircle it except on the southern or cliff side. There are fourteen of them, all but four occupied for some purpose or other. Corblets is a most handsome and impressive private residence; Essex – that is to say Fort Essex or Essex Castle – is a collection of flats, and so is Château à l'Etoc; while Clonque is owned by the Landmark Trust; Raz Island – once much coveted by J.A. – is a restaurant cut off from the main island by high tides; Albert is used by the local cadet force, Doyle by the scouts and guides; Grosnez is the headquarters of the Department of Works responsible for the impressively long breakwater; Platte Saline is a gravel works; the huge Tourgis is falling into the ruin of disuse; there is some attempt to preserve Houmet Herbé, and for some time attempts were made to rebuild Quesnard; Les Houmeaux Florains is quite frankly a ruin; and the Nunnery, which stands on the site of what was probably the earliest defence work on the island, is pleasingly residential.

As the description of Toby Herivel's morning circuit will have indicated, there are plenty of hostelries – five have been added since his walking days – and there are eating places on virtually all levels of food and cost. It is, though, definitely not – repeat, not – a candyfloss or tripperish island and every attempt has been made, with reasonable if not complete success, to maintain that state of affairs. Nevertheless, its numerous beaches are never crowded and they are happily safe for children. There are enough shops to meet ordinary people's demands, though their prices are higher than on the mainland. It is a good place to seek refreshment for, except on Sundays, pubs and hotel bars may open from ten in the morning to one o'clock the next morning. Channel Jumper, which produces sweaters and cardigans and woollen goods in general, is now the only industrial base apart from the gravel works at Platte Saline. To be honest about it, the island is not harnessed to industry, rather it is gently hitched to idleness.

After Valerie's death, J.A. realized just how helpless he had become so far as companionship was concerned. The selfish independent of the cricket tours had become a man who needed a wife as he had never dreamt he would. In April 1977 he married Patricia Hoare, who looks after him and who not merely types this autobiography for him, but actually contrives to keep and file its motley pages.

Pat is tall, with dark, curly hair, green eyes and extremely English features. She walks a lot, bowling along in preference to riding or driving. He had first met her as a secretary at Lord's many years before, and eventually persuaded her to come and be his secretary. They married, she completed Robert's upbringing in a happy three-cornered household, with frequent, and also happy, visits from Timothy. He, physically rather like his maternal grandfather, grew up to be quick-moving and athletic – a capable long-distance runner – and a good, practical journalist, direct and thinking. The publisher of this book has agreed that, if J.A. does not stay around long enough to finish it, Timothy will do so. He will do it competently.

J.A. leans upon Pat increasingly. As he has aged, so his need for her, and his wider needs, have multiplied. Through this autobiography their relationship has grown through affection to understanding; his reliance upon her is great.

He has always been a family man, brought up in the deep affection of his mother and father, wanting back from his wives the love that he has given them. He is also, perhaps somewhat exaggeratedly, fond of his sons, and makes heavy emotional demands upon them, which they meet with a mixture of amusement and affection.

He does not think for a moment that this passage has done justice to his people, nor to his feelings for them. A mere versifier is not capable of communicating that depth of feeling. That would require a true poet, and the narrow of true love poetry shows how few real poets there are in that respect. Shakespeare, in a single sonnet, could express more emotion of this quality than most could cram into a book.

At the start of 1987 'Tricia, Timothy's wife, produced a son – the physically impressive Lucas – which has enabled the old man to dote even further; for his weakness for his own children, and now grandchild, at least, is deep, and he owes a great debt of gratitude to the three women who have made his adult life fine enough to escape destruction from its tragedies of death. He has realized, with time and mature feeling, that for many things – including, especially, in his case, books and pictures – he is no more than a caretaker able to pass on material riches in complete trust.

He has made money and amassed possessions, though he would happily have exchanged both for the lives he has lost. Now, on this island, he can regret his sins and count his blessings. He lives in no little comfort, with a wife converted from some austerity of table into the kind of cook who can offer the sort of food which comforts an old man's age. Here, too, he has found friends, all of them younger – by much or little – than himself, who have helped to make retirement fairly painless. No one, of course, can take away the sorrows of old age.

INDEX

Walford, M. M., 130
Walker, W., 62–3
Wallace, W. M., 189
Walsh, J. E., 161, 180
Waqar Hassan 230
Wardle, J. H., 162, 221–4, 230–1, 235, 238, 240, 248, 252, 260
Warner, P. F., 230
Warwickshire CCC 131–2, 148, 168, 189, 192, 200, 219
Washbrook, C., 124, 126, 128–9, 144–5, 148–9, 160, 164–8, 178–81, 183, 191, 198–9, 261–3
Watkins, A. J., 148, 168–9, 171, 173, 178, 215–16
Watson, F. B., 54
Watson, 'Tiny', 76–7, 80–1
Watson, W., 127, 211, 221–3, 251–2, 261, 281
Webster, Tom, 54, 230
Weekes, E. de C., 196–9, 271
Wellard, A. W., 179, 230
Wellings, E. M., 192
Wells, H. G., 93

West Indians in England (1928) 55–7 (1950) 196–9 (1957) 269–74
Westerman, Percy F., 49
Whistler, Laurence, 115, 157
White, A. F. T., 141
White, Crawford, 192
White, Gilbert, 35
White, T. H., 292
Wickets, Tries and Goals 193–5
Wilcox, D. R., 63
Willis, George, 44, 65, 67
Wilshin, Sunday, 108, 137
Wilson, A. E., 132
Wilson, J. V., 126, 240
Wilson, J. W., 258
Winrow, F. H., 123
Winslow, P. L., 247, 250, 252, 254
Wisden Cricketers' Almanack 49
Wisdom, Tom, 229
Witty, John, 112
Wodehouse, P. G., 93
Wolfe, Jabez, 14

Woods, Rev. Theodore, 14
Wooller, W., 171–2, 192, 194, 261
Woolley, F. E., 52, 230
Worcestershire CCC 117, 141, 161, 197, 220, 284
Workers' Educational Association 96
Worrell, F. M. M. 196–9, 269, 271–3
Wright, D. V. P., 124, 144–5, 149, 166, 178–9
Wyatt, R. E. S., 161, 230
Wynne, O. E., 181

Yardley, N. W. D., 127, 143–6, 148, 160, 166, 168–9, 177
Yarnold, H., 141
Yorkshire CCC 125, 127, 145, 147, 162, 171–2, 192, 197, 200, 214, 220, 249, 256
Young, Andrew, 157
Young, J. A., 147, 166–7, 182